Making Choices

Readings in Economics

Edited by Ray Notgrass and John Notgrass
with Bethany Poore

Making Choices
Edited by Ray Notgrass and John Notgrass
with Bethany Poore

ISBN 978-1-60999-095-4

Cover and interior design by Mary Evelyn McCurdy

Printed in the United States of America

Notgrass Company
975 Roaring River Road
Gainesboro, TN 38562

1-800-211-8793
www.notgrass.com

Table of Contents

Introduction

Making Choices is a compilation of historic documents, speeches, essays, and other writings, all of which further our understanding of economics. We created it for students to use in conjunction with the text *Exploring Economics*. The student who is using that text will find these readings assigned at the end of the appropriate lessons.

The order of the documents reflects the order in which they are assigned in *Exploring Economics*. The purpose of this collection is to give the reader handy access to significant original documents and to highlight the experience, opinions, and ideas of others so that the reader can develop his or her own informed thinking about economics. We have used excerpts of some documents, indicated by ellipses.

You might not agree with all of the opinions presented in this collection. The same is true for us. Notgrass History does not endorse every person or idea included in this volume. The authors of these readings, as do all people, have differing opinions about economics, the way people should use money, appropriate decisions in business, and many other topics. It is a good exercise to read material that challenges your thinking and helps you clarify what you believe, even if you do not agree with the author. Sometimes you may come to realize that your outlook and opinions need to change.

Economics is not merely a group of theories and numbers, stuck on paper or locked in big bank buildings. Economics happens when you (and people across the globe) earn money, give to a church and charities, choose where to shop and what to buy, prepare for a career, save and invest money, run a business, comply with government rules, pay taxes—in other words, when you are living life. Understanding economics is well worth your time. You will benefit yourself, your future family, and the local and global economy. Most importantly, you will be a better steward of God's resources that He has entrusted to your care.

Ray Notgrass

I, Pencil

Leonard Read (1958)

Leonard Read (1898-1983) established the Foundation for Economic Education in 1946 (www.fee.org). This organization promotes individual liberty, free markets, and property rights. Read wrote this essay in 1958. The Imprimis *introduction to the essay invites the reader to "Wonder at the countless bits of human know-how and natural materials spontaneously organized by our global market economy into the making of a simple wooden pencil. . . . And wonder, most of all, at the everyday miracles made possible by a political and economic system that dares to have faith in free men."*

I am a lead pencil—the ordinary wooden pencil familiar to all boys and girls and adults who can read and write. (My official name is "Mongol 482." My many ingredients are assembled, fabricated, and finished by Eberhard Faber Pencil Company, Wilkes-Barre, Pennsylvania.)

Writing is both my vocation and my avocation; that's all I do.

You may wonder why I should write a genealogy. Well, to begin with, my story is interesting. And, next, I am a mystery—more so than a tree or a sunset or even a flash of lightning. But, sadly, I am taken for granted by those who use me, as if I were a mere incident and without background. This supercilious attitude relegates me to the level of the commonplace. This is a species of the grievous error in which mankind cannot too long persist without peril. For, as a wise man observed, "We are perishing for want of wonder, not for want of wonders" (Chesterton).

I, Pencil, simple though I appear to be, merit your wonder and awe, a claim I shall attempt to prove. In fact, if you can understand me—no, that's too much to ask of anyone—if you can become aware of the miraculousness which I symbolize, you can help save the freedom mankind is so unhappily losing. I have a profound lesson to teach. And I can teach this lesson better than can an automobile or an airplane or a mechanical dishwasher because—well, because I am seemingly so simple.

Simple? Yet, not a single person on the face of this earth knows how to make me. This sounds fantastic, doesn't it? Especially when it is realized that there are about one and one-half billion of my kind produced in the U.S.A. each year.

Pick me up and look me over. What do you see? Not much meets the eye—there's some wood, lacquer, the printed labeling, graphite lead, a bit of metal, and an eraser.

Innumerable Antecedents

Just as you cannot trace your family tree back very far, so is it impossible for me to name and explain all my antecedents. But I would like to suggest enough of them to impress upon you the richness and complexity of my background.

My family tree begins with what in fact is a tree, a cedar of straight grain that grows in Northern California and Oregon. Now contemplate all the saws and trucks and rope and the countless other gear used in harvesting and carting the cedar logs to the railroad siding. Think of all the persons and the numberless skills that went into their fabrication: the mining of ore, the making of steel and its refinement into saws, axes, motors; the growing of hemp and bringing it through all the stages to heavy and strong rope; the logging camps with their beds and mess halls, the cookery and the raising of all the foods. Why, untold thousands of persons had a hand in every cup of coffee the loggers drink!

The logs are shipped to a mill in San Leandro, California. Can you imagine the individuals who make flat cars and rails and railroad engines and who construct and install the communication systems incidental thereto? These legions are among my antecedents.

Consider the millwork in San Leandro. The cedar logs are cut into small, pencil-length slats less than one-fourth of an inch in thickness. These are kiln dried and then tinted for the same reason women put rouge on their faces. People prefer that I look pretty, not a pallid white. The slats are waxed and kiln dried again. How many skills went into the making of the tint and the kilns, into supplying the heat, the light and power, the belts, motors, and all the other things a mill requires? Sweepers in the mill among my ancestors? Yes, and included are the men who poured the concrete for the dam of a Pacific Gas & Electric Company hydroplant which supplies the mill's power! Don't overlook the ancestors present and distant who have a hand in transporting sixty carloads of slats across the nation from California to Wilkes-Barre!

Moving cedar logs at a wood products mill in Oregon

Complicated Machinery

Once in the pencil factory—$4,000,000 in machinery and building, all capital accumulated by thrifty and saving parents of mine—each slat is given eight grooves by a complex machine, after which another machine lays leads in every other slat, applies glue, and places another slat atop—a lead sandwich, so to speak. Seven brothers and I are mechanically carved from this "wood-clinched" sandwich.

My "lead" itself—it contains no lead at all—is complex. The graphite is mined in Ceylon. Consider these miners and those who make their many tools and the

Sigiriya, Sri Lanka (formerly Ceylon)

makers of the paper sacks in which the graphite is shipped and those who make the string that ties the sacks and those who put them aboard ships and those who make the ships. Even the lighthouse keepers along the way assisted in my birth—and the harbor pilots.

The graphite is mixed with clay from Mississippi in which ammonium hydroxide is used in the refining process. Then wetting agents are added such as sulfonated tallow—animal fats chemically reacted with sulfuric acid. After passing through numerous machines, the mixture finally appears as endless extrusions—as from a sausage grinder—cut to size, dried, and baked for several hours at 1,850 degrees Fahrenheit. To increase their strength and smoothness the leads are then treated with a hot mixture which includes candelilla wax from Mexico, paraffin wax, and hydrogenated natural fats.

My cedar receives six coats of lacquer. Do you know all of the ingredients of lacquer? Who would think that the growers of castor beans and the refiners of castor oil are a part of it? They are. Why, even the processes by which the lacquer is made a beautiful yellow involves the skills of more persons than one can enumerate!

Observe the labeling. That's a film formed by applying heat to carbon black mixed with resins. How do you make resins and what, pray, is carbon black?

My bit of metal—the ferrule—is brass. Think of all the persons who mine zinc and copper and those who have the skills to make shiny sheet brass from these products of nature. Those black rings on my ferrule are black nickel. What is black nickel and how is it applied? The complete story of why the center of my ferrule has no black nickel on it would take pages to explain.

Then there's my crowning glory, inelegantly referred to in the trade as "the plug," the part man uses to erase the errors he makes with me. An ingredient called "factice" is what does the erasing. It is a rubber-like product made by reacting rape seed oil from the Dutch East Indies with sulfur chloride. Rubber, contrary to the common notion, is only for binding purposes. Then, too, there are numerous vulcanizing and accelerating agents. The pumice comes from Italy; and the pigment which gives "the plug" its color is cadmium sulfide.

Oil production field worker in Azerbaijan (2009)

Vast Web of Know-How

Does anyone wish to challenge my earlier assertion that no single person on the face of this earth knows how to make me?

Actually, millions of human beings have had a hand in my creation, no one of whom even knows more than a very few of the others. Now, you may say that I go too far in relating the picker of a coffee berry in far off Brazil and food growers elsewhere to my creation; that this is an extreme position. I shall stand by my claim. There isn't a single person in all these millions, including the president of the pencil company, who contributes more than a tiny, infinitesimal bit of know-how. From the standpoint of know-how the only difference between the miner of graphite in Ceylon and the logger in Oregon is in the type of know-how. Neither the miner nor the logger can be dispensed with, any more than can the chemist at the factory or the worker in the oil field—paraffin being a by-product of petroleum.

Here is an astounding fact: Neither the worker in the oil field nor the chemist nor the digger of graphite or clay nor any who mans or makes the ships or trains or trucks nor the one who runs the machine that does the knurling on my bit of metal nor the president of the company performs his singular task because he wants me. Each one wants me less, perhaps, than does a child in the first grade. Indeed, there are some among this vast multitude who never saw a pencil nor would they know how to use one. Their motivation is other than me. Perhaps it is something like this: Each of these millions sees that he can thus exchange his tiny know-how for the goods and services he needs or wants. I may or may not be among these items.

No Human Master Mind

There is a fact still more astounding: The absence of a master mind, of anyone dictating or forcibly directing these countless actions which bring me into being. No trace of such

Utah's Bingham Canyon Mine, also known as the Kennecott Copper Mine, is the largest man-made excavation on earth.

a person can be found. Instead, we find the Invisible Hand at work. This is the mystery to which I earlier referred.

It has been said that "only God can make a tree." Why do we agree with this? Isn't it because we realize that we ourselves could not make one? Indeed, can we even describe a tree? We cannot, except in superficial terms. We can say, for instance, that a certain molecular configuration manifests itself as a tree. But what mind is there among men that could even record, let alone direct, the constant changes in molecules that transpire in the life span of a tree? Such a feat is utterly unthinkable!

I, Pencil, am a complex combination of miracles; a tree, zinc, copper, graphite, and so on. But to these miracles which manifest themselves in Nature an even more extraordinary miracle has been added: the configuration of creative human energies—millions of tiny know-hows configurating naturally and spontaneously in response to human necessity and desire and in the absence of any human master-minding! Since only God can make a tree, I insist that only God could make me. Man can no more direct these millions of know-hows to bring me into being than he can put molecules together to create a tree.

The above is what I meant when writing, "If you can become aware of the miraculousness which I symbolize, you can help save the freedom mankind is so unhappily losing." For, if one is aware that these know-hows will naturally, yes, automatically, arrange themselves into creative and productive patterns in response to human necessity and demand—that is, in the absence of governmental or any other coercive master-minding—then one will possess an absolutely essential ingredient for freedom: a faith in free men. Freedom is impossible without this faith.

Once government has had a monopoly of a creative activity such, for instance, as the delivery of the mails, most individuals will believe that the mails could not be efficiently delivered by men acting freely. And here is the reason: Each one acknowledges that he himself doesn't know how to do all the things incident to mail delivery. He also recognizes that no other individual could do it. These assumptions are correct. No individual possesses enough know-how to perform a nation's mail delivery any more than any individual possesses enough know-how to make a pencil. Now, in the absence of a faith in free men—in the unawareness that millions of tiny know-hows would naturally and miraculously form and cooperate to satisfy this necessity—the individual cannot help but reach the erroneous conclusion that the mail can be delivered only by governmental "master-minding."

Testimony Galore

If I, Pencil, were the only item that could offer testimony on what men can accomplish when free to try, then those with little faith would have a fair case. However, there is testimony galore; it's all about us and on every hand. Mail delivery is exceedingly simple when compared, for instance, to the making of an automobile or a calculating machine or a grain combine or a milling machine, or to tens of thousands of other things.

Delivery? Why, in this area where men have been left free to try, they deliver the human voice around the world in less than one second; they deliver an event visually and in motion to any person's home when it is happening; they deliver 150 passengers from Seattle to Baltimore in less than four hours; they deliver gas from Texas to one's range or furnace in New York at unbelievably low rates and without subsidy; they deliver each four pounds of oil from the Persian Gulf to our Eastern Seaboard—halfway around the world—for less money than the government charges for delivering a one-ounce letter across the street!

Leave Men Free

The lesson I have to teach is this: Leave all creative energies uninhibited. Merely organize society to act in harmony with this lesson. Let society's legal apparatus remove all obstacles the best it can. Permit these creative know-hows freely to flow. Have faith that free men will respond to the Invisible Hand. This faith will be confirmed. I, Pencil, seemingly simple though I am, offer the miracle of my creation as testimony that this is a practical faith, as practical as the sun, the rain, a cedar tree, the good earth.

Reprinted by permission from **Imprimis**, *the national speech digest of Hillsdale College, www.hillsdale.edu.*

The Wealth of Nations
Adam Smith (1776)

The publication of An Inquiry into the Nature and Causes of the Wealth of Nations *by Scottish philosopher Adam Smith is usually cited as the beginning of the modern study of economics. The excerpts below highlight some of Smith's main points in the book.*

The annual labour of every nation is the fund which originally supplies it with all the necessaries and conveniences of life which it annually consumes, and which consist always either in the immediate produce of that labour, or in what is purchased with that produce from other nations.

According therefore as this produce, or what is purchased with it, bears a greater or smaller proportion to the number of those who are to consume it, the nation will be better or worse supplied with all the necessaries and conveniences for which it has occasion.

But this proportion must in every nation be regulated by two different circumstances; first, by the skill, dexterity, and judgment with which its labour is generally applied; and, secondly, by the proportion between the number of those who are employed in useful labour, and that of those who are not so employed. Whatever be the soil, climate, or extent of territory of any particular nation, the abundance or scantiness of its annual supply must, in that particular situation, depend upon those two circumstances.

The abundance or scantiness of this supply, too, seems to depend more upon the former of those two circumstances than upon the latter. Among the savage nations of hunters and fishers, every individual who is able to work, is more or less employed in useful labour, and endeavours to provide, as well as he can, the necessaries and conveniences of life, for himself, or such of his family or tribe as are either too old, or too young, or too infirm to go a-hunting and fishing. Such nations, however, are so miserably poor that, from mere want, they are frequently reduced, or, at least, think themselves reduced, to the necessity sometimes of directly destroying, and sometimes of abandoning their infants, their old people, and those afflicted with lingering diseases, to perish with hunger, or to be devoured by wild beasts. Among civilised and thriving nations, on the contrary, though a great number of people do not labour at all, many of whom consume the produce of ten times, frequently of a hundred times more labour than the greater part of those who work; yet the produce of the whole labour of the society is so great that all are often abundantly supplied, and a workman, even of the lowest and poorest order, if he is frugal and industrious, may enjoy a greater share of the necessaries and conveniences of life than it is possible for any savage to acquire.

Workers weed a carrot field in Elgin, Moray, Scotland (2014)

The causes of this improvement, in the productive powers of labour, and the order, according to which its produce is naturally distributed among the different ranks and conditions of men in the society, make the subject of the first book of this Inquiry. . . .

The greatest improvement in the productive powers of labour, and the greater part of the skill, dexterity, and judgment with which it is anywhere directed, or applied, seem to have been the effects of the division of labour.

The effects of the division of labour, in the general business of society, will be more easily understood by considering in what manner it operates in some particular manufactures. It is commonly supposed to be carried furthest in some very trifling ones; not perhaps that it really is carried further in them than in others of more importance: but in those trifling manufactures which are destined to supply the small wants of but a small number of people, the whole number of workmen must necessarily be small; and those employed in every different branch of the work can often be collected into the same workhouse, and placed at once under the view of the spectator. In those great manufactures, on the contrary, which are destined to supply the great wants of the great body of the people, every different branch of the work employs so great a number of workmen that it is impossible to collect them all into the same workhouse. We can seldom see more, at one time, than those employed in one single branch. Though in such manufactures, therefore, the work may really be divided into a much greater number of parts than in those of a more trifling nature, the division is not near so obvious, and has accordingly been much less observed.

To take an example, therefore, from a very trifling manufacture; but one in which the division of labour has been very often taken notice of, the trade of the pin-maker; a workman not educated to this business (which the division of labour has rendered a distinct trade), nor acquainted with the use of the machinery employed in it (to the invention of which the same division of labour has probably given occasion), could scarce, perhaps, with his utmost industry, make one pin in a day, and certainly could not make twenty. But in the way in which this business is now carried on, not only the whole work is a peculiar trade, but it is divided into a number of branches, of which the greater part are likewise peculiar trades. One man draws out the wire, another straights it, a third cuts it, a fourth points it, a fifth grinds it at the top for receiving the head; to make the head requires two or three distinct operations; to put it on is a peculiar business, to whiten the pins is another; it is even a trade by itself to put them into the paper; and the important business of making a pin is, in this manner, divided into about eighteen distinct operations, which, in some manufactories, are all performed by distinct hands, though in others the same man will sometimes perform two or three of them. I have seen a small manufactory of this kind where ten men only were employed, and where some of them consequently performed two or three distinct operations. But though they were very poor, and therefore but indifferently accommodated with the necessary machinery, they could, when they exerted themselves, make among them about twelve pounds of pins in a day. There are in a pound upwards of four thousand pins of a middling size. Those ten persons, therefore, could make among them upwards of forty-eight thousand pins in a day. Each person, therefore, making a tenth part of forty-eight thousand pins, might be considered as making four thousand eight hundred pins in a day. But if they had all wrought separately and independently, and without any of them having been educated to this peculiar business, they certainly could not each of them have made twenty, perhaps not one pin in a day; that is, certainly, not the two hundred and fortieth, perhaps not the four thousand eight hundredth part of what they are at present capable of performing, in consequence of a proper division and combination of their different operations.

In every other art and manufacture, the effects of the division of labour are similar to what they are in this very trifling one. . . .

This division of labour, from which so many advantages are derived, is not originally the effect of any human wisdom, which foresees and intends that general opulence to which it gives occasion. It is the necessary, though very slow and gradual consequence of a certain propensity in human nature which has in view no such extensive utility; the propensity to truck, barter, and exchange one thing for another. . . .

In civilised society [the individual] stands at all times in need of the cooperation and assistance of great multitudes, while his whole life is scarce sufficient to gain the friendship of a few persons. In almost every other race of animals each individual, when it is grown up to maturity, is entirely independent, and in its natural state has occasion for the assistance of no other living creature. But man has almost constant occasion for the help of his brethren, and it is in vain for him to expect it from their benevolence only. He will be more likely to prevail if he can interest their self-love in his favour, and show them that it is for their own advantage to do for him what he requires of them. Whoever offers to another a bargain of any kind, proposes to do this. Give me that which I want, and you shall have this which you want, is the meaning of every such offer; and it is in this manner that we obtain from one another the far greater part of those good offices which we stand in need of. It is not from the benevolence of the butcher, the brewer, or the baker that we expect our dinner, but from their regard to their own interest. We address ourselves, not to their humanity but to their self-love, and never talk to them of our own necessities but of their advantages. . . .

As it is by treaty, by barter, and by purchase that we obtain from one another the greater part of those mutual good offices which we stand in need of, so it is this same trucking disposition which originally gives occasion to the division of labour. In a tribe of hunters or shepherds a particular person makes bows and arrows, for example, with more readiness and dexterity than any other. He frequently exchanges them for cattle or for venison with his companions; and he finds at last that he can in this manner get more cattle and venison than if he himself went to the field to catch them. From a regard to his own interest, therefore, the making of bows and arrows grows to be his chief business, and he becomes a sort of armourer. Another excels in making the frames and covers of their little huts or movable houses. He is accustomed to be of use in this way to his neighbours, who reward him in the same manner with cattle and with venison, till at last he finds it his interest to dedicate himself entirely to this employment, and to become a sort of house-carpenter. In the same manner a third becomes a smith or a brazier, a fourth a tanner or dresser of hides or skins, the principal part of the clothing of savages. And thus the certainty of being able to exchange all that surplus part of the produce of his own labour,

Pueblo man holding bows and arrows (c. 1908)

which is over and above his own consumption, for such parts of the produce of other men's labour as he may have occasion for, encourages every man to apply himself to a particular occupation, and to cultivate and bring to perfection whatever talent or genius he may possess for that particular species of business. . . .

As it is the power of exchanging that gives occasion to the division of labour, so the extent of this division must always be limited by the extent of that power, or, in other words, by the extent of the market. When the market is very small, no person can have any encouragement to dedicate himself entirely to one employment, for want of the power to exchange all that surplus part of the produce of his own labour, which is over and above his own consumption, for such parts of the produce of other men's labour as he has occasion for.

There are some sorts of industry, even of the lowest kind, which can be carried on nowhere but in a great town. A porter, for example, can find employment and subsistence in no other place. A village is by much too narrow a sphere for him; even an ordinary market town is scarce large enough to afford him constant occupation. In the lone houses and very small villages which are scattered about in so desert a country as the Highlands of Scotland, every farmer must be butcher, baker and brewer for his own family. In

Traditional Wheelwright Shop in Shropshire, England

such situations we can scarce expect to find even a smith, a carpenter, or a mason, within less than twenty miles of another of the same trade. The scattered families that live at eight or ten miles distance from the nearest of them must learn to perform themselves a great number of little pieces of work, for which, in more populous countries, they would call in the assistance of those workmen. Country workmen are almost everywhere obliged to apply themselves to all the different branches of industry that have so much affinity to one another as to be employed about the same sort of materials. A country carpenter deals in every sort of work that is made of wood; a country smith in every sort of work that is made of iron. The former is not only a carpenter, but a joiner, a cabinet-maker, and even a carver in wood, as well as a wheel-wright, a plough-wright, a cart and waggon maker. The employments of the latter are still more various. It is impossible there should be such a trade as even that of a nailer in the remote and inland parts of the Highlands of Scotland. Such a workman at the rate of a thousand nails a day, and three hundred working days in the year, will make three hundred thousand nails in the year. But in such a situation it would be impossible to dispose of one thousand, that is, of one day's work in the year.

As by means of water-carriage a more extensive market is opened to every sort of industry than what land-carriage alone can afford it, so it is upon the sea-coast, and along the banks of navigable rivers, that industry of every kind naturally begins to subdivide and improve itself, and it is frequently not till a long time after that those improvements extend themselves to the inland parts of the country. . . .

When the division of labour has been once thoroughly established, it is but a very small part of a man's wants which the produce of his own labour can supply. He supplies the far greater part of them by exchanging that surplus part of the produce of his own labour, which is over and above his own consumption, for such parts of the produce of other men's labour as he has occasion for. Every man thus lives by exchanging, or becomes in some measure a merchant, and the society itself grows to be what is properly a commercial society.

Bakery in Rosenberg, Germany (2015)

But when the division of labour first began to take place, this power of exchanging must frequently have been very much clogged and embarrassed in its operations. One man, we shall suppose, has more of a certain commodity than he himself has occasion for, while another has less. The former consequently would be glad to dispose of, and the latter to purchase, a part of this superfluity. But if this latter should chance to have nothing that the former stands in need of, no exchange can be made between them. The butcher has more meat in his shop than he himself can consume, and the brewer and the baker would each of them be willing to purchase a part of it. But they have nothing to offer in exchange, except the different productions of their respective trades, and the butcher is already provided with all the bread and beer which he has immediate occasion for. No exchange can, in this case, be made between them. He cannot be their merchant, nor they his customers; and they are all of them thus mutually less serviceable to one another. In order to avoid the inconveniency of such situations, every prudent man in every period of society, after the first establishment of the division of labour, must naturally have endeavoured to manage his affairs in such a manner as to have at all times by him, besides the peculiar produce of his own industry, a certain quantity of some one commodity or other, such as he imagined few people would be likely to refuse in exchange for the produce of their industry.

Many different commodities, it is probable, were successively both thought of and employed for this purpose. In the rude ages of society, cattle are said to have been the common instrument of commerce; and, though they must have been a most inconvenient one, yet in old times we find things were frequently valued according to the number of cattle which had been given in exchange for them. The armour of Diomede, says Homer, cost only nine oxen; but that of Glaucus cost an hundred oxen. Salt is said to be the common instrument of commerce and exchanges in Abyssinia; a species of shells in some parts of the coast of India; dried cod at Newfoundland; tobacco in Virginia; sugar in some of our West India colonies; hides or dressed leather in some other countries; and there is at this day a village in Scotland where it is not uncommon, I am told, for a workman to carry nails instead of money to the baker's shop or the alehouse.

In all countries, however, men seem at last to have been determined by irresistible reasons to give the preference, for this employment, to metals above every other commodity. Metals can not only be kept with as little loss as any other commodity, scarce anything being less perishable than they are, but they can likewise, without any loss, be divided into any number of parts, as by fusion those parts can easily be reunited again; a quality which no other equally durable commodities possess, and which more than any other quality renders them fit to be the instruments of commerce and circulation. The man who wanted to buy salt, for example, and had nothing but cattle to give in exchange for it, must have been obliged to buy salt to the value of a whole ox, or a whole sheep at a time. He could seldom buy less than this, because what he was to give for it could seldom be divided without loss; and if he had a mind to buy more, he must, for the same reasons, have been obliged to buy double or triple the quantity, the value, to wit, of two or three oxen, or of two or three sheep. If, on the contrary, instead of sheep or oxen, he had metals to give in exchange for it, he could easily proportion the quantity of the metal to the precise quantity of the commodity which he had immediate occasion for.

Different metals have been made use of by different nations for this purpose. Iron was the common instrument of commerce among the ancient Spartans; copper among the ancient Romans; and gold and silver among all rich and commercial nations. . . .

Those metals seem originally to have been made use of for this purpose in rude bars, without any stamp or coinage. Thus we are told by Pliny, upon the authority of Timaeus, an ancient historian, that, till the time of Servius Tullius, the Romans had no coined money, but made use of unstamped bars of copper, to purchase whatever they had occasion for. These bars, therefore, performed at this time the function of money.

The use of metals in this rude state was attended with two very considerable inconveniencies; first, with the trouble of weighing; and, secondly, with that of assaying them. In the precious metals, where a small difference in the quantity makes a great difference in the value, even the business of weighing, with proper exactness, requires at least very accurate weights and scales. The weighing of gold in particular is an operation of some nicety. In the coarser metals, indeed, where a small error would be of little consequence, less accuracy would, no doubt, be necessary. Yet we should find it excessively troublesome, if every time a poor man had occasion either to buy or sell a farthing's worth of goods, he was obliged to weigh the farthing. The operation of assaying is still more difficult, still more tedious, and, unless a part of the metal is fairly melted in the crucible, with proper dissolvents, any conclusion that can be drawn from it, is extremely uncertain. Before the institution of coined money, however, unless they went through this tedious and difficult operation, people must always have been liable to the grossest frauds and impositions, and instead of a pound weight of pure silver, or pure copper, might receive in exchange for their goods an adulterated composition of the coarsest and cheapest materials, which had, however, in their outward appearance, been made to resemble those metals. To prevent such abuses, to facilitate exchanges, and thereby to encourage all sorts of industry and commerce, it has been found necessary, in all countries that have made any considerable advances towards improvement, to affix a public stamp upon certain quantities of such particular metals as were in those countries commonly made use of to purchase goods. Hence the origin of coined money, and of those public offices called mints; institutions exactly of the same nature with those of the aulnagers* and stamp-masters of woolen and linen cloth. All of them are equally meant to ascertain, by means of a public stamp, the quantity and uniform goodness of those different commodities when brought to market. . . .

As every individual, therefore, endeavours as much as he can both to employ his capital in the support of domestic industry, and so to direct that industry that its produce may be of the greatest value; every individual necessarily labours to render the annual revenue of the society as great as he can. He generally, indeed, neither intends to promote the public interest, nor knows how much he is promoting it. By preferring the support of domestic to that of foreign industry, he intends only his own security; and by directing that industry in such a manner as its produce may be of the greatest value, he intends only his own gain, and he is in this, as in many other cases, led by an invisible hand to promote an end which was no part of his intention. Nor is it always the worse for the society that it was no part of it. By pursuing his own interest he frequently promotes that of the society more effectually than when he really intends to promote it. I have never known much good done by those who affected to trade for the public good. It is an affectation, indeed, not very common among merchants, and very few words need be employed in dissuading them from it. . . .

---

* *government inspectors*

Every system which endeavours, either by extraordinary encouragements to draw towards a particular species of industry a greater share of the capital of the society than what would naturally go to it, or, by extraordinary restraints, force from a particular species of industry some share of the capital which would otherwise be employed in it, is in reality subversive of the great purpose which it means to promote. It retards, instead of accelerating, the progress of the society towards real wealth and greatness; and diminishes, instead of increasing, the real value of the annual produce of its land and labour.

All systems either of preference or of restraint, therefore, being thus completely taken away, the obvious and simple system of natural liberty establishes itself of its own accord. Every man, as long as he does not violate the laws of justice, is left perfectly free to pursue his own interest

Statue of Adam Smith in Edinburgh, Scotland

his own way, and to bring both his industry and capital into competition with those of any other man, or order of men. The sovereign is completely discharged from a duty, in the attempting to perform which he must always be exposed to innumerable delusions, and for the proper performance of which no human wisdom or knowledge could ever be sufficient; the duty of superintending the industry of private people, and of directing it towards the employments most suitable to the interest of the society. According to the system of natural liberty, the sovereign has only three duties to attend to; three duties of great importance, indeed, but plain and intelligible to common understandings: first, the duty of protecting the society from violence and invasion of other independent societies; secondly, the duty of protecting, as far as possible, every member of the society from the injustice or oppression of every other member of it, or the duty of establishing an exact administration of justice; and, thirdly, the duty of erecting and maintaining certain public works and certain public institutions which it can never be for the interest of any individual, or small number of individuals, to erect and maintain; because the profit could never repay the expense to any individual or small number of individuals, though it may frequently do much more than repay it to a great society. . . .

Socialism, Capitalism, and the Bible

Ronald H. Nash (1985)

Ronald Nash received a doctorate from Syracuse University and authored numerous books. He was a professor of philosophy and religion at Western Kentucky University; Reformed Theological Seminary in Maitland, Florida; and Southern Baptist Theological Seminary in Louisville, Kentucky. Nash died in 2006. This essay presents the idea that free market capitalism, not socialism, best accomplishes Biblical teachings.

In the Christian church today, one can find a small but growing army of Protestants and Roman Catholics who have entered into an uncritical alliance with the political Left. The so-called liberation theologians not only promote a synthesis of Marxism and Christianity, but attempt to ground their recommended restrictions of economic and political freedom on their interpretation of the biblical ethic. A growing number of my own religious fellowship (those theologically conservative Protestants known as evangelicals) appear to stop just short of the more radical pronouncements of the liberation thinkers. These evangelicals of the Left are convinced that the biblical ethic obliges them to condemn capitalism and endorse the politics of statism and the economics of socialism.

Many writings from the Christian Left illustrate what can be called the prooftext method. What these writers normally do is isolate some vague passage (usually one from the Old Testament) that pertains to an extinct culture situation or practice. They then proceed to deduce some complex economic or political program from that text.

My approach to the subject rejects the prooftext method and proceeds via three main steps. First, a Christian should acquire a clear and complete picture of the Christian worldview. What basic views about God, humankind, morality, and society are taught or implied by Scripture? Second, he should put his best effort into discovering the truth about economic and political systems. He should try to clarify what capitalism and socialism really are (not what the propagandists say they are); he should try to discover how each system works or, as in the case of socialism, whether it can work. He should identify the strengths and weaknesses of each system. Third, he should compare his economic options to the standard of biblical morality, and ask which system is more consistent with the entire Christian worldview.

Palmer Chapel in the Great Smoky Mountains of North Carolina

Creator and Freedom; Morality and Sin

We can begin, then, by noting several relevant aspects of the biblical worldview:

1. Certainly the biblical worldview implies that since God is the creator of all that exists, He ultimately is the rightful owner of all that exists. Whatever possessions a human being may acquire, he holds them temporarily as a steward of God and is ultimately accountable to God for how he uses them. However omnipresent greed and avarice may be in the human race, they are clearly incompatible with the moral demands of the biblical worldview.

2. The biblical worldview also contains important claims about human rights and liberties. All human beings have certain natural rights inherent in their created nature and have certain moral obligations to respect the rights of others. The possibility of human freedom is not a gift of government but a gift from God.

The Old Testament tended to focus on the economic and social dimensions of freedom. But gradually, as one moves into the New Testament, a more spiritual dimension of freedom assumes dominance. Freedom in the New Testament is deliverance from bondage to sin and is available only to those who come to know God's truth through Christ and enter into a saving relationship with Christ.

Some interesting parallels between the biblical account of spiritual freedom and political-economic freedom should be noted. For one thing, freedom always has God as its ultimate ground. For another, freedom must always exist in relationship to law. The moral law of God identifies definite limits beyond which human freedom under God should not pass. Liberty should never be turned into license.

3. The moral system of the Bible is another key element of the Christian worldview. While the Ten Commandments do not constitute the entire biblical ethic, they are a good place to begin. But it is important to notice other dimensions of the biblical ethic that have relevance for our subject. For example, Christians on the Left insist that the biblical ethic condemns individual actions and social structures that oppress people, harm people and favor some at the expense of others. I agree. Where I disagree, however, is with the next step taken by the Leftists. They claim that capitalism inevitably and necessarily encourages individual actions and produces social structures that oppress and harm people. On this point, they are dead wrong. Fortunately, the question as to which system actually harms or helps different classes of people is an empirical and not a normative matter. The Leftists simply have their facts wrong.

4. One final aspect of the Christian worldview must be mentioned: the inescapable fact of human sin and depravity. No economic or political system that assumes the essential goodness of human nature or holds out the dream of a perfect earthly society can possibly be consistent with the biblical worldview.

Peaceful or Violent Exchange?

Now we must examine the three major economic systems that compete for attention: capitalism, socialism and somewhere between, the hybrid known as interventionism or the mixed economy.

One dominant feature of capitalism is economic freedom, the right of people to exchange things voluntarily, free from force, fraud, and theft. Socialism, on the other hand, seeks to replace the freedom of the market with a group of central planners who exercise control over essential market functions. There are degrees of socialism as there are degrees of capitalism in the real world. But basic to any form of socialism is distrust of or contempt for the market process and the desire to replace the freedom of the market with some form of centralized control. Generally speaking, as one moves along the continuum of socialism to capitalism, one finds the following: the more freedom a socialist allows, the closer his position is to interventionism; the more freedom an interventionist allows, the closer his position is to capitalism. The crux is the extent to which human beings will be permitted to exercise their own choices in the economic sphere of life.

I will say nothing more about that deplorable economic system known as interventionism, a hopeless attempt to stop on a slippery slope where no stop is possible. The only way the half-hearted controls of the interventionist can work is if they become the total controls of the socialist. Anything less will result in the kind of troubled and self-damaging economy we have had for the past several decades in the United States.

I shall attempt to get a clearer fix on the real essence both of capitalism and socialism and then see which is more compatible with the biblical worldview. The best starting point for this comparison is a distinction made most recently by the American economist, Walter Williams. According to Williams, there are two and only two ways in which something may be exchanged. He called them *the peaceful means of exchange and the violent means of exchange.*

The peaceful means of exchange may be summed up in the phrase, "If you do something good for me, then I'll do something good for you." When capitalism is understood correctly, it epitomizes the peaceful means of exchange. The reason people exchange in a real market is because they believe the exchange is good for them. They take advantage of an opportunity to obtain something they want more in exchange for something they desire less. Capitalism then should be understood as a voluntary system of relationships that utilizes the peaceful means of exchange.

But exchange can also take place by means of force and violence. In this violent means of exchange, the basic rule of thumb is: "Unless you do something good for me, I'll do something bad to you." This turns out to be the controlling principle of socialism. Socialism means far more than centralized control of the economic process. It entails the introduction of coercion into economic exchange in order to facilitate the attainment of the goals of the elite who function as the central planners. One of the great ironies of

Christian socialism is that its proponents in effect demand that the State get out its weapons and force people to fulfill the demands of Christian love. Even if we fail to notice any other contrast between capitalism and socialism, we already have a major difference to relate to the biblical ethic. One system stresses voluntary and peaceful exchange while the other depends on coercion and violence.

Military monument from the Socialist era stands in front of modern buildings in Durres, Albania (2015)

Some Christian socialists object to the way I have set this up. They profess contempt for the more coercive forms of state-socialism on exhibit in communist countries. They would like us to believe that a more humane, non-coercive kind of socialism is possible. They would like us to believe that there is a form of socialism, not yet tried anywhere on earth, where the central ideas are cooperation and community and where coercion and dictatorship are precluded. But they provide very little information about the workings of this more utopian kind of socialism, and they ignore the fact that however humane and voluntary their socialism is supposed to become after it has been put into effect, it will take massive amounts of coercion and theft to get things started.

Socialist Falsehoods, Capitalist Facts

To that paradox, add one more: the fact that socialists need capitalism in order to survive. Unless socialists make allowance for some free markets which provide the pricing information that alone makes rational economic activity possible, socialist economies would have even more problems than those for which they are already notorious. Consequently, socialism is a gigantic fraud which attacks the market at the same time it is forced to utilize the market process.

But critics of the market try to shift attention away from their own embarrassing problems to claims that capitalism must be abolished or restricted because it is unjust or because it restricts important human freedoms. Capitalism is supposed to be unchristian because it allegedly gives a predominant place to greed and other unchristian values. It is alleged to increase poverty and the misery of the poor while, at the same time, it makes a few rich at the expense of the many. Socialism, on the other hand, is portrayed as the economic system of people who really care for the less fortunate members of society. Socialism is represented as the economics of compassion. Socialism is also recommended on the ground that it encourages other basic Christian values such as community.

Sign outside the Republican National Convention in Cleveland, Ohio (2016)

If these claims were true, they would constitute a serious problem for anyone anxious to show that capitalism is compatible with the biblical ethic. But, of course, the claims are not true. People who make such charges have their facts wrong or are aiming at the wrong target. The "capitalism" they accuse of being inhumane is a caricature. The system that in fact produces the consequences they deplore turns out to be not capitalism, but interventionism.

Capitalism is not economic anarchy. It recognizes several necessary conditions for the kinds of voluntary relationships it recommends. One of these presuppositions is the existence of inherent human rights, such as the right to make decisions, the right to be free, the right to hold property, and the right to exchange what one owns for something else. Capitalism also presupposes a system of morality. Capitalism should be thought of as a system of voluntary relationships within a framework of laws which protect people's rights against force, fraud, theft, and violations of contracts. "Thou shalt not steal" and "Thou shalt not lie" are part of the underlying moral constraints of the system. Economic exchanges can hardly be voluntary if one participant is coerced, deceived, defrauded, or robbed.

Allowing for Human Weakness

Once we grant that consistency with the biblical doctrine of sin is a legitimate test of political and economic systems, it is relatively easy to see how well democratic capitalism scores in this regard. The limited government willed to Americans by the Founding Fathers was influenced in large measure by biblical considerations about human sin. If one of the more effective ways of mitigating the effects of human sin in society is dispersing and decentralizing power, the conservative view of government is on the right track. So too is the conservative vision of economics.

The free market is consistent with the biblical view of human nature in another way. It recognizes the weaknesses of human nature and the limitations of human knowledge. No one can possibly know enough to manage a complex economy. No one should ever be trusted with this power. However, in order for socialism to work, socialism requires a class of omniscient planners to forecast the future, to set prices and to control production. In the free market system, decisions are not made by an omniscient bureaucratic elite but made across the entire economic system by countless economic agents.

At this point, of course, collectivists will raise another set of objections. Capitalism, they will counter, may make it difficult for economic power to be consolidated in the hands of the state; but it only makes it easier for vast concentrations of wealth and power to be vested in the hands of private individuals and companies. But the truth turns out to be something quite different from this widely accepted myth. It is not the free market that produces monopolies; rather it is governmental intervention with the market that creates the conditions that encourage monopoly.

As for another old charge, that capitalism encourages greed, the truth is just the reverse. The mechanism of the market neutralizes greed as selfish individuals are forced to find ways of servicing the needs of those with whom they wish to exchange. As we know, various people often approach economic exchanges with motives and objectives that fall short of the biblical ideal. But no matter how base or selfish a person's motives may be, so long as the rights of the other parties are protected, the greed of the first individual cannot harm them. As long as greedy individuals are prohibited from introducing force, fraud, and theft into the exchange process, their greed must be channeled into the discovery of products or services for which people are willing to exchange their holdings. Every person in a market economy has to be other-directed.

New Religion of the Left

Finally, some examples of the way in which attempts to ground American liberalism and interventionism or Latin American liberationism on the Bible involve serious distortions of the biblical message.

For instance, consider how radical American evangelicals on the Left abuse the biblical notion of justice. The basic idea in the Old Testament notion of justice is righteousness and fairness. But it is essential to the Leftist's cause that he read into biblical pronouncements about justice, contemporary notions of distributive justice. When the Bible says that Noah was a just man, it does not mean that he would have voted the straight Democratic ticket. It means simply that he was a righteous man.

Likewise, many Christians on the Left seek to reinterpret Jesus' earthly mission in exclusively economic and political terms. In their view, Jesus came primarily to deliver those who were poor and oppressed in a material sense. But every member of the human race is poor in the sense of being spiritually bankrupt. Jesus came to end our spiritual poverty by making available the righteousness that God demands and that only God can provide.

It is heresy to state that God's love for people varies in proportion to their wealth and social class. It is nonsense to suggest that all the poor are good and all the rich are evil. Once we eliminate the semantic game-playing by which some refer to a non-coercive voluntary utopian type of socialism, it becomes clear that socialism is incompatible with a truly free society. Edmund Opitz has seen this clearly:

As History's vice-regent, the Planner is forced to view men as mass; which is to deny their full stature as persons with rights endowed by the Creator, gifted with free will, possessing the capacity to order their own lives in terms of their convictions. The man who has the authority and the power to put the masses through their paces, and to punish nonconformists, must be ruthless enough to sacrifice a person to a principle . . . a commissar who believes that each person is a child of God will eventually yield to a commissar whose ideology is consonant with the demands of his job.

And so, Opitz concludes, "Socialism needs a secular religion to sanction its authoritarian politics, and it replaces the traditional moral order by a code which subordinates the individual to the collective." All of this is justified in the cause of improving economic well-being and in the name of compassion.

The Choice I Make

I think I have said enough to allow me, at least, to make a reasoned choice between capitalism and socialism on the basis of each system's compatibility to the biblical worldview. The alternative to free exchange is violence. Capitalism is a mechanism that allows natural human desires to be satisfied in a nonviolent way. Little can be done to prevent human beings from wanting to be rich. But what capitalism does is channel that desire into peaceful means that benefit many besides those who wish to improve their own situation.

Which choice then should I, as a Christian, make in the selection between capitalism and socialism? Capitalism is quite simply the most moral system, the most effective system, and the most equitable system of economic exchange. When capitalism, the system of free economic exchange, is described fairly, there can be no question that it, rather than socialism or interventionism, comes closer to matching the demands of the biblical ethic.

Reprinted by permission from Imprimis, *the national speech digest of Hillsdale College, www.hillsdale.edu.*

Precepts of Ptah-Hotep

(Egyptian, c. 2000 bc)

These excerpts come from an ancient Egyptian text ascribed to a government official named Ptah-Hotep. Ptah is the name for one of the Egyptian gods. The document contains advice for young men on proper behavior, including in work and financial matters. This translation is from Charles F. Horne's The Sacred Books and Early Literature of the East *(1917).*

Inspire not men with fear, else Ptah will fight against you in the same manner. If any one asserts that he lives by such means, Ptah will take away the bread from his mouth; if any one asserts that he enriches himself thereby, Ptah says: I may take those riches to myself. If any one asserts that he beats others, Ptah will end by reducing him to impotence. Let no one inspire men with fear; this is the will of Ptah. Let one provide sustenance for them in the lap of peace; it will then be that they will freely give what has been torn from them by terror.

If you are a farmer, gather the crops in the field which the great Ptah has given you, do not boast in the house of your neighbors; it is better to make oneself dreaded by one's deeds. As for him who, master of his own way of acting, being all-powerful, seizes the goods of others like a crocodile in the midst even of watchment, his children are an object of malediction, of scorn, and of hatred on account of it, while his father is grievously distressed, and as for the mother who has borne him, happy is another rather than herself. But a man becomes a god when he is chief of a tribe which has confidence in following him.

Ancient Egyptian Artwork

Be active during the time of your existence, do no more than is commanded. Do not spoil the time of your activity; he is a blameworthy person who makes a bad use of his moments. Do not lose the daily opportunity of increasing that which your house possesses. Activity produces riches, and riches do not endure when it slackens.

Disturb not a great man; weaken not the attention of him who is occupied. His care is to embrace his task, and he strips his person through the love which he puts into it. That transports men to Ptah, even the love for the work which they accomplish. Compose then your face even in trouble, that peace may be with you, when agitation is with . . . These are the people who succeed in what they desire.

Teach others to render homage to a great man. If you gather the crop for him among men, cause it to return fully to its owner, at whose hands is your subsistence. But the gift of affection is worth more than the provisions with which your back is covered. For that which the great man receives from you will enable your house to live, without speaking of the maintenance you enjoy, which you desire to preserve; it is thereby that he extends a beneficent hand, and that in your home good things are added to good things. Let your love pass into the heart of those who love you; cause those about you to be loving and obedient.

If you have become great after having been little, if you have become rich after having been poor, when you are at the head of the city, know how not to take advantage of the fact that you have reached the first rank, harden not your heart because of your elevation; you are become only the administrator, the prefect, of the provisions which belong to Ptah. Put not behind you the neighbor who is like you; be unto him as a companion.

A Model of Christian Charity

John Winthrop (1630)

The Puritans saw the entire socioeconomic structure as being from God. John Winthrop delivered a message in 1630 to those who were settling the Massachusetts Bay colony. This is an excerpt from that sermon (often remembered for its reference to the colony as a "City on a Hill").

John Winthrop

God Almighty in His most holy and wise providence, hath so disposed of the condition of mankind, as in all times some must be rich, some poor, some high and eminent in power and dignity; others mean and in subjection.

Reason: First, to hold conformity with the rest of His works, being delighted to show forth the glory of His wisdom in the variety and difference of the creatures, and the glory of His power in ordering all these differences for the preservation and good of the whole, and the glory of His greatness, that as it is the glory of princes to have many officers, so this great King will have many stewards, counting Himself more honored in dispensing His gifts to man by man, than if He did it by His own immediate hands.

Reason: Secondly, that He might have the more occasion to manifest the work of His Spirit: first upon the wicked in moderating and restraining them, so that the rich and mighty should not eat up the poor, nor the poor and despised rise up against their superiors and shake off their yoke. Secondly, in the regenerate, in exercising His graces in them, as in the great ones, their love, mercy, gentleness, temperance, etc., and in the poor and inferior sort, their faith, patience, obedience, etc.

Reason: Thirdly, that every man might have need of others, and from hence they might be all knit more nearly together in the bond of brotherly affection. From hence it appears plainly that no man is made more honorable than another, or more wealthy, etc., out of any particular and singular respect to himself, but for the glory of his Creator and the common good of the creature, man.

Therefore God still reserves the property of these gifts to Himself as Ezekiel 16:17. He there calls wealth, His gold and His silver. In Proverbs 3:9, He claims their service as His due, "Honor the Lord with thy riches," etc.—All men being thus (by divine providence) ranked into two sorts, rich and poor; under the first are comprehended all such as are able to live comfortably by their own means duly improved; and all others are poor according to the former distribution.

The Use of Money

John Wesley (1744)

John Wesley (1703-1791) was a founding leader of the Methodist movement in England. His sermons, full of references to Scripture, provided practical guidance on living in obedience to Christ. This sermon was published in a printed collection in 1771.

"I say unto you, Make unto yourselves friends of the mammon of unrighteousness; that, when ye fail, they may receive you into the everlasting habitations." Luke 16:9.

1. Our Lord, having finished the beautiful parable of the Prodigal Son, which he had particularly addressed to those who murmured at his receiving publicans and sinners, adds another relation of a different kind, addressed rather to the children of God. "He said unto his disciples," not so much to the scribes and Pharisees to whom he had been speaking before, —"There was a certain rich man, who had a steward, and he was accused to him of wasting his goods. And calling him, he said, Give an account of thy stewardship, for thou canst be no longer steward." (Luke 16:1, 2.) After reciting the method which the bad steward used to provide against the day of necessity, our Saviour adds, "His lord commended the unjust steward" namely, in this respect, that he used timely precaution; and subjoins this weighty reflection, "The children of this world are wiser in their generation than the children of light:" (Luke 16:8) Those who seek no other portion than this world "are wiser" (not absolutely; for they are one and all the veriest fools, the most egregious madmen under heaven; but, "in their generation," in their own way; they are more consistent with themselves; they are truer to their acknowledged principles; they more steadily pursue their end) "than the children of light;"—than they who see "the light of the glory of God in the face of Jesus Christ." Then follow the words above recited: "And I,"—the only-begotten Son of God, the Creator, Lord, and Possessor of heaven and earth and all that is therein; the Judge of all, to whom ye are to "give an account of your stewardship," when ye "can be no longer

John Wesley

stewards;" "I say unto you," — learn in this respect, even of the unjust steward, — "make yourselves friends," by wise, timely precaution, "of the mammon of unrighteousness." "Mammon" means riches or money. It is termed "the mammon of unrighteousness," because of the unrighteous manner wherein it is frequently procured, and wherein even that which was honestly procured is generally employed. "Make yourselves friends" of this, by doing all possible good, particularly to the children of God; "that, when ye fail," — when ye return to dust, when ye have no more place under the sun, — those of them who are gone before "may receive you," may welcome you, into the "everlasting habitations."

2. An excellent branch of Christian wisdom is here inculcated by our Lord on all his followers, namely, the right use of money — a subject largely spoken of, after their manner, by men of the world; but not sufficiently considered by those whom God hath chosen out of the world. These, generally, do not consider, as the importance of the subject requires, the use of this excellent talent. Neither do they understand how to employ it to the greatest advantage; the introduction of which into the world is one admirable instance of the wise and gracious providence of God. It has, indeed, been the manner of poets, orators, and philosophers, in almost all ages and nations, to rail at this, as the grand corrupter of the world, the bane of virtue, the pest of human society. Hence nothing so commonly heard, as:

Nocens ferrum, ferroque nocentius aurum:
And gold, more mischievous than keenest steel.

Hence the lamentable complaint,
Effodiuntur opes, irritamenta malorum.
Wealth is dug up, incentive to all ill.

Nay, one celebrated writer gravely exhorts his countrymen, in order to banish all vice at once, to "throw all their money into the sea:"
. . . in mare proximum [. . .]
Summi materiem mali!

But is not all this mere empty rant? Is there any solid reason therein? By no means. For, let the world be as corrupt as it will, is gold or silver to blame? "The love of money," we know, "is the root of all evil;" but not the thing itself. The fault does not lie in the money, but in them that use it. It may be used ill: and what may not? But it may likewise be used well: It is full as applicable to the best, as to the worst uses. It is of unspeakable service to all civilized nations, in all the common affairs of life: It is a most compendious instrument of transacting all manner of business, and (if we use it according to Christian wisdom) of doing all manner of good. It is true, were man in a state of innocence, or were all men "filled with the Holy Ghost," so that, like the infant Church at Jerusalem, "no man counted anything he had his own," but "distribution was made to everyone as he had need," the use of it would be superseded; as we cannot conceive there is anything of the kind among the inhabitants of heaven. But, in the present state of mankind, it is an excellent gift of God, answering the noblest ends. In the hands of his children, it is food for the hungry, drink for the thirsty, raiment for the naked: It gives to the traveller and the stranger where to lay his head. By it we may supply the place of an husband to the widow, and of a father to the fatherless. We maybe a defence for the oppressed, a means of health to the sick, of ease to them that are in pain; it may be as eyes to the blind, as feet to the lame; yea, a lifter up from the gates of death!

3. It is therefore of the highest concern that all who fear God know how to employ this valuable talent; that they be instructed how it may answer these glorious ends, and in the highest degree. And, perhaps, all the instructions which are necessary for this may be reduced to three plain rules, by the exact observance whereof we may approve ourselves faithful stewards of "the mammon of unrighteousness."

Part I.

In Sections 1-6 of Part I, Wesley argues that those engaged in a honest, respectable business should gain all they can without injuring their body or mind or hurting their neighbor physically, financially, or spiritually.

7. These cautions and restrictions being observed, it is the bounden duty of all who are engaged in worldly business to observe that first and great rule of Christian wisdom with respect to money, "Gain all you can." Gain all you can by honest industry. Use all possible diligence in your calling. Lose no time. If you understand yourself and your relation to God and man, you know you have none to spare. If you understand your particular calling as you ought, you will have no time that hangs upon your hands. Every business will afford some employment sufficient for every day and every hour. That wherein you are placed, if you follow it in earnest, will leave you no leisure for silly, unprofitable diversions. You have always something better to do, something that will profit you, more or less. And "whatsoever thy hand findeth to do, do it with thy might." Do it as soon as possible: No delay! No putting off from day to day, or from hour to hour! Never leave anything till to-morrow, which you can do to-day. And do it as well as possible. Do not sleep or yawn over it: Put your whole strength to the work. Spare no pains. Let nothing be done by halves, or in a slight and careless manner. Let nothing in your business be left undone if it can be done by labour or patience.

8. Gain all you can, by common sense, by using in your business all the understanding which God has given you. It is amazing to observe, how few do this; how men run on in the same dull track with their forefathers. But whatever they do who know not God, this is no rule for you. It is a shame for a Christian not to improve upon them, in whatever he

takes in hand. You should be continually learning, from the experience of others, or from your own experience, reading, and reflection, to do everything you have to do better to-day than you did yesterday. And see that you practise whatever you learn, that you may make the best of all that is in your hands.

Part II.

1. Having gained all you can, by honest wisdom and unwearied diligence, the second rule of Christian prudence is, "Save all you can." Do not throw the precious talent into the sea: Leave that folly to heathen philosophers. Do not throw it away in idle expenses, which is just the same as throwing it into the sea. Expend no part of it merely to gratify the desire of the flesh, the desire of the eye, or the pride of life.

2. Do not waste any part of so precious a talent merely in gratifying the desires of the flesh; in procuring the pleasures of sense of whatever kind; particularly, in enlarging the pleasure of tasting. I do not mean, avoid gluttony and drunkenness only: An honest heathen would condemn these. But there is a regular, reputable kind of sensuality, an elegant epicurism, which does not immediately disorder the stomach, nor (sensibly, at least) impair the understanding. And yet (to mention no other effects of it now) it cannot be maintained without considerable expense. Cut off all this expense! Despise delicacy and variety, and be content with what plain nature requires.

3. Do not waste any part of so precious a talent merely in gratifying the desire of the eye by superfluous or expensive apparel, or by needless ornaments. Waste no part of it in curiously adorning your houses; in superfluous or expensive furniture; in costly pictures, painting, gilding, books; in elegant rather than useful gardens. Let your neighbours, who know nothing better, do this: "Let the dead bury their dead." But "what is that to thee?" says our Lord: "Follow thou me." Are you willing? Then you are able so to do.

Gold Bars

4. Lay out nothing to gratify the pride of life, to gain the admiration or praise of men. This motive of expense is frequently interwoven with one or both of the former. Men are expensive in diet, or apparel, or furniture, not barely to please their appetite, or to gratify their eye, their imagination, but their vanity too. "So long as thou dost well unto thyself, men will speak good of thee." So long as thou art "clothed in purple and fine linen, and farest sumptuously" every day," no doubt many will applaud thy elegance of taste, thy generosity and hospitality. But do not buy their applause so dear. Rather be content with the honour that cometh from God.

5. Who would expend anything in gratifying these desires if he considered that to gratify them is to increase them? Nothing can be more certain than this: Daily experience shows, the more they are indulged, they increase the more. Whenever, therefore, you expend anything to please your taste or other senses, you pay so much for sensuality. When you lay out money to please your eye, you give so much for an increase of curiosity,—for a stronger attachment to these pleasures which perish in the using. While you are purchasing anything which men use to applaud, you are purchasing more vanity. Had you not then enough of vanity, sensuality, curiosity before? Was there need of any addition? And would you pay for it, too? What manner of wisdom is this? Would not the literally throwing your money into the sea be a less mischievous folly?

6. And why should you throw away money upon your children, any more than upon yourself, in delicate food, in gay or costly apparel, in superfluities of any kind? Why should you purchase for them more pride or lust, more vanity, or foolish and hurtful desires? They do not want any more; they have enough already; nature has made ample provision for them: Why should you be at farther expense to increase their temptations and snares, and to pierce them through with more sorrows?

7. Do not leave it to them to throw away. If you have good reason to believe that they would waste what is now in your possession in gratifying and thereby increasing the desire of the flesh, the desire of the eye, or the pride of life at the peril of theirs and your own soul, do not set these traps in their way. Do not offer your sons or your daughters unto Belial, any more than unto Moloch. Have pity upon them, and remove out of their way what you may easily foresee would increase their sins, and consequently plunge them deeper into everlasting perdition! How amazing then is the infatuation of those parents who think they can never leave their children enough! What! cannot you leave them enough of arrows, firebrands, and death? Not enough of foolish and hurtful desires? Not enough of pride, lust, ambition vanity? not enough of everlasting burnings? Poor wretch! thou fearest where no fear is. Surely both thou and they, when ye are lifting up your eyes in hell, will have enough both of the "worm that never dieth," and of "the fire that never shall be quenched!"

8. "What then would you do, if you was in my case? If you had a considerable fortune to leave?" Whether I would do it or no, I know what I ought to do: This will admit

of no reasonable question. If I had one child, elder or younger, who knew the value of money; one who I believed, would put it to the true use, I should think it my absolute, indispensable duty to leave that child the bulk of my fortune; and to the rest just so much as would enable them to live in the manner they had been accustomed to do. "But what, if all your children were equally ignorant of the true use of money?" I ought then (hard saying! who can hear it?) to give each what would keep him above want, and to bestow all the rest in such a manner as I judged would be most for the glory of God.

Part III.

1. But let not any man imagine that he has done anything, barely by going thus far, by "gaining and saving all he can," if he were to stop here. All this is nothing, if a man go not forward, if he does not point all this at a farther end. Nor, indeed, can a man properly be said to save anything, if he only lays it up. You may as well throw your money into the sea, as bury it in the earth. And you may as well bury it in the earth, as in your chest, or in the Bank of England. Not to use, is effectually to throw it away. If, therefore, you would indeed "make yourselves friends of the mammon of unrighteousness," add the Third rule to the two preceding. Having, First, gained all you can, and, Secondly saved all you can, Then "give all you can."

2. In order to see the ground and reason of this, consider, when the Possessor of heaven and earth brought you into being, and placed you in this world, he placed you here not as a proprietor, but a steward: As such he entrusted you, for a season, with goods of various kinds; but the sole property of these still rests in him, nor can be alienated from him. As you yourself are not your own, but his, such is, likewise, all that you enjoy. Such is your soul and your body, not your own, but God's. And so is your substance

in particular. And he has told you, in the most clear and express terms, how you are to employ it for him, in such a manner, that it may be all an holy sacrifice, acceptable through Christ Jesus. And this light, easy service, he has promised to reward with an eternal weight of glory.

3. The directions which God has given us, touching the use of our worldly substance, may be comprised in the following particulars. If you desire to be a faithful and a wise steward, out of that portion of your Lord's goods which he has for the present lodged in your hands, but with the right of resuming whenever it pleases him, First, provide things needful for yourself; food to eat, raiment to put on, whatever nature moderately requires for preserving the

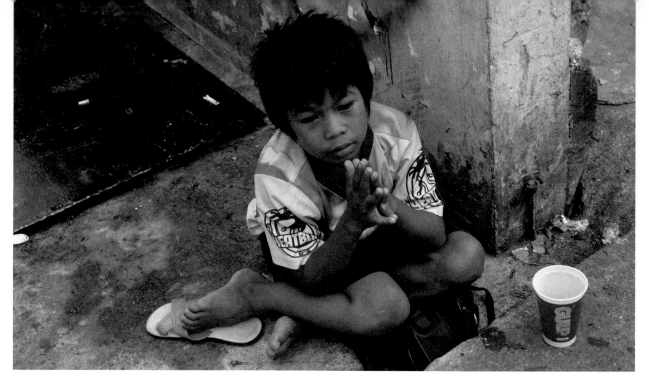

Young beggar on the street in Bangkok, Thailand (2014)

body in health and strength. Secondly, provide these for your wife, your children, your servants, or any others who pertain to your household. If when this is done there be an overplus left, then "do good to them that are of the household of faith." If there be an overplus still, "as you have opportunity, do good unto all men." In so doing, you give all you can; nay, in a sound sense, all you have: For all that is laid out in this manner is really given to God. You "render unto God the things that are God's," not only by what you give to the poor, but also by that which you expend in providing things needful for yourself and your household.

4. If, then, a doubt should at any time arise in your mind concerning what you are going to expend, either on yourself or any part of your family, you have an easy way to remove it. Calmly and seriously inquire, "(1.) In expending this, am I acting according to my character? Am I acting herein, not as a proprietor, but as a steward of my Lord's goods? (2.) Am I doing this in obedience to his Word? In what Scripture does he require me so to do? (3.) Can I offer up this action, this expense, as a sacrifice to God through Jesus Christ? (4.) Have I reason to believe that for this very work I shall have a reward at the resurrection of the just?" You will seldom need anything more to remove any doubt which arises on this head; but by this four-fold consideration you will receive clear light as to the way wherein you should go.

5. If any doubt still remain, you may farther examine yourself by prayer according to those heads of inquiry. Try whether you can say to the Searcher of hearts, your conscience not condemning you, "Lord, thou seest I am going to expend this sum on that food, apparel, furniture. And thou knowest, I act herein with a single eye as a steward of thy goods, expending this portion of them thus in pursuance of the design thou hadst in entrusting

me with them. Thou knowest I do this in obedience to the Lord, as thou commandest, and because thou commandest it. Let this, I beseech thee, be an holy sacrifice, acceptable through Jesus Christ! And give me a witness in myself that for this labour of love I shall have a recompense when thou rewardest every man according to his works." Now if your conscience bear you witness in the Holy Ghost that this prayer is well-pleasing to God, then have you no reason to doubt but that expense is right and good, and such as will never make you ashamed.

6. You see then what it is to "make yourselves friends of the mammon of unrighteousness," and by what means you may procure, "that when ye fail they may receive you into the everlasting habitations." You see the nature and extent of truly Christian prudence so far as it relates to the use of that great talent, money. Gain all you can, without hurting either yourself or your neighbour, in soul or body, by applying hereto with unintermitted diligence, and with all the understanding which God has given you;—save all you can, by cutting off every expense which serves only to indulge foolish desire; to gratify either the desire of flesh, the desire of the eye, or the pride of life; waste nothing, living or dying, on sin or folly, whether for yourself or your children;—and then, give all you can, or, in other words, give all you have to God. Do not stint yourself, like a Jew rather than a Christian, to this or that proportion. "Render unto God," not a tenth, not a third, not half, but all that is God's, be it more or less; by employing all on yourself, your household, the household of faith, and all mankind, in such a manner, that you may give a good account of your stewardship when ye can be no longer stewards; in such a manner as the oracles of God direct, both by general and particular precepts; in such a manner, that whatever ye do may be "a sacrifice of a sweet-smelling savour to God," and that every act may be rewarded in that day when the Lord cometh with all his saints.

7. Brethren, can we be either wise or faithful stewards unless we thus manage our Lord's goods? We cannot, as not only the oracles of God, but our own conscience beareth witness. Then why should we delay? Why should we confer any longer with flesh and blood, or men of the world? Our kingdom, our wisdom is not of this world: Heathen custom is nothing to us. We follow no men any farther than they are followers of Christ. Hear ye him. Yea, to-day, while it is called to-day, hear and obey his voice! At this hour, and from this hour, do his will: Fulfil his word, in this and in all things! I entreat you, in the name of the Lord Jesus, act up to the dignity of your calling! No more sloth! Whatsoever your hand findeth to do, do it with your might! No more waste! Cut off every expense which fashion, caprice, or flesh and blood demand! No more covetousness! But employ whatever God has entrusted you with, in doing good, all possible good, in every possible kind and degree to the household of faith, to all men! This is no small part of "the wisdom of the just." Give all ye have, as well as all ye are, a spiritual sacrifice to Him who withheld not from you his Son, his only Son: So "laying up in store for yourselves a good foundation against the time to come, that ye may attain eternal life!"

Letter 4 of the
Letters from a Farmer in Pennsylvania

John Dickinson (1768)

In 1767 the British Parliament passed the Townshend Acts that imposed taxes on the American colonies for the purpose of raising revenue. Many Americans believed that Parliament could enact taxes to regulate trade but not simply to raise revenue. Later that year, Pennsylvania attorney John Dickinson began publishing a series of letters in opposition to the Townshend Acts. In the letters he expressed the objections that many colonists had to paying taxes imposed on them by the British government. The taxes called for in the Townshend Acts were eventually repealed, except for the tax on tea.

My dear Countrymen,

An objection, I hear, has been made against my second letter, which I would willingly clear up before I proceed. "There is," say these objectors, "a material difference between the Stamp Act and the late act for laying a duty on paper, etc. that justifies the conduct of those who opposed the former, and yet are willing to submit to the latter. The duties imposed by the Stamp Act were internal taxes; but the present are external, and therefore the parliament may have a right to impose them."

To this I answer with a total denial of the power of parliament to lay upon these colonies any "tax" whatever.

This point, being so important to this, and to succeeding generations, I wish to be clearly understood.

To the word "tax," I annex that meaning which the constitution and history of England require to be annexed to it; that is—that it is an imposition on the subject, for the sole purpose of levying money.

In the early ages of our monarchy, certain services were rendered to the crown for the general good. These were personal: But in process of time, such institutions being found inconvenient, gifts and grants of their own property were made by the people, under the several names of aids, tallages, talks, taxes and subsidies, etc. These were made, as may be collected even from the names, for public service upon "need and necessity." All these sums were levied upon the people by virtue of their voluntary gift. Their intention was to support the national honor and interest. Some of those grants comprehended duties arising from trade; being imports on merchandizes. These Lord Chief Justice Coke classes under "subsidies," and "parliamentary aids." They are also called "customs." But whatever the name was, they were always considered as gifts of the people to the crown, to be employed for public uses.

Commerce was at a low ebb, and surprising instances might be produced how little it was attended to for a succession of ages. The terms that have been mentioned, and, among the rest, that of "tax," had obtained a national, parliamentary meaning, drawn from the principles of the constitution, long before any Englishman thought of imposition of duties, for the regulation of trade.

Whenever we speak of "taxes" among Englishmen, let us therefore speak of them with reference to the principles on which, and the intentions with which, they have been established. This will give certainty to our expression, and safety to our conduct: But if, when we have in view the liberty of these colonies, we proceed in any other course, we pursue a juno indeed, but shall only catch a cloud.

In the national, parliamentary sense insisted on, the word "tax" was certainly understood by the congress at New York, whose resolves may be said to form the American "bill of rights."

The third, fourth, fifth, and sixth resolves, are thus expressed.

III. "That it is inseparably essential to the freedom of a people, and the undoubted right of Englishmen, that NO TAX be imposed on them, except with their own consent, given personally, or by their representatives."

IV. "That the people of the colonies are not, and from their local circumstances, cannot be represented in the house of commons in Great Britain."

V. "That the only representatives of the people of the colonies, are the persons chosen therein by themselves; and that NO TAXES ever have been, or can be constitutionally imposed on them, but by their respective legislatures."

VI. "That all supplies to the crown, being free gifts of the people, it is unreasonable, and inconsistent with the principles and spirit of the British constitution, for the people of Great Britain to grant to his Majesty the property of the colonies."

Here is no distinction made between internal and external taxes. It is evident from the short reasoning thrown into these resolves, that every imposition "to grant to his Majesty the property of the colonies," was thought a "tax"; and that every such imposition, if laid any other way, than "with their consent, given personally, or by their representatives," was not only "unreasonable, and inconsistent with the principles and spirit of the British constitution," but destructive "to the freedom of a people."

This language is clear and important. A "tax" means an imposition to raise money. Such persons therefore as speak of internal and external "taxes," I pray may pardon me, if I object to that expression, as applied to the privileges and interests of these colonies. There may be internal and external impositions, founded on different principles, and having different tendencies; every "tax" being an imposition, though every imposition is not a "tax." But all taxes are founded on the same principle; and have the same tendency.

External impositions, for the regulation of our trade, do not "grant to his Majesty the property of the colonies." They only prevent the colonies acquiring property, in things not necessary, in a manner judged to be injurious to the welfare of the whole empire. But the last statute respecting us, "grants to his Majesty the property of the colonies," by laying duties on the manufactures of Great Britain which they must take, and which she settled them, on purpose that they should take.

What tax can be more internal than this? Here is money drawn, without their consent, from a society, who have constantly enjoyed a constitutional mode of raising all money among themselves. The payment of this tax they have no possible method of avoiding; as they cannot do without the commodities on which it is laid, and they cannot manufacture these commodities themselves. Besides, if this unhappy country should be so lucky as to elude this act, by getting parchment enough, in the place of paper, or by reviving the ancient method of writing on wax and bark, and by inventing something to serve instead of glass, her ingenuity would stand her in little stead; for then the parliament would have nothing to do but to prohibit such manufactures, or to lay a tax on hats and woolen cloths, which they have already prohibited the colonies from supplying each other with; or on instruments and tools of steel and iron, which they have prohibited the provincials from manufacturing at all: And then, what little gold and silver they have, must be torn from their hands, or they will not be able, in a short time, to get an ax for cutting their firewood, nor a plough for raising their food. In what respect, therefore, I beg leave to ask, is the late act preferable to the Stamp Act, or more consistent with the liberties of the colonies? For my own part, I regard them both with equal apprehension; and think they ought to be in the same manner opposed.

[Dickinson closed with a Latin phrase which translated:]

We have a statute, laid up for future use, like a sword in the scabbard.

A Farmer

John Dickinson

Letters to John P. Nicholson

Sam Watkins (1882)

Samuel R. Watkins was born in 1839 in Columbia, Tennessee. He enlisted in the First Tennessee Regiment of the Confederate army in 1861 and surrendered with it in North Carolina in 1865. Twenty years after the Civil War began, his local newspaper published his memoirs. Cumberland Presbyterian Publishing House in Nashville printed a book version in 1882.

John P. Nicholson was born in 1842 in Philadelphia, Pennsylvania. He served in the Union army throughout the war, rising to the rank of Lieutenant Colonel. Nicholson's father was a bookbinder, and John made it his mission to help people remember what had happened during the Civil War. In addition to collecting weapons and other physical objects, Nicholson collected written recollections of the conflict.

Watkins and Nicholson had served on opposing sides during the war, and they even participated in some of the same battles in northern Georgia. After Co. Aytch *was released, Sam Watkins contacted John Nicholson with the following letter on June 23, 1882.*

Sam Watkins

Dear Sir

I send you a circular of a new book just issued, the same being anecdotes and incidents of a private soldier. A Gen. Marcus J. Wright* thought perhaps by sending you a circular that you might desire a copy of Co. Aytch.

Should you desire a copy, I would be grateful to receive an order from you. There might be something in these memoirs of a private soldier (my own) that might contribute to a genuine history of those stormy days & times. I would be pleased to hear from you.

> I am very Resp[ectfully]
> Sam R Watkins

Richardson replied with his order two days later, and Watkins sent this letter with the books on June 28. (The hardback version of Co. Aytch *sold for $1.50 and the paperback version for 75 cents.)*

---

* *Marcus Joseph Wright was a Confederate general from Tennessee. He worked with the U.S. War Department to collect Confederate records for* The War of the Rebellion, *issued in multiple volumes between 1881 and 1901.*

Dear Sir

Your favor of June 25 enclosing check for $1.50 is at hand for which please accept my thanks.

I send you two copies of "Co. Aytch" paperback & regret my inability to send the same untrimed as you request.

I assure you that I appreciate your kind favor. Coming from the source which it does. And I trust that you may be fully compensated by being interested and entertained by its perusal.

And further Col. Nicholson if you can speak a word in favor of the book you will do an act of philanthropy & charity for me, for I am a very poor man & a cripple & have a wife & eight children & an old grandmother dependent upon me for their daily bread, & any favor shown me I will be grateful for. I am very Resp. Sam R Watkins

Nicholson did "speak a word in favor" of Watkins' book, and the two men continued to correspond. Watkins wrote this letter to Nicholson on August 17.

Dear Friend

Your kind favor of the 13th is at hand, for which please accept my thanks.

Please allow me to say that your kindness to me has done me more good in assisting the sale of my book than any one else. And for this kindness I assure you that I am grateful & trust that God will bless you a thousand fold.

I have sent books ordered as directed & circulars as directed.

I am doing very well and much of my success is due to you & should opportunity ever present whereby I can show you my appreciation, you will find your favors have not been unworthily bestowed.

I am very Respectfully
Sam R Watkins

Sam Watkins never fully recovered from the physical hardship he experienced during the war: wounds, exposure, and deprivation. He died in 1901. John Nicholson remained active in veterans groups, particularly the Military Order of the Loyal Legion. He was also Chairman of the Gettysburg National Military Park Commission from 1893 until his death in 1922.

Free to Choose:
A Conversation with Milton Friedman
(2006)

Milton Friedman (1912-2006) received a doctorate from Columbia University in 1946. He taught at the University of Chicago and later worked with the Hoover Institution at Stanford University. Friedman received the Nobel Prize in Economics in 1976. Dr. Friedman and his wife, Rose (also an economist), published Free to Choose, *a defense and explanation of free-market ideas, in 1980. A ten-part PBS series by the same title featuring the Friedmans also aired that year. One of his main areas of study was the influence of monetary policy on the economy. He discussed this and other issues in this interview with Hillsdale College president Larry Arnn a few months before Friedman's death.*

LARRY ARNN: In *Free to Choose,* in the chapter on "The Tyranny of Controls," you argue that protectionism and government intervention in general breed conflict and that free markets breed cooperation. How do you reconcile this statement with the fact that we think of free markets as being competitive?

MILTON FRIEDMAN: They are competitive, but they are competitive over a broad range. The question is, how do you make money in a free market? You only make money if you can provide someone with something he or she is willing to pay for. You can't make money any other way. Therefore, in order to make money, you have to promote cooperation. You have to do something that your customer wants you to do. You don't do it because he orders you to. You don't do it because he threatens to hit you over the head if you don't. You do it because you offer him a better deal than he can get anywhere else. Now that's promoting cooperation. But there are other people who are trying to sell to him, too. They're your competitors. So there is competition among sellers, but cooperation between sellers and buyers.

Milton Friedman

LA: In the chapter on "The Tyranny of Controls," you seem gloomy about the prospects for India. Why?

MF: I was in India in 1955 on behalf of the American government to serve as an economic adviser to the minister of finance. I concluded then that India had tremendous potential, but none of it was being achieved. That fact underlies the passage you are referring to in *Free to Choose*. Remember, *Free to Choose* aired in January 1980, and as of that time there had been no progress in India. The population had grown, but the standard of living was as low as it had been in 1955. Now, in the past ten or fifteen years, there has been movement in India, and maybe those hidden potentials I saw in 1955 will finally be achieved. But, there is still great uncertainty there.

LA: In that same chapter, you wrote the following about China: "Letting the genie of . . . initiative out of the bottle even to this limited extent will give rise to political problems that, sooner or later, are likely to produce a reaction toward greater authoritarianism. The opposite outcome, the collapse of communism and its replacement by a market system, seems far less likely." What do you think about that statement today?

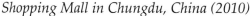

Shopping Mall in Chungdu, China (2010)

MF: I'm much more optimistic about China today than I was then. China has made great progress since that time. It certainly has not achieved complete political freedom, but it has come closer. It certainly has a great deal more economic freedom. I visited China for the first time in 1980 right after the publication of *Free to Choose*. I had been invited by the government to lecture on how to stop inflation, among other things. China at that time was in a pretty poor state. The hotel we stayed in showed every sign of being run by a communist regime. We returned to China twice, and each time, the changes were tremendous. In 1980, everybody was wearing the dull and drab Mao costume; there were bicycles all over the place and very few cars. Eight years later, we started to see some color in the clothes, there were things available for sale that hadn't been available before, and free markets were breaking out all over the place. China has continued to grow at a dramatic rate. But in the section of *Free to Choose* you refer to, I talked about the political conflict that was coming—and that broke out in Tiananmen Square. The final outcome in China will not be decided until there is a showdown between the political tyranny on the one hand and economic freedom on the other—they cannot coexist.

LA: Let me ask you about demographic trends. Columnist Mark Steyn writes that in ten years, 40 percent of young men in the world are going to be living in oppressed Muslim countries. What do you think the effect of that is going to be?

MF: What happens will depend on whether we succeed in bringing some element of greater economic freedom to those Muslim countries. Just as India in 1955 had great but unrealized potential, I think the Middle East is in a similar situation today. In part this is because of the curse of oil. Oil has been a blessing from one point of view, but a curse from another. Almost every country in the Middle East that is rich in oil is a despotism.

LA: Why do you think that is so?

MF: One reason, and one reason only—the oil is owned by the governments in question. If that oil were privately owned and thus someone's private property, the political outcome would be freedom rather than tyranny. This is why I believe the first step following the 2003 invasion of Iraq should have been the privatization of the oil fields. If the government had given every individual over 21 years of age equal shares in a corporation that had the right and responsibility to make appropriate arrangements with foreign oil companies for the purpose of discovering and developing Iraq's oil reserves, the oil income would have flowed in the form of dividends to the people—the shareholders—rather than into government coffers. This would have provided an income to the whole people of Iraq and thereby prevented the current disputes over oil between the Sunnis, Shiites and Kurds, because oil income would have been distributed on an individual rather than a group basis.

LA: Many Middle Eastern societies have a kind of tribal or theocratic basis and long-held habits of despotic rule that make it difficult to establish a system of contract between strangers. Is it your view that the introduction of free markets in such places could overcome those obstacles?

MF: Eventually, yes. I think that nothing is so important for freedom as recognizing in the law each individual's natural right to property, and giving individuals a sense that they own something that they're responsible for, that they have control over, and that they can dispose of.

LA: Is there an area here in the United States in which we have not been as aggressive as we should in promoting property rights and free markets?

MF: Yes, in the field of medical care. We have a socialist-communist system of distributing medical care. Instead of letting people hire their own physicians and pay them, no one pays his or her own medical bills. Instead, there's a third party payment system. It is a communist system and it has a communist result. Despite this, we've had numerous miracles in medical science. From the discovery of penicillin, to new surgical techniques, to MRIs and CAT scans, the last 30 or 40 years have been a period of miraculous change in medical science. On the other hand, we've seen costs skyrocket. Nobody is happy: physicians don't like it, patients don't like it. Why? Because none of them are responsible for themselves. You no longer have a situation in which a patient chooses a physician, receives a service, gets charged, and pays for it. There is no direct relation between the patient and the physician. The physician is an employee of an insurance company or an employee of the government. Today, a third party pays the bills. As a result, no one who visits the doctor asks what the charge is going to be—somebody else is going to take care of that. The end result is third party payment and, worst of all, third party treatment.

LA: Following the recent expansion in prescription drug benefits and Medicare, what hope is there for a return to the free market in medical care?

MF: It does seem that markets are on the defensive, but there is hope. The expansion of drug benefits was accompanied by the introduction of health savings accounts—HSAs.

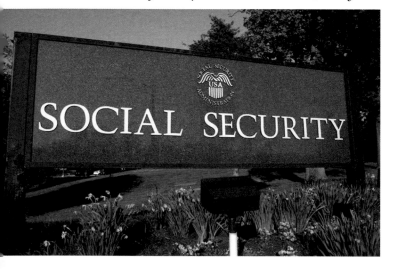

Social Security Headquarters in Woodlawn, Maryland

That's the one hopeful sign in the medical area, because it's a step in the direction of making people responsible for themselves and for their own care. No one spends somebody else's money as carefully as he spends his own.

LA: On the subject of Social Security, let me read to you a passage from *Free to Choose*: "As we have gone through the literature on Social Security, we have been shocked at the arguments that have been used to defend the program. Individuals who would not lie to their children, their friends, their colleagues, whom all of us would trust implicitly in the most important personal dealings, have propagated a false view of Social Security. Their intelligence and exposure to contrary views make it hard to believe that they have done so unintentionally and innocently. Apparently they have regarded themselves as an elite group within society that knows what is good for other people better than those people do for themselves." What do you think of these words today?

MF: I stick by every word there. But there has been progress since then. Let me explain: *Free to Choose* was produced and shown on television for the first time in January 1980. President Reagan was elected in November 1980. To get a clear picture of what has happened since the publication of *Free to Choose*, we really need to look at what happened before and after the election of Ronald Reagan. Before Reagan, non-defense government spending—on the federal, state and local levels—as a percentage of national income was rising rapidly. Between the early 1950s and 1980, we were in a period of what I would call galloping socialism that showed no signs of slowing. Following the election of Ronald Reagan, there was an abrupt and immediate halt to this expansion of government. But even under Reagan, government spending as a percentage of national income didn't come down: It has held constant from that time to now. Although the early years of the current Bush presidency did see spending increases, national income has risen, too. We have achieved some success at our first task: stopping the growth of government. The second task is to shrink government spending and make government smaller. We haven't done that yet, but we are making some progress. I should also mention as a cautionary tale that, prior to Reagan, the number of pages in the Federal Register was on the rise, but Reagan succeeded in reducing this number substantially. However, once Reagan was out of office, the number of pages in the Register began to rise even more quickly. We have not really succeeded in that area.

There have been real changes in our society since *Free to Choose* was published. I'm not attributing them to *Free to Choose*—I'm not saying that's the reason—but in general, there has been a complete change in public opinion. This change is probably due as much to the collapse of the Soviet Union as it is to what Friedrich Hayek or Milton Friedman or somebody else wrote. Socialism used to mean the ownership and operation of the means of production, but nobody gives it that meaning today. There is no country in the world attempting to be socialist in that sense except North Korea. And perhaps Russia is moving

---

The monument titled "Socialist Revolution and Socialist Construction" was constructed in the North Korean capitol of Pyongyang in 1972.

in that direction. Conversely, opinion has not shifted far enough in terms of the dangers of big government and the deleterious effects it can have, and that's where we're facing future problems. This clarifies the task facing institutions such as Hillsdale College: We must make clear that the only reason we have our freedom is because government is so inefficient. If the government were efficient in spending the approximately 40 percent of our income that it currently manages, we would enjoy less freedom than we do today.

LA: In *Free to Choose* you discuss Abraham Lincoln's "House Divided" speech, which you relate to the great task that the American people face. Like Lincoln, you argue that a house divided against itself cannot stand: America is going to be a government intervention country or it's going to be a free market country, but it cannot continue indefinitely as a mixture of both. Do you still believe that?

MF: Yes, I very much believe that, and I believe that we've been making some headway since *Free to Choose* appeared. However, even though it is real headway compared to what was happening before, we are mostly holding ground.

LA: What do you think are the major factors behind the economic growth we have experienced since the publication of *Free to Choose*?

MF: Economic growth since that time has been phenomenal, which has very little to do with most of what we've been talking about in terms of the conflict between government and private enterprise. It has much more to do with the technical problem of establishing sound monetary policy. The economic situation during the past 20 years has been unprecedented in the history of the world. You will find no other 20-year period in which prices have been as stable—relatively speaking—in which there has been as little variability in price levels, in which inflation has been so well-controlled, and in which output has gone up as regularly. You hear all this talk about economic difficulties, when the fact is we are at the absolute peak of prosperity in the history of the world. Never before have so many people had as much as they do today. I believe a large part of that is to be attributed to better monetary policy. The improved policy is a result of the acceptance of the view that inflation is a monetary phenomenon, not a real phenomenon. We have accepted the view that central banks are primarily responsible for maintaining stable prices and nothing else.

LA: Do you think the Great Depression was triggered by bad monetary policy at a crucial moment?

MF: Absolutely. Unfortunately, it is still the case that if you ask people what caused the Great Depression, nine out of ten will probably tell you it was a failure of business. But it's absolutely clear that the Depression was a failure of government and not a failure of business.

LA: You don't think the Smoot-Hawley tariff caused the Depression?

MF: No. I think the Smoot-Hawley tariff was a bad law. I think it did harm. But the Smoot-Hawley tariff by itself would not have made one quarter of the labor force unemployed. However, reducing the quantity of money by one third did make a quarter of the labor force unemployed. When I graduated from undergraduate college in 1932, I was baffled by the fact that there were idle machines and idle men and you couldn't get them together. Those men wanted to cooperate; they wanted to work; they wanted to produce what they wore; and they wanted to produce the food they ate. Yet something had gone wrong: The government was mismanaging the money supply.

LA: Do you think our government has learned its lesson about how to manage the money supply?

MF: I think that the lesson has been learned, but I don't think it will last forever. Sooner or later, government will want to raise funds without imposing taxes. It will want to spend money it does not have. So I hesitate to join those who are predicting two percent inflation for the next 20 years. The temptation for government to lay its hands on that money is going to be very hard to resist. The fundamental problem is that you shouldn't have an institution such as the Federal Reserve, which depends for its success on the abilities of its chairman. My first preference would be to abolish the Federal Reserve, but that's not going to happen.

Senator Smoot and Representative Hawley on the steps of the United States Capitol address a large gathering who presented petitions for tax reductions

LA: I want to talk now about education and especially about vouchers, because I know they are dear to your heart. Why do you think teachers unions oppose vouchers?

MF: The president of the National Education Association was once asked when his union was going to do something about students. He replied that when the students became members of the union, the union would take care of them. And that was a correct answer. Why? His responsibility as president of the NEA was to serve the members of his union, not to serve public purposes. I give him credit: The trade union has been very effective in serving its members. However, in the process, they've destroyed American education. But you see, education isn't the union's function. It's our fault for allowing the union to pursue its agenda. Consider this fact: There are two areas in the United States that suffer from the same disease—education is one and health care is the other. They both suffer from the disease that takes a system that should be bottom-up and converts it into a system that is top-down. Education is a simple case. It isn't the public purpose to build brick schools and have students taught there. The public purpose is to

Geography class in a Washington, D.C. school (c. 1899)

provide education. Think of it this way: If you want to subsidize the production of a product, there are two ways you can do it. You can subsidize the producer or you can subsidize the consumer. In education, we subsidize the producer—the school. If you subsidize the student instead—the consumer—you will have competition. The student could choose the school he attends and that would force schools to improve and to meet the demands of their students.

LA: Although you discuss many policy issues in *Free to Choose*, you have turned much of your attention to education, and to vouchers as a method of education reform. Why is that your focus?

MF: I don't see how we can maintain a decent society if we have a world split into haves and have-nots, with the haves subsidizing the have-nots. In our current educational system, close to 30 percent of the youngsters who start high school never finish. They are condemned to low-income jobs. They are condemned to a situation in which they are going to be at the bottom. That leads in turn to a divisive society; it leads to a stratified society rather than one of general cooperation and general understanding. The effective literacy rate in the United States today is almost surely less than it was 100 years ago. Before government had any involvement in education, the majority of youngsters were schooled, literate, and able to learn. It is a disgrace that in a country like the United States, 30 percent of youngsters never graduate from high school. And I haven't even mentioned those who drop out in elementary school. It's a disgrace that there are so many people who can't read and write. It's hard for me to see how we can continue to maintain a decent and free society if a large subsection of that society is condemned to poverty and to handouts.

LA: Do you think the voucher campaign is going well?

MF: No. I think it's going much too slowly. What success we have had is almost entirely in the area of income-limited vouchers. There are two kinds of vouchers: One is a charity voucher that is limited to people below a certain income level. The other is an education voucher, which, if you think of vouchers as a way of transforming the educational industry, is available to everybody. How can we make vouchers available to everybody? First, education ought to be a state and local matter, not a federal matter. The 1994 Contract with America called for the elimination of the Department of Education.

Since then, the budget for the Department of Education has tripled. This trend must be reversed. Next, education ought to be a parental matter. The responsibility for educating children is with parents. But in order to make it a parental matter, we must have a situation in which parents are free to choose the schools their children attend. They aren't free to do that now. Today the schools pick the children. Children are assigned to schools by geography—by where they live. By contrast, I would argue that if the government is going to spend money on education, the money ought to travel with the children. The objective of such an expenditure ought to be educated children, not beautiful buildings. The way to accomplish this is to have a universal voucher. As I said in 1955, we should take the amount of money that we're now spending on education, divide it by the number of children, and give that amount of money to each parent. After all, that's what we're spending now, so we might as well let parents spend it in the form of vouchers.

LA: I have one more question for you. You describe a society in which people look after themselves because they know the most about themselves, and they will flourish if you let them. You, however, are a crusader for the rights of others. For example, you say in *Free to Choose*—and it's a very powerful statement—a tiny minority is what matters. So is it one of the weaknesses of the free market that it requires certain extremely talented and disinterested people who can defend it?

MF: No, that's not right. The self-interest of the kind of people you just described is promoting public policy. That's what they're interested in doing. For example, what was my self-interest in economics? My self-interest to begin with was to understand the real mystery and puzzle that was the Great Depression. My self-interest was to try to understand why that happened, and that's what I enjoyed doing—that was my self-interest. Out of that I grew to learn some things—to have some knowledge. Following that, my self-interest was to see that other people understood the same things and took appropriate action.

LA: Do you define self-interest as what the individual wants?

MF: Yes, self-interest is what the individual wants. Mother Teresa, to take one example, operated on a completely self-interested basis. Self-interest does not mean narrow self-interest. Self-interest does not mean monetary self-interest. Self-interest means pursuing those things that are valuable to you but which you can also persuade others to value. Such things very often go beyond immediate material interest.

LA: Does that mean self-interest is a synonym for self-sacrifice?

MF: If you want to see how pervasive this sort of self-interest is that I'm describing, look at the enormous amount of money contributed after Hurricane Katrina. That was a tremendous display of self-interest: The self-interest of people in that case was to help others. Self-interest, rightly understood, works for the benefit of society as a whole.

Reprinted by permission from Imprimis, *the national speech digest of Hillsdale College, www.hillsdale.edu.*

Letter to Eli Whitney Sr.

Eli Whitney Jr. (1793)

Eli Whitney was born in 1765. He worked in his father's nail manufacturing workshop during the Revolutionary War. Whitney graduated from Yale in 1792. He went south and ended up at the plantation of Catharine Greene, widow of Revolutionary War general Nathanael Greene.

Eli Whitney to Eli Whitney, Senr

New Haven, Sept. 11th, 1793.

Dear Parent,

I received your letter of the 16th of August with peculiar satisfaction and delight. It gave me no small pleasure to hear of your health and was very happy to be informed that your health and that of the family has been so good since I saw you. I have fortunately just heard from you by Mr. Robbinson who says you were well when he left Westboro sooner than I now fear will be in my power. I presume, sir, you are desirous to hear how I have spent my time since I left College. This I conceive you have a right to know and that it is my duty to inform you and should have done it before this time; but I thought I could do it better by verbal communication than by writing, and expecting to see you soon, I omitted it. As I now have a safe and direct opportunity to send by Mr. Robbinson, I will give you a summary account of my southern expedition.

I went from N. York with the family of the late Major General Greene to Georgia. I went immediately with the family to their Plantation about twelve miles from Savannah with an expectation of spending four or five days and then proceed into Carolina to take the school as I have mentioned in former letters. During this time I heard much said of the extreme difficulty in ginning Cotton, that is, separating it from its seeds. There were a number of very respectable Gentlemen at Mrs. Greene's who all agreed that if a machine could be invented which would clean the cotton with expedition, it would be a great thing both to the Country and to the inventor. I involuntarily happened to be thinking on the subject and struck out a plan of a Machine in my mind, which I communicated to Miller, (who is agent to the Executors of Genl. Greene and resides in the family, a man of respectability and property) he was pleased with the Plan and said if I would pursue it and try an experiment to see if it would answer, he would be at the whole expense, I should loose nothing but my time, and if I succeeded we would share the profits. Previous to this I found I was like[ly] to be disappointed in my school, that is, instead of a hundred, I found I could get only fifty Guineas a year. I however held the refusal of the school untill I tried some experiments. In about ten Days I made a little model, for which I was offered, if I would give up all right and title to it, a Hundred Guineas. I concluded to relinquish my school and turn my attention to perfecting the Machine. I made one before I came away which required the labor of one man to turn it and with which one man will clean ten times as much cotton as he can in any other way before known and also cleanse it much better than in the usual mode. This machine may be turned by water or with a horse, with the greatest ease, and one may and a horse will do more than fifty men with the old machine. It makes the labor fifty times less, without throwing any class of People out of business.

I returned to the Northward for the purpose of having a machine made on a large scale and obtaining a patent

Eli Whitney Jr.

for the invention. I went to Philadelphia soon after I arrived, made myself acquainted with the steps necessary to obtain a Patent, took several of the steps with Secretary of State Mr. Jefferson agreed to send the Pattent to me as soon as it could be made out—so that I apprehended no difficulty in obtaining the Patent—Since I have been here I have employed several workmen in making machines and as soon as my business is such that I can leave it a few days, I shall come to Westboro'. I think it is probable I shall go to Philadelphia again before I come to Westboro', and when I do come I shall be able to stay but few days. I am certain I can obtain a patent in England. As soon as I have got a Patent in America, I shall go with the machine which I am not making, to Georgia, where I shall stay a few weeks to see it at work. From thence I expect to go to England, where I shall probably continue two or three years. How advantageous this business will eventually prove to me, I cannot say. It is generally said by those who know anything about it, that I shall make a Fortune by it. I have not expectation that I shall make an independent fortune by it, but think I had better pursue it than any other business into which I can enter. Something which cannot be foreseen may frustrate my expectations and defeat my Plan; but I am now so sure of success that ten thousand dollars, if I saw the money counted out to me, would not tempt me to give up my right and relinquish the object. I wish you, sir, not to show this letter not communicate anything of its contents to any body except My Brothers and Sister, _enjoining_ it on them to keep the whole a _profound secret_.

Mr. Robbinson came into town yesterday and goes out tomorrow, this has been such a bustling time that I have not had opportunity to say six words to him. I have told him nothing of my business—perhaps he will hear something about it from some body else in town. But only two or three of my friends know what I am about tho' there are many surmises in town—if Mr. Robbinson says anything about it, you can tell him I wrote you concerning it, but wished not to have it mentioned. I have been considerably out of health since I wrote you last; but now feel tolerably well. I should write to my Brothers and Sister but fear I shall not have time—hope they will accept my good wishes for their happiness and excuse me.

> With respects to Mama I am,
>> kind Parent, your most obt. Son
>>> Eli Whitney, Junr.

Illustration of slaves using the first cotton gin from Harper's Weekly *(1869)*

Letter to Eli Whitney Jr.

Thomas Jefferson (1793)

Thomas Jefferson served as Secretary of State under President George Washington. He was also appointed to the board of the U.S. patent office, created in 1790. After receiving Eli Whitney's patent application, Jefferson replied with this letter that mixes official business with personal inquiries about the cotton gin.

Germantown   Nov. 16, 1793

Sir

Your favor of October 15, inclosing a drawing of your cotton gin, was received on the 6th inst. The only requisite of the law now uncomplied with is the forwarding a model which being received your patent may be made out and delivered to your order immediately.

As the State of Virginia, of which I am, carries on household manufactures of cotton to a great extent, as I also do myself, and one of our great embarrassments is the cleaning the cotton of the seed, I feel considerable interest in the success of your invention for family use. Permit me therefore to ask information from you on these points, has the machine been thoroughly tried to the ginning of cotton, or is it as yet but a machine of theory? What quantity of cotton has it cleaned on an average of several days & worked by hand & by how many hands? What will be the cost of one of them made to be worked by hand? Favorable answers to these questions would induce me to engage one of them to be forwarded to Richmond for me. Wishing to hear from you on the subject, I am Sir

You most obedt servt

Thomas Jefferson

P.S. is this the machine advertised the last year by Pearce at the Patterson Manufactory?[*]

Mr. Eli Whitney.   Connecticut. New Haven.

In March 1794, Whitney brought the requested model to Jefferson for a demonstration and obtained his patent. At first Whitney and his business partner Phineas Miller did not want to sell the machines. They offered to rent their use to plantation owners who would pay in cotton. Other people entered the market by building and selling competing cotton gins. Whitney spent the next ten years dealing with legal disputes with other gin manufacturers. These efforts largely failed, and Whitney himself never profited from the invention.

---

[*] *William Pearce was a British mechanic working in the United States who had also developed a device for ginning cotton.*

Letters to Theodore and Martha Roosevelt

Theodore Roosevelt Jr. (1876-1878)

Theodore Roosevelt entered Harvard College in September 1876, one month before his 18th birthday. It was the first time he had been away from his family. While he was at school, Roosevelt exchanged many letters with his parents and siblings. He wrote this letter in reply to his father a few weeks after he left home to attend Harvard.

Cambridge, October 22, 1876

Dearest Father Your letter with the slip of paper containing an account of your speech has only just come to hand. Was not Mr Cuders letter ever so kind? I have also received a letter from Uncle Jimmie Bulloch, which was so sweet and touching that it really almost made me feel like crying. I enclose it to you. I have appreciated greatly the numbers of letters I have received from home and have appreciated still more their contents. I do not think there is a fellow in College who has a family that love him as much as you all do me, and I am sure that there is no one who has a Father who is also his best and most

Theodore Roosevelt Jr.

intimate friend, as you are mine. I have kept the first letter you wrote me and shall do my best to deserve your trust. I do not find it nearly so hard as I expected not to drink and smoke, many of the fellows backing me up. For example, out of the eleven other boys at the table where I am, no less than seven do not smoke and four drink nothing stronger than beer.

I wish you would send in a petition for me to attend the Congregational church here. I do not intend to wait until Christmas before taking a mission class, but shall go into some such work as soon as I get settled at the Church.

My expenses have been very heavy hitherto, with paying my room rent in advance, buying my clothing, etc., but at the worst I will not have to draw upon you till about Christmas time, and I may not have to do it then.

With best love to all I am,
Your Loving Son

P.S. Send back Uncle Jimmie's letter when you have finished.

The younger Roosevelt sent this letter to his father the next spring.

Darling Father, I am spending my Easter vacation with the Minots, who with their usual kindness asked me to do so. I did not go home for I knew I would never be able to study there. I have been working pretty steadily, having finished during the last five days the first book of Horace, the sixth book of Homer, and the Apology of Socrates. In the afternoon some of the boys usually came out to see me, and we spent that time in the open air, and on Saturday evening I went to a party, but during the rest of the time I have worked pretty faithfully. I spent today, Sunday, with the Welds, and went to

Martha and Theodore Roosevelt

their church where, although it was a Unitarian church, I heard a really remarkably good sermon about the attributes of a Christian. Minot Weld takes a great interest in farming, and his livestock were really very interesting.

I have enjoyed all your letters very much, and my conscience reproaches me greatly for not writing you before, but as you may imagine I have had to study pretty hard to make up for lost time, and a letter with me is quite a serious work.

Your Loving Son

Theodore Roosevelt Sr. died in February of 1878, and the younger Theodore wrote these next two letters to his mother that year. In the first, he quotes from that first letter he received from his father while at school.

Cambridge, March 24, 1878

Darling Motherling, I am writing to you today before I go to church; it is a lovely mild morning outside, but not very clear. We have had very bad weather lately, and I have been more fortunate than most of the boys in escaping without catching cold. I have just been looking over a letter of my dear Father's in which he wrote me "Take care of your morals first, your health next and finally your studies." I do not think I ever could do anything wrong while I have his letters; but it seems very sad never to write to him.

I had a three hour examination yesterday; of course I do not yet know what mark I got in it. I shall be home two weeks from next Friday. Give my best love to Bamie and Pussie.*

Your Loving Son

P.S. This bill is all right; I have already paid my bill, which was different. This was your Xmas present to me.

---

* *Theodore's sisters Anna and Corinne*

Darling, Beloved, Little Motherling, I have just loved your dear, funny pathetic little letter; and I am now going to write you the longest letter I ever write and if it is still rather short, you must recollect that it takes Teddy boy a long time to write.

I have enjoyed Charlie's being here extremely, and I think I have been of some service to him. We always go to prayers together. For his own sake I have not been much with him in the daytime, after the first one or two days; but every evening we spend a good part of the time together, in my room or his. His room, by the way, is very homelike and tasteful; but of course it is not yet as cosy as mine is. He is just the same honest, good old fellow as ever, and, unless I am very much mistaken, is going to make a thorough success in every way of college.

My studies do not come very well this year, as I have to work nearly as hard on Saturday as on any other day that is, seven or eight hours. Some of them are extremely interesting, however; especially Political Economy and Metaphysics. These are both rather hard, requiring a good deal of work, but they are even more interesting than my Natural History courses; and all the more so, from the fact that I radically disagree on many points with the men whose books we are reading (Mill and Ferrier). One of my zoological courses is rather dry; but the other I like very much, though it necessitates ten or twelve hours work a week. My German is not very interesting, but I expect my Italian will be when I get farther on.

For exercise I have hitherto relied chiefly on walking, but today I have regularly begun sparring. I have practised a good deal with my rifle, walking to and from the range which is nearly three miles off; my scores have been fair, although not very good. Funnily enough, I have enjoyed quite a burst of popularity since I came back, having been elected into several different clubs.

My own friends have as usual been perfect trumps, and I have been asked to spend Sunday with at least half a dozen of them. Next Saturday Dick Saltonstall is going to drive me over in his tilbury to call on Miss Bessie Whitney; but I shall have to come back to Cambridge to spend Sunday, owing to several reasons Sunday school, etc. But I shall probably spend the following Sunday with him and the Sunday after that I shall probably be with you all.

I indulged in a luxury the other day, buying the "Library of British Poets," and I like my purchase very much; but I have been so busy that I have hardly had time to read it yet. I shall really have to have a new bookcase, for I have nowhere to put all my books. I have not seen Miss Jeannie Hooper yet, but I am going to call on her tomorrow or the day after. We have had quite a cold snap, and I have put on my winter flannels, but I may have to take them off soon, if this weather continues. Have my gun sent in town and cleaned; do'n't take the cartridges in yet. With best love to all I am

Your Loving Son

The Market and Human Values

John Davenport (1975)

John Davenport graduated from Yale in 1926. He was a writer and economic journalist who worked at Barron's Weekly *and* Fortune *magazines and wrote for many other publications. He wrote* The U.S. Economy *in 1964. Davenport died in 1987 at the age of 82. Here Mr. Davenport reminds us that the successful working of the free market, as he puts it, "requires a framework of law, order, and ethical consensus that involves fundamentally an affirmation of certain human values."*

May 1975 *Imprimis*

. . . I am . . . honored to be included in what has become known as the Ludwig von Mises Lecture Series, though this strikes me as inviting a boy (if an old boy) to do a man's work. After all, I am only a working journalist, whereas it is not too much to say that von Mises was a foremost economist of our times, though his role as such was never publicly acknowledged by what we may call The Establishment. He was the leading champion of the free market economy in this century. He was a devastating critic not only of Marxian socialism but of that "soft socialism" which infects so much of our thinking today. He was finally a scholar and a gentleman—a scholar ever ready to bring a vast store of learning to the principles he believed in, and a gentleman in the sense that while he did not suffer fools gladly, he never lost an Old World courtesy and graciousness which he displayed toward friends and foes alike.

I trust this spirit of tolerance is brooding over this meeting tonight as I examine two different aspects of von Mises' thought. The first part of my task is relatively easy. It is to run over rapidly the chief arguments for the market type of economy and to dispose of some of the chief criticisms that are made of it. But the second and main part of my assignment is more difficult and controversial. It is to explore the underpinnings which seem to me necessary to maintain this kind of economy in a hostile world. And here my thesis will be that while the market is self-sustaining in an economic sense, it is not necessarily self-sustaining in a moral sense. It requires a framework of law, order, and ethical consensus that involves fundamentally an affirmation of certain human values. The market is not an end in itself, but the means to higher ends. Definition of these ends leads us inevitably into the domain of philosophy and metaphysics.

Two and One-Half Cheers for the Market

This may appear a brash statement in a so-called scientific age, but the importance of values is really implicit in the arguments which protagonists of the market make for this form of social organization. Let us briefly run over the position. It should not have taken

Selling eggs at a market in Kigali, Rwanda

the Arab sheiks to remind us that by definition all economic goods are scarce, whereas the hunger of man for those goods is well-nigh infinite. In this situation some means must be found for allocating scarce resources—be they work, materials or capital—to human wants. There are basically two ways in which this may be done. In the first place, we might conceive of some all-wise government which would plan out in advance what goods would be produced each year according to some master chart or plan. This is the road taken by Marxian socialism, and to my horror I see it is still being taken seriously by various intellectuals who want to set up a master-planning agency in Washington.

The trouble with such a system, of course, is that government officials are not all-wise when it comes to knowing what people want, and furthermore that the only way by which government can enforce its plans is by using some form of coercion. Economic planning in this sense cannot be squared with human freedom. It cannot even be squared, as von Mises has brilliantly shown, with rational choice and decision. It is easy for governments to decide that their people will probably want some bread to eat. They will also want shoes to put on their feet. But how much bread? How many shoes? These are the questions which officials cannot really answer.

By contrast, a market economy solves the problem of allocation smoothly and efficiently. Assuming that there is a given income distribution, consumers bid for what they want via the price mechanism. This gives them a vote in the economic arena which may be just as important as, and perhaps more important than, their vote at the ballot box. The price system is really a sophisticated signalling system which indicates what should be produced, and in what quantities. The wage system is likewise a signalling device which indicates where labor is most productive. Were labor "taken out of the market," as organized labor has declared it ought to be, we would be left without guide or rudder to determine how the world's work should be accomplished. Finally, profits—the difference between final prices and costs—are the evanescent margin of return that goes to producers and entrepreneurs for bringing labor, materials and capital together before goods can be sold. In a growing economy someone must undertake this risk, and it is far better that it be diffused among individual entrepreneurs and corporations than concentrated in the hands of bureaucrats, whose mistakes in judging human needs are apt to be monumental.

It may come as a surprise to you that even the late John Maynard Keynes had no quarrel with this proposition and concluded his famous *General Theory of Employment, Interest and Money* with a ringing apologia for the market's virtues. Where Keynes broke with the classical tradition was on the question of whether the market is economically self-sustaining. Following Jean Baptiste Say, most economists before Keynes' time had assumed that production in the market creates its own demand: it is the shoes which the shoemaker makes that constitute his real purchasing power for food produced by the farmer. The heart of the General Theory is its attack on Say's law of markets and on the grounds that in a capitalist society, people will attempt to save more than they invest. From this it followed that governments must step in to fill the gap by spending and extending easy credit, if we would maintain full use of our resources.

This was, to say the least, music to the ears of politicians who for thirty-odd years have been presenting us with ever-rising government expenditures and budget deficits. With what results? With the result that inflation has predictably grown apace, while unemployment is still very much with us. . . . The truth seems to be that debasement of the currency and government efforts to pump up so-called "aggregate demand" are a self-defeating process. They may sometimes restore prosperity for a while, but in the end we suffer the worst of both worlds—namely stagflation. It is a tribute to von Mises that he never accepted the Keynesian analysis and hence never accepted its conclusions. He held that society needs a stable currency and that government may have a part in creating it. But given this framework, his position was that unemployed resources are not the result of market forces but rather the result of blockage by powerful labor unions, minimum wage laws, and other forms of government interference. Were he alive today, I suspect that his prescription would be far different from and far simpler than the ideas currently circulating in Congress and in the White House. He would propose elimination of monopoly practices in both industry and labor, combined with a cut in, or elimination of, that most foolish of all taxes—namely the corporate profit tax.

The Limits of Neutrality

I trust that by now I have convinced you that I am a good free marketeer in the Misesian sense of the word. . . . I would like now to advance up more slippery slopes. Granted that the free market is a buttress of liberty, a coordinator of free and spontaneous collaboration, and that given proper adjustment of prices, costs and profits, it has no inherent tendency to run down—granted all this, is it a self-sustaining mechanism in a deeper sense? Can we safely argue for the virtues of the market without paying some attention to virtue itself in the ethical meaning of that word? Can the market succeed without the commitment of society and a nation to certain fundamental values that lie beyond the margin of supply and demand and so-called "indifference curves"?

And here we come to a paradox that involves the very nature of economics and the task of the economist. Von Mises and the Austrian school of economics which he represented freed us from viewing economics as some kind of spurious physical science. Economics, as von Mises made plain in his great book, *Human Action*, is not the study of physical wealth, as some earlier economists had believed. It is fundamentally the study of human choice and preferences in the face of scarce resources; and such choice is obviously psychological in nature. Human behavior is purposive in character, and purposes involving judgment of the future, as well as of the past, cannot be reduced to outward events which can be studied under the microscope. Purposes, it would seem evident, involve ends and values. And yet it was a prime tenet of von Mises' teaching, and certainly is a prime tenet of most modern economists, that economics is value free. Economics studies human choice, but when it comes to human choices it does not pass judgment. To put it bluntly, if men choose to buy cocaine instead of Coca-Cola, that is to be lamented from a social point of view. But the economist qua economist is supposed to keep his mouth shut.

Now I find that this doctrine of ethical neutrality in modern economics has something to be said for it. Economists are busy enough nowadays explaining the intricacies of supply and demand (of oil, for instance) and further explaining the intricacies of the modern money system without getting themselves involved in moral judgments. They perform a highly useful function in explaining that if a man or a nation follows course A, the consequence B is apt to follow. All of us, including government officials, do need to know the probable consequences of alternative lines of action, whether these relate to our personal lives or to social issues, such as rent control, environmental protection, or the inflation of the currency. Yet I also find this doctrine of ethical neutrality on the part of economists a puzzling and at times highly dangerous one. For one thing, few economists, and least of all my libertarian friends, are really able to stick to it. They are, in fact, constantly telling us what we ought to do rather than what we do. Indeed, the whole case for free enterprise and the market economy rests on moral evaluations—that freedom and collaboration are good, and that coercion, in general, is bad.

Moreover, I would remind you that even the most devoted of free marketeers, who are against most interferences by government in the price-profit system, still assume that some governmental framework is necessary if the market is to perform its functions. The market requires the enforcement of property rights and of contract. It assumes a framework of law which has its foundation deep within a moral public consensus. It requires a viable monetary system through which all prices, wages, and profits are registered. Government is involved here whether it adopts some form of gold standard or whether, following the advice of the Chicago school of thought, it adopts some fixed rule for enlarging the money supply, defined in terms of currency and checking accounts. Even if we assume that gold coins will circulate again, still the king's head or the American eagle will presumably be stamped on the coins.

The Market Depends on Order

In short, the market system is dependent upon a right and just political order, and such an order, as Aristotle saw long ago, depends on our making up our minds as to what constitutes justice and other forms of the Good. I conclude that while economists may abstain, if they like, from passing judgment on individual acts of human choice, they cannot possibly remain neutral when it comes to defining the kind of economic and political order which makes freedom of individual choice possible. Perhaps we should allow them the privilege of wearing two hats, so to speak, donning one when they play the role of the economist, but putting on the other when they speak as concerned citizens. But I confess I am not too fond of hat tricks, especially when the same bald or bushy head is discovered beneath the felt!

More seriously, I wish that economists would abstain from making highly dangerous philosophic statements in their efforts to defend their alleged scientific neutrality. If you ask many of them today (not necessarily the followers of von Mises) why they are

Interior of a JUSCO store in Shenzhen, China (2016)

ethically neutral, their answer all too often will be that ethical judgments are, by their nature, "subjective" whereas economic judgments are "objective." Now this is a very dangerous statement. If all that is meant by it is that ethical judgments are psychological and non-physical facts, well and good. But if what is meant is that ethical judgments are *ipso facto* capricious and not subject to general moral laws, then we are in very serious trouble indeed. For in this case, we would be left with no common standards and criteria for evaluating human actions. We would be left in a world where all that could guide us would be the attitude, "You do your thing, and I'll do mine."

But I submit that this business of "you do your thing and I'll do mine" is really an invitation to anarchy or worse, if there be anything worse. It is first cousin to that Relativism and Logical Positivism (i.e., only the measurable is real) which afflict the modern world and which have undermined the very intellectual foundations of what Walter Lippmann once called the Good Society. In the Good Society it must be assumed that there are enduring standards for judging the good, the beautiful, and the true. Indeed, without belief in truth, science itself becomes impossible. In this matter it seems to me that some thinkers of the Middle Ages were far ahead of our latter-day philosophers and economists. For they posited a "natural order" which included not only the so-called facts of nature, as we observe them, but also certain moral laws that were just as real as the facts of nature, even though they could not be observed by the human eye (or the modern microscope). It is my contention that if we are to have the kind of economy free marketeers say they want, and the kind of limited government which most of us want, then some such comprehensive Natural Order must be assumed. In short, we must reconnect economics with philosophy in both branches of the latter subject—with metaphysics, the study of the Real; and with ethics, the study of the Good.

Center portion of a carrot seen through a microscope

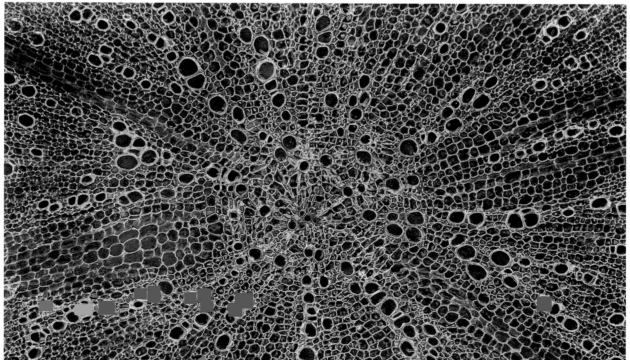

"Get You Wisdom"

Now all this is pretty deep stuff, and I must apologize for having led you into it. Yet my remarks have been dictated by the very nature of the topic assigned. The assignment was not just to defend the market system of economy. It was to try to indicate that we cannot get very far in that defense without considering human values, and that once that Pandora's box is opened we are up against questions as old as Plato and Aristotle.

I would commend both men to your attention, especially Aristotle, who after all wrote the first short treatise on economics as part of a much broader synthesis. For Aristotle economics was part of politics, and politics in its turn flowed out of ethics. And that, when you come to think about it, is more or less how the Founding Fathers of this country proceeded. Madison, Jefferson and Hamilton did not begin by defining a full-blown economic system. On the contrary, they began with certain assumptions about the nature of man, that in the language of the Declaration, "all men are endowed by their Creator with certain inalienable rights." From that assumption flowed their concept of limited rather than unlimited government. And from that assumption flowed an economic system which, while dependent on government for its basic framework, nevertheless took from government the decisions of how the world's work should be performed and how resources—human, material, and capital—should be allocated.

Today this order of priorities has been strangely reversed. We have a vast body of so-called economic knowledge and statistics which is kept in one compartment of our thinking. Then we have our so-called "political scientists" who argue to and fro about the nature of government. Finally, we still do have our philosophers, though . . . their discussion is too often clouded by exercises in symbolic logic or arid studies of semantics and linguistics. Never mind. I hold that there still is a great philosophic tradition, and that some acquaintance with Greek and medieval philosophy will serve you well in your comprehension of modern economics.

I would add furthermore that you will not understand our civilization without exploring that other great tradition which has shaped it—namely Christianity. As Edmund Opitz has argued in his brilliant book, *Religion and Capitalism: Allies, Not Enemies*, there should be no quarrel between the deepest insights of religion and the kind of free economy we wish to preserve against the inroads of the all-powerful state. On the contrary, it is where secularism and materialism have taken deepest hold, as in Communist Russia, that the free economy has been all but eliminated. Religion, Marx held, was the "opium of the people." What force is to reinforce the Good? And what force is to stand up against the princes, principalities and dictators of this our modern secular world? . . .

Reprinted by permission from **Imprimis**, *the national speech digest of Hillsdale College, www.hillsdale.edu.*

Interview with Soviet Refugee
Harvard Project on the Soviet Social System (1950s)

In the early years of the Cold War, sociologist Alex Inkeles and social psychologist Raymond Bauer, both of Harvard University, wanted to study the Soviet social system. Their research idea led to hundreds of interviews with Soviet refugees who had fled to West Germany, Austria, and the United States. These excerpts are from interviews with a woman who had worked as a bookkeeper in a government bank for twelve years. At the time of her interview in 1950, she was 37.

What did your husband do?

My husband held various jobs—he was a longshoreman, a machinist, a captain of small boats, an electrician, he can do everything. He really is very clever, maybe I should not praise him, but he does know everything, he thinks about all that goes on in the world. You should interview him. (*The above words were repeated by the respondent again and again. The question of whether her husband would agree to come, etc. was discussed at the end of the various sessions. During the later sessions she stressed the point that her husband knew so much more than she did, that she was really ignorant, etc. She expressed repeatedly her admiration for "intelligentsia," implying that she herself did not really belong to it, but would have liked to.*)

Was there anything else in Soviet life which made it especially easy or difficult for you to raise your children?

It was hard that women had to work for material necessity. It was so difficult to do something for the children. I took my boy to the nursery in the morning—the nursery was at the bank—when he was a little older he used to cry till he was blue in his face, when he saw me leaving. I used to come away in tears. Especially the law that women could not stop working even if they wanted to was hard.

How did your family get along materially in the last years of your stay in the Soviet Union?

We paid so much for our room, that inspite of my good salary and my husband's stipend we never could come out even at the end of the month. The last two days of the month we had to borrow money. My husband graduated from the university in 1941.

We could not buy clothes and shoes. My husband wore shoes made out of material (*tapochki*) and galoshes on top of them. Shoes cost from 375 to 425 rubles. His stipend was 175 rubles minus 10%. If you ordered shoes in a government store you had to stand in queue every night and every morning for about 6 or 9 months, if you missed one time you lost your place. The shoes there cost 40 to 60 rubles. But of course I could not do it. I always had to pay more for everything I bought. Some students used to buy pieces of material, then sell them on the black market, and live for that money for a while, till they heard that something else could be bought.

Soviet banknote issued in 1938

We had one little room—it was a little hut in a yard (*mazanka*) which belonged to the man who owned the house. Maybe it was a former bathhouse. We had a little stove in it. When the fire was going it became unbearably hot. But in the morning the ink was frozen. Three of us lived in this room. My husband's mother had a room of her own in a different place; his sister also lived alone. It was difficult to get the coal too. It was normed—if you missed your turn in the queue they would deliver the coal to you, but, again, you had to pay more.

Did the abolition of rationing have any effect on your family? (Refers to the abolition of rationing in 1935.)

It was difficult anyway. The food just was not there. At one time you could not find anything else on the shelves but tooth powder and dried mustard. But one thing was there in plenty, always, and that was vodka. You could always buy vodka.

What do you think was your position compared to other families in the Soviet Union?

Like an average family. Many lived much worse. The workers—some of them lived like beggars. I always remember one family in the yard where our hut was; there were 5 children, but only one at a time could get out, because they had one pair of shoes and their mother's jacket between them.

Now think of the family among your acquaintances which lived better than any other. In what circumstances did they live?

I knew some from the office. The husband of one woman was in the NKVD*, the husband of the other worked at a bread factory. He could make "geschafte." I visited her once, she lived much better than we did, but they also had one room only. She did help me to get bread when the times were very hard. You can't imagine the degree of poverty you can see there. . . .

Now I should like to ask you about the relations of your work to your family life. How did your work affect your family life?

I went to work while still in my teens, my mother was at home, and like all mothers, she saw to it that I could get some rest at home.

How did the members of your family feel toward your work?

I had to work, I had no choice. I had younger brothers. I felt, after Father had died, that they had a greater right to learn. But of course I did want to study very much.

The NKVD was a Soviet law enforcement agency that provided traditional police protection and also conducted political repression activities for the ruling party.

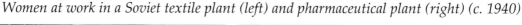

Women at work in a Soviet textile plant (left) and pharmaceutical plant (right) (c. 1940)

In the thirties did you ever think that you were working too hard?

No, not in the youth. My young sister worked as a longshoreman, she lost her leg when she was 19 years old. You had to serve your period as a worker—from 2 to 5 years in order to be allowed to study. You could attend the evening courses any time. But they did not give you any special training. You had no chance at all. If you had no old woman at home who took care of the household you could, but not otherwise.

What moment was the happiest for your family during the thirties?

There were not any, after the thirties. No good years at all. Later, after rationing system was abolished, there were things to buy, but no money to buy anything.

Can you indicate any event or date in your life that marked a turning point in your attitude to the Soviet regime?

Personally I did not have, there was always this feeling—five year plans, loans, constructions. Particularly bad was the law that you could not leave your job.

What Soviet measure had the most positive consequences for your family life in the thirties?

Nothing. '32 and '33 were very hard years.

Do you think that there is social equality for men and women in the Soviet Union?

Only the right to work *(laughs)*. Women became more enslaved than they have been before.

How do you imagine the future development of the Soviet family?

Everything is getting worse and worse, as far as I can learn from the radio. You know, even women and teenagers had to work in the mines.

This interview is reproduced with the permission of Harvard University. The transcript is from the Harvard Project on the Soviet Social System. Schedule A, Vol. 5, Case 49 (interviewer H.B., type A3). Female, 37, Great Russian, Bookkeeper in State Bank. Widener Library, Harvard University Library. Pages 20-23 (seq. 20-23). Accessed October 5, 2016. Persistent Link http://nrs.harvard.edu/urn-3:FHCL:941013?n=20

Principles of Economics
Alfred Marshall (1890)

Alfred Marshall (1842-1924) was a leading English economist. His wife Mary Paley Marshall (1850-1944) was also an economist (she had once been his student), and the two of them worked together. Marshall believed that the diligent study and application of economics could help improve society by reducing poverty and providing new opportunity. He wrote, "The growth of mankind in numbers, in health and strength, in knowledge, ability, and in richness of character is the end of all our studies: but it is an aim to which economics can do no more than contribute some important elements." The following excerpt on "Wealth" is from Principles of Economics, *Chapter 2 of Book Two.*

1. All wealth consists of desirable things; that is, things which satisfy human wants directly or indirectly: but not all desirable things are reckoned as wealth. The affection of friends, for instance, is an important element of wellbeing, but it is not reckoned as wealth, except by a poetic licence. Let us then begin by classifying desirable things, and then consider which of them should be accounted as elements of wealth.

In the absence of any short term in common use to represent all desirable things, or things that satisfy human wants, we may use the term Goods for that purpose.

Desirable things or goods are Material, or Personal and Immaterial. Material goods consist of useful material things, and of all rights to hold, or use, or derive benefits from material things, or to receive them at a future time. Thus they include the physical gifts of nature, land and water, air and climate; the products of agriculture, mining, fishing, and manufacture; buildings, machinery, and implements; mortgages and other bonds; shares in public and private companies, all kinds of monopolies, patent-rights, copyrights; also rights of way and other rights of usage. Lastly, opportunities of travel, access to good scenery, museums, etc. are the embodiment of material facilities, external to a man; though the faculty of appreciating them is internal and personal.

A man's non-material goods fall into two classes. One consists of his own qualities and faculties for action and for enjoyment; such for instance as business ability, professional skill, or the faculty of deriving recreation from reading or music. All these lie within himself and are called internal. The second class are called external because they consist of relations beneficial to him with other people. Such, for instance, were the labour dues and personal services of various kinds which the ruling classes used to require from their serfs and other dependents. But these have passed away; and the chief instances of such relations beneficial to their owner now-a-days are to be found in the good will and business connection of traders and professional men.

Again, goods may be transferable or non-transferable. Among the latter are to be classed a person's qualities and faculties for action and enjoyment (i.e. his internal goods); also such part of his business connection as depends on personal trust in him and cannot

Commercial fishing boat in Alaska

be transferred, as part of his vendible good will; also the advantages of climate, light, air, and his privileges of citizenship and rights and opportunities of making use of public property.

Those goods are free, which are not appropriated and are afforded by nature without requiring the effort of man. The land in its original state was a free gift of nature. But in settled countries it is not a free good from the point of view of the individual. Wood is still free in some Brazilian forests. The fish of the sea are free generally: but some sea fisheries are jealously guarded for the exclusive use of members of a certain nation, and may be classed as national property. Oyster beds that have been planted by man are not free in any sense; those that have grown naturally are free in every sense if they are not appropriated; if they are private property they are still free gifts from the point of view of the nation. But, since the nation has allowed its rights in them to become vested in private persons, they are not free from the point of view of the individual; and the same is true of private rights of fishing in rivers. But wheat grown on free land and the fish that have been landed from free fisheries are not free: for they have been acquired by labour.

2. We may now pass to the question which classes of a man's goods are to be reckoned as part of his wealth. The question is one as to which there is some difference of opinion, but the balance of argument as well as of authority seems clearly to incline in favour of the following answer.

When a man's wealth is spoken of simply, and without any interpretation clause in the context, it is to be taken to be his stock of two classes of goods.

In the first class are those material goods to which he has (by law or custom) private rights of property, and which are therefore transferable and exchangeable. These it will be remembered include not only such things as land and houses, furniture and machinery, and other material things which may be in his single private ownership, but also any shares in public companies, debenture bonds, mortgages and other obligations which he may hold requiring others to pay money or goods to him. On the other hand, the debts which he owes to others may be regarded as negative wealth; and they must be subtracted from his gross possessions before his true net wealth can be found.

Services and other goods, which pass out of existence in the same instant that they come into it, are, of course, not part of the stock of wealth.

In the second class are those immaterial goods which belong to him, are external to him, and serve directly as the means of enabling him to acquire material goods. Thus it excludes all his own personal qualities and faculties, even those which enable him to earn his living; because they are internal. And it excludes his personal friendships, in so far as they have no direct business value. But it includes his business and professional connections, the organization of his business, and—where such things exist—his property in slaves, in labour dues, etc.

This use of the term Wealth is in harmony with the usage of ordinary life: and, at the same time, it includes those goods, and only those, which come clearly within the scope of economic science, as defined in Book I; and which may therefore be called economic goods. For it includes all those things, external to a man, which (i) belong to him, and do not belong equally to his neighbours, and therefore are distinctly his; and which (ii) are directly capable of a money measure,—a measure that represents on the one side the efforts and sacrifices by which they have been called into existence, and, on the other, the wants which they satisfy.

3. A broader view of wealth may indeed be taken for some purposes; but then recourse must be had to a special interpretation clause, to prevent confusion. Thus, for instance, the carpenter's skill is as direct a means of enabling him to satisfy other people's material wants, and therefore indirectly his own, as are the tools in his work-basket; and perhaps it may be convenient to have a term which will include it as part of wealth in a broader use. Pursuing the lines indicated by Adam Smith, and followed by most continental economists, we may define personal wealth so as to include all those energies, faculties, and habits which directly contribute to making people industrially efficient; together with those business connections and associations of any kind, which we have already reckoned as part of wealth in the narrower use of the term. Industrial faculties have a further claim to be regarded as economic in the fact that their value is as a rule capable of some sort of indirect measurement.

The question whether it is ever worth while to speak of them as wealth is merely one of convenience, though it has been much discussed as if it were one of principle.

Confusion would certainly be caused by using the term "wealth" by itself when we desire to include a person's industrial qualities. "Wealth" simply should always mean external wealth only. But little harm, and some good seems likely to arise from the occasional use of the phrase "material and personal wealth."

4. But we still have to take account of those material goods which are common to him with his neighbours; and which therefore it would be a needless trouble to mention when comparing his wealth with theirs; though they may be important for some purposes, and especially for comparisons between the economic conditions of distant places or distant times.

These goods consist of the benefits which he derives from living in a certain place at a certain time, and being a member of a certain state or community; they include civil and military security, and the right and opportunity to make use of public property and institutions of all kinds, such as roads, gaslight, etc., and rights to justice or to a free education. The townsman and the countryman have each of them for nothing many advantages which the other either cannot get at all, or can get only at great expense. Other things being equal, one person has more real wealth in its broadest sense than another, if the place in which the former lives has a better climate, better roads, better water, more wholesome drainage; and again better newspapers, books, and places of amusement and instruction. House-room, food and clothing, which would be insufficient in a cold climate, may be abundant in a warm climate: on the other hand, that warmth which lessens men's physical needs, and makes them rich with but a slight provision of material wealth, makes them poor in the energy that procures wealth.

Many of these things are collective goods. i.e. goods, which are not in private ownership. And this brings us to consider wealth from the social, as opposed to the individual point of view.

5. Let us then look at those elements of the wealth of a nation which are commonly ignored when estimating the wealth of the individuals composing it. The most obvious forms of such wealth are public material property of all kinds, such as roads and canals, buildings and parks, gasworks and waterworks; though unfortunately many of them have been secured not by public savings, but by public borrowings, and there is the heavy "negative" wealth of a large debt to be set against them.

Homeless man in Honolulu, Hawaii (2015)

London and the River Thames

But the Thames has added more to the wealth of England than all its canals, and perhaps even than all its railroads. And though the Thames is a free gift of nature (except in so far as its navigation has been improved), while the canal is the work of man, yet we ought for many purposes to reckon the Thames a part of England's wealth.

German economists often lay stress on the non-material elements of national wealth; and it is right to do this in some problems relating to national wealth, but not in all. Scientific knowledge indeed, wherever discovered, soon becomes the property of the whole civilized world, and may be considered as cosmopolitan rather than as specially national wealth. The same is true of mechanical inventions and of many other improvements in the arts of production; and it is true of music. But those kinds of literature which lose their force by translation, may be regarded as in a special sense the wealth of those nations in whose language they are written. And the organization of a free and well-ordered State is to be regarded for some purposes as an important element of national wealth.

But national wealth includes the individual as well as the collective property of its members. And in estimating the aggregate sum of their individual wealth, we may save some trouble by omitting all debts and other obligations due to one member of a nation from another. For instance, so far as the English national debt and the bonds of an English railway are owned within the nation, we can adopt the simple plan of counting the railway itself as part of the national wealth, and neglecting railway and government bonds altogether. But we still have to deduct for those bonds etc. issued by the English Government or by private Englishmen, and held by foreigners; and to add for those foreign bonds etc. held by Englishmen.

Cosmopolitan wealth differs from national wealth much as that differs from individual wealth. In reckoning it, debts due from members of one nation to those of another may conveniently be omitted from both sides of the account. Again, just as rivers are important elements of national wealth, the ocean is one of the most valuable properties of the world. The notion of cosmopolitan wealth is indeed nothing more than that of national wealth extended over the whole area of the globe.

Individual and national rights to wealth rest on the basis of civil and international law, or at least of custom that has the force of law. An exhaustive investigation of the economic conditions of any time and place requires therefore an inquiry into law and custom; and economics owes much to those who have worked in this direction. But its boundaries are already wide; and the historical and juridical bases of the conceptions of property are vast subjects which may best be discussed in separate treatises.

6. The notion of Value is intimately connected with that of Wealth; and a little may be said about it here. "The word value," says Adam Smith, "has two different meanings, and sometimes expresses the utility of some particular object and sometimes the power of purchasing other goods which the possession of that object conveys." But experience has shown that it is not well to use the word in the former sense.

The value, that is the exchange value, of one thing in terms of another at any place and time, is the amount of that second thing which can be got there and then in exchange for the first. Thus the term value is relative, and expresses the relation between two things at a particular place and time.

Civilized countries generally adopt gold or silver or both as money. Instead of expressing the values of lead and tin, and wood, and corn and other things in terms of one another, we express them in terms of money in the first instance; and call the value of each thing thus expressed its price. If we know that a ton of lead will exchange for fifteen sovereigns at any place and time, while a ton of tin will exchange for ninety sovereigns, we say that their prices then and there are £15 and £90 respectively, and we know that the value of a ton of tin in terms of lead is six tons then and there.

The price of every thing rises and falls from time to time and place to place; and with every such change the purchasing power of money changes so far as that thing goes. If the purchasing power of money rises with regard to some things, and at the same time falls equally with regard to equally important things, its general purchasing power (or its power of purchasing things in general) has remained stationary. This phrase conceals some difficulties, which we must study later on. But meanwhile we may take it in its popular sense, which is sufficiently clear and we may throughout this volume neglect possible changes in the general purchasing power of money. Thus the price of anything will be taken as representative of its exchange value relatively to things in general, or in other words as representative of its general purchasing power.

But if inventions have increased man's power over nature very much, then the real value of money is better measured for some purposes in labour than in commodities. This difficulty however will not much affect our work in the present volume, which is only a study of the "Foundations" of economics.

Finance and Society

Janet Yellen (2015)

Janet Yellen (b. 1946) became the first woman to serve as Chair of the Board of Governors of the Federal Reserve System in 2014. She had previously been Vice Chair of the Federal Reserve and President of the Federal Reserve Bank of San Francisco. Yellen delivered these remarks at the "Finance and Society" conference, sponsored by the Institute for New Economic Thinking, in Washington D.C.

Let me begin by thanking the organizers for inviting me to participate in this important dialogue on the role of finance in society. The financial sector is vital to the economy. A well-functioning financial sector promotes job creation, innovation, and inclusive economic growth. But when the incentives facing financial firms are distorted, these firms may act in ways that can harm society. Appropriate regulation, coupled with vigilant supervision, is essential to address these issues.

Unfortunately, in the years preceding the financial crisis, all too many firms took on risks they could neither measure nor manage. Leverage, interconnectedness, and maturity and liquidity transformation escalated to dangerous levels across the financial system. The result was the most severe financial crisis and economic downturn since the Great Depression. Almost 9 million Americans lost their jobs, roughly twice as many lost their homes, and all too many households ended up underwater on their mortgages and overburdened with debt. To be sure, some individuals and families borrowed unwisely, but too often financial institutions encouraged the behavior that resulted in such excessive debt.

In my remarks today I will discuss some important reasons why the incentives facing financial institutions were distorted and the steps that regulators are taking to realign those incentives.

The Important Role of the Financial Sector

Before discussing the incentives that contributed to the buildup of risk at financial institutions, I would like to highlight the important contributions that the financial sector makes to the economy and society. First and foremost, financial institutions channel society's scarce savings to productive investments, thereby promoting business formation and job creation. Access to capital is important for all firms, but it is particularly vital for startups and young firms, which often lack a sufficient stream of earnings to increase employment and internally finance capital spending. Indeed, research shows that more highly developed financial systems disproportionately benefit entrepreneurship.

The financial sector also helps households save for retirement, purchase homes and cars, and weather unexpected developments. Many financial innovations, such as the increased availability of low-cost mutual funds, have improved opportunities for households to participate in asset markets and diversify their holdings. Expanded credit access has helped households maintain living standards when suffering job loss, illness, or other unexpected contingencies. Technological innovations have increased the ease and convenience with which individuals make and receive payments.

The contribution of the financial sector to household risk management and business investment, as well as the significant contribution of financial-sector

Henry Wells and William Fargo founded Wells Fargo in 1852. The company now operates over 6,000 banking locations in the United States, including the one pictured above in Yountville, California.

development to economic growth, has been documented in many studies. Such research shows that, across countries and over time, financial development, up to a point, has disproportionately benefited the poor and served to alleviate economic inequality.

Distorted Incentives in the Financial Sector

Despite these benefits, as we have seen, actions by financial institutions have the potential to inflict harm on society. Instead of promoting financial security through prudent mortgage underwriting, the financial sector prior to the crisis facilitated a bubble in the housing market and too often encouraged households to take on mortgages they neither understood nor could afford. Recent research has raised important questions about the benefits and costs of the rapid growth of the financial services industry in the United States over the past 40 years.

A combination of responses to distorted incentives by players throughout the financial system created an environment conducive to a crisis. Excessive leverage placed institutions at great risk of insolvency in the event that severe, albeit low-probability, problems materialized. Overreliance on fragile short-term funding by many institutions left the system vulnerable to runs. And excessive risk-taking increased the probability that severe problems would, in fact, materialize. Moreover, regulators—and the structure of the regulatory system itself—did not keep up with changes in the financial sector and were insufficiently attuned to systemic risks. Once concerns began to develop about escalating losses at large firms, insufficient liquidity and capital interacted in an adverse feedback loop. Funding pressures contributed to "fire sales" of financial assets and losses, reducing capital levels and heightening liquidity pressures—culminating in the near collapse of the financial system in late 2008.

Federal Reserve Bank of New York

Capital and liquidity

Several factors encouraged excessive leverage, including market perceptions that some institutions were "too big to fail." Eight Financial institutions also had an incentive to engage in regulatory arbitrage, moving assets to undercapitalized off-balance-sheet vehicles. The complexity of the largest banking organizations also may have impeded market discipline. In addition, financial intermediation outside of the traditional banking sector grew rapidly in the years up to 2007, leaving gaps in the regulatory umbrella. And conflicts in the incentives facing managers, shareholders, and creditors may have induced banks to increase leverage.

To strengthen banks' resilience, the Federal Reserve and the other banking agencies have substantially increased capital requirements. Regulatory minimums for capital relative to risk-weighted assets are significantly higher, and capital requirements now focus on the highest-quality capital, such as common equity. In addition to risk-based standards, bank holding companies and depositories face a leverage ratio requirement. Also, significantly higher capital standards—both risk-weighted and leverage ratios—are being applied to the most systemically important banking organizations. Such surcharges are appropriate because of the substantial harm that the failure of a systemic institution would inflict on the financial system and the economy. Higher capital standards provide large, complex institutions with an incentive to reduce their systemic footprint. We are also employing annual stress tests to gauge large institutions' ability to weather a very severe downturn and distress of counterparties and, importantly, continue lending to households and businesses. Firms that do not meet these standards face restrictions on dividends and share buybacks. As a result of these changes, for the largest banks, Tier 1 common equity—the highest-quality form of capital—has more than doubled since the financial crisis.

New liquidity regulations will also improve incentives in the financial system. Prior to the crisis, institutions' incentives to rely on short-term borrowing to fund investments in riskier or less liquid instruments were distorted in two important ways. First, many investors were willing to accept a very low interest rate on short-term liabilities of financial institutions or on securitizations without demanding adequate compensation for severe-but-unlikely risks, such as a temporary loss of market liquidity. Perhaps these firms expected government support or simply considered illiquidity a very remote possibility. Second, institutions' attempts to shift their holdings once concerns about credit or liquidity risk arose created a fire-sale dynamic that amplified declines in market values, causing unanticipated spillovers onto other institutions and across markets.

Recently implemented regulations aim to strengthen liquidity. For example, a new liquidity coverage ratio requires internationally active banking organizations to hold sufficient high-quality liquid assets to meet their projected net cash outflows during a 30-day stress period. A new process—the Comprehensive Liquidity Analysis and Review—sets supervisory expectations for liquidity-risk management and evaluates institutions' practices against these benchmarks. A proposal for a net stable funding ratio would require better liquidity management at horizons beyond that covered by the liquidity coverage ratio. A proposed capital surcharge for the largest firms would discourage overreliance on short-term wholesale funding. Also, the Securities and Exchange Commission has adopted changes in regulations that may help avoid future runs on prime money market mutual funds (that is, money funds that invest primarily in corporate debt securities). And reforms in the triparty repo market have reduced risks associated with intraday exposures.

Large, complex institutions and too big to fail

In the aftermath of the crisis, the Congress tasked the banking regulators with challenging and changing the perception that any financial institution is too big to fail by ensuring that even very large banking organizations can be resolved without harming financial stability. Steps are under way to achieve this objective. In particular, banking organizations are required to prepare "living wills"—plans for their rapid and orderly resolution in the event of insolvency. Regulators are considering requiring that bank holding companies have sufficient total loss-absorbing capacity, including long-term debt, to enable them to be wound down without government support. In addition, the Federal Deposit Insurance Corporation has designed a strategy that it could deploy (known as Single Point of Entry) to resolve a systemically important institution in an orderly manner.

The crisis also revealed that risk management at large, complex financial institutions was insufficient to handle the risks that some firms had taken. Compensation systems all too frequently failed to appropriately account for longer-term risks undertaken by employees. And lax controls in some cases contributed to unethical and illegal behavior by banking organizations and their employees. The Federal Reserve has made improving risk management and internal controls a top priority. For example, the Comprehensive Capital Analysis and Review, which includes the stress tests that I mentioned, also involves an evaluation to ensure firms have a sound process in place for measuring and monitoring the risks they are taking and for matching their capital levels to those risks. Also, supervisors from the Fed and other agencies have pressed firms to improve their internal controls and to make their boards of directors more directly responsible for compensation decisions and employee conduct.

Changes to Regulatory and Supervisory Focus

As I noted, the financial crisis revealed weaknesses in our nation's system for supervising and regulating the financial industry. Prior to the crisis, regulatory agencies, including the Federal Reserve, focused on the safety and soundness of individual firms—as required by their legislative mandate at the time—rather than the stability of the financial system as a whole. Our regulatory system did not provide any supervisory watchdog with responsibility for identifying and addressing risks associated with activities and institutions that were outside the regulatory perimeter. The rapid growth of the "shadow" nonbank financial sector left significant gaps in regulation.

In response, the Dodd-Frank Wall Street Reform and Consumer Protection Act of 2010 (Dodd-Frank Act) expanded the mandate and authority of the Federal Reserve to allow it to consider risks to financial stability in supervising financial firms under its charge. Within the Federal Reserve System, we have reorganized our supervision of the most systemically important institutions to emphasize what we call a "horizontal perspective," which examines institutions as a group and in comparative terms, focusing on their interaction with the broader financial system. We also created a new office within the Fed to identify emerging risks to stability in the broader financial system—both the bank and nonbank financial sectors—and to develop policies to mitigate systemic risk. The Dodd-Frank Act created the interagency Financial Stability Oversight Council, chaired by the Treasury Secretary, and the Federal Reserve is a member. It is charged with identifying systemically important financial institutions and systemically risky activities that are not subject to consolidated supervision and designating those institutions and activities for appropriate supervision. And it is charged with encouraging greater information sharing and policy coordination across financial regulatory agencies.

Where We Stand

My topic is broad, and my time is short. Let me end with three thoughts. First, I believe that we and other supervisory agencies have made significant progress in addressing incentive problems within the financial sector, especially within the banking sector. Second, policymakers, including those of us at the Federal Reserve, remain watchful for areas in need of further action or in which the steps taken to date need to be adjusted. And, third, engagement with the broader public is crucial to ensuring that any future steps move our financial system closer to where it should be. Active debate and discussion of these issues at this conference and in other forums is important to improve our understanding of the challenges that remain.

Federal Reserve Bank of Atlanta

The Candlemakers' Petition
Frederic Bastiat (1845)

The French political writer Frederic Bastiat (1801-1850) published this supposed petition to the French National Assembly in 1845 to ridicule the idea of favorable regulations and tariff protection for a particular industry instead of a policy of free trade. "Albion" is a reference to Great Britain, a long-time rival of France. The petition humorously says that the sun shows respect for Great Britain because it is a foggy island and thus the people there must buy more candles.

A PETITION From the Manufacturers of Candles, Tapers, Lanterns, Sticks, Street Lamps, Snuffers, and Extinguishers, and from Producers of Tallow, Oil, Resin, Alcohol, and Generally of Everything Connected with Lighting.

To the Honorable Members of the Chamber of Deputies.

Gentlemen:

You are on the right track. You reject abstract theories and have little regard for abundance and low prices. You concern yourselves mainly with the fate of the producer. You wish to free him from foreign competition, that is, to reserve the domestic market for domestic industry.

We come to offer you a wonderful opportunity for your—what shall we call it? Your theory? No, nothing is more deceptive than theory. Your doctrine? Your system? Your principle? But you dislike doctrines, you have a horror of systems, as for principles, you deny that there are any in political economy; therefore we shall call it your practice—your practice without theory and without principle.

We are suffering from the ruinous competition of a rival who apparently works under conditions so far superior to our own for the production of light that he is flooding the domestic market with it at an incredibly low price; for the moment he appears, our sales cease, all the consumers turn to him, and a branch of French industry whose ramifications are innumerable is all at once reduced to complete stagnation. This rival, which is none other than the sun, is waging war on us so mercilessly we suspect he is being stirred up against us by perfidious Albion (excellent diplomacy nowadays!), particularly because he has for that haughty island a respect that he does not show for us.

We ask you to be so good as to pass a law requiring the closing of all windows, dormers, skylights, inside and outside shutters, curtains, casements, bull's-eyes, deadlights, and blinds—in short, all openings, holes, chinks, and fissures through which the light of the sun is wont to enter houses, to the detriment of the fair industries with which, we are proud to say, we have endowed the country, a country that cannot, without betraying ingratitude, abandon us today to so unequal a combat.

Be good enough, honorable deputies, to take our request seriously, and do not reject it without at least hearing the reasons that we have to advance in its support.

Eguisheim, Alsace, France

First, if you shut off as much as possible all access to natural light, and thereby create a need for artificial light, what industry in France will not ultimately be encouraged?

If France consumes more tallow, there will have to be more cattle and sheep, and, consequently, we shall see an increase in cleared fields, meat, wool, leather, and especially manure, the basis of all agricultural wealth.

If France consumes more oil, we shall see an expansion in the cultivation of the poppy, the olive, and rapeseed. These rich yet soil-exhausting plants will come at just the right time to enable us to put to profitable use the increased fertility that the breeding of cattle will impart to the land.

Our moors will be covered with resinous trees. Numerous swarms of bees will gather from our mountains the perfumed treasures that today waste their fragrance, like the flowers from which they emanate. Thus, there is not one branch of agriculture that would not undergo a great expansion.

The same holds true of shipping. Thousands of vessels will engage in whaling, and in a short time we shall have a fleet capable of upholding the honor of France and of gratifying the patriotic aspirations of the undersigned petitioners, chandlers, etc.

But what shall we say of the specialities of Parisian manufacture? Henceforth you will behold gilding, bronze, and crystal in candlesticks, in lamps, in chandeliers, in candelabra sparkling in spacious emporia compared with which those of today are but stalls.

There is no needy resin-collector on the heights of his sand dunes, no poor miner in the depths of his black pit, who will not receive higher wages and enjoy increased prosperity.

It needs but a little reflection, gentlemen, to be convinced that there is perhaps not one Frenchman, from the wealthy stockholder of the Anzin Company to the humblest vendor of matches, whose condition would not be improved by the success of our petition.

We anticipate your objections, gentlemen; but there is not a single one of them that you have not picked up from the musty old books of the advocates of free trade. We defy you to utter a word against us that will not instantly rebound against yourselves and the principle behind all your policy.

Will you tell us that, though we may gain by this protection, France will not gain at all, because the consumer will bear the expense?

We have our answer ready:

You no longer have the right to invoke the interests of the consumer. You have sacrificed him whenever you have found his interests opposed to those of the producer. You have done so in order to encourage industry and to increase employment. For the same reason you ought to do so this time too.

Indeed, you yourselves have anticipated this objection. When told that the consumer has a stake in the free entry of iron, coal, sesame, wheat, and textiles, "Yes," you reply, "but the producer has a stake in their exclusion." Very well, surely if consumers have a stake in the admission of natural light, producers have a stake in its interdiction.

"But," you may still say, "the producer and the consumer are one and the same person. If the manufacturer profits by protection, he will make the farmer prosperous. Contrariwise, if agriculture is prosperous, it will open markets for manufactured goods." Very well, If you grant us a monopoly over the production of lighting during the day, first of all we shall buy large amounts of tallow, charcoal, oil, resin, wax, alcohol, silver, iron, bronze, and crystal to supply our industry; and, moreover, we and our numerous suppliers, having become rich, will consume a great deal and spread prosperity into all areas of domestic industry.

Candle making

Will you say that the light of the sun is a gratuitous gift of Nature, and that to reject such gifts would be to reject wealth itself under the pretext of encouraging the means of acquiring it?

But if you take this position, you strike a mortal blow at your own policy; remember that up to now you have always excluded foreign goods because and in proportion as they approximate gratuitous gifts. You have only half as good a reason for complying with the demands of other monopolists as you have for granting our petition, which is in complete accord with your established policy; and to reject our demands precisely because they are better founded than anyone else's would be tantamount to accepting the equation: + x + = -; in other words, it would be to heap absurdity upon absurdity.

Labor and Nature collaborate in varying proportions, depending upon the country and the climate, in the production of a commodity. The part that Nature contributes is always free of charge; it is the part contributed by human labor that constitutes value and is paid for.

If an orange from Lisbon sells for half the price of an orange from Paris, it is because the natural heat of the sun, which is, of course, free of charge, does for the former what the latter owes to artificial heating, which necessarily has to be paid for in the market.

Thus, when an orange reaches us from Portugal, one can say that it is given to us half free of charge, or, in other words, at half price as compared with those from Paris.

Now, it is precisely on the basis of its being semigratuitous (pardon the word) that you maintain it should be barred. You ask: "How can French labor withstand the competition of foreign labor when the former has to do all the work, whereas the latter has to do only half, the sun taking care of the rest?" But if the fact that a product is half free of charge leads you to exclude it from competition, how can its being totally free of charge induce you to admit it into competition? Either you are not consistent, or you should, after excluding what is half free of charge as harmful to our domestic industry, exclude what is totally gratuitous with all the more reason and with twice the zeal.

To take another example: When a product—coal, iron, wheat, or textiles—comes to us from abroad, and when we can acquire it for less labor than if we produced it ourselves, the difference is a gratuitous gift that is conferred up on us. The size of this gift is proportionate to the extent of this difference. It is a quarter, a half, or three-quarters of the value of the product if the foreigner asks of us only three-quarters, one-half, or one-quarter as high a price. It is as complete as it can be when the donor, like the sun in providing us with light, asks nothing from us. The question, and we pose it formally, is whether what you desire for France is the benefit of consumption free of charge or the alleged advantages of onerous production. Make your choice, but be logical; for as long as you ban, as you do, foreign coal, iron, wheat, and textiles, in proportion as their price approaches zero, how inconsistent it would be to admit the light of the sun, whose price is zero all day long!

U.S. Customs and Border Protection

(2016)

U.S. Customs and Border Protection (CBP) is the unified border agency within the Department of Homeland Security charged with the management, control and protection of our nation's borders at and between the official ports of entry. These press releases from the CBP highlight different aspects of the agency's work during one week in August

Border Patrol Rescues 32 Locked in a Cold Storage Trailer

Release Date: August 27, 2016

LAREDO, Texas – On Aug. 24, 2016, at approximately 10:10 p.m., Border Patrol agents from the Laredo Sector Border Patrol discovered and rescued multiple individuals at the Interstate Highway 35 Checkpoint.

Border Patrol agents assigned to the Border Patrol Checkpoint on Interstate Highway 35 encountered a cold storage Peterbilt Tractor-trailer at the primary inspection lane. After a service canine alerted to possible narcotics or humans concealed within the vehicle, agents performed an x-ray scan using the Vehicle and Cargo Inspection System (VACIS).

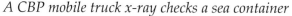

A CBP mobile truck x-ray checks a sea container

Border Patrol agents observed several people within the trailer, quickly unsealed the doors and found them trapped inside with no apparent means to escape. A total of 32 people from Mexico and Central America were rescued.

"We are fortunate that our Border Patrol agents found these people in time to prevent possible serious injury and a loss of life. We ask the community to report suspicious activity. Together we can stop smugglers, who have no regard for human life, from exploiting these persons' desperate desire to enter the Unites States," said Chief Patrol Agent Mario Martinez.

The Laredo Sector Border Patrol will continue to warn against the dangers of people crossing illegally into the United States through our Border Safety Initiative (BSI). BSI is a humanitarian, bi-national strategy designed to reduce migrant deaths, educate and inform potential migrants of the dangers and hazards of crossing the border illegally, and to respond to those who are in life-threatening situations.

The case has been turned over to Homeland Security Investigations (HSI), Laredo Office for further investigation.

CBP agriculture specialists nab pests, invasive seeds in North Dakota
Release Date: August 30, 2016

PORTAL, North Dakota—U.S. Customs and Border Protection (CBP) Office of Field Operations agriculture specialists discovered multiple pests and invasive seeds while conducting inspections of rail containers at the Portal Port of Entry rail facility.

Earlier this month, agriculture specialists normally assigned to work in Pembina, North Dakota, and International Falls, Minnesota, joined staff at the Portal Port of Entry and conducted a two-day special enforcement operation.

Over the two days, several rail containers that had been targeted for inspection were examined, which revealed several unwanted pests and invasive seeds. A total of 55 different pests were submitted for identification. CBP agriculture specialists regularly inspect commercial shipments to see if they meet

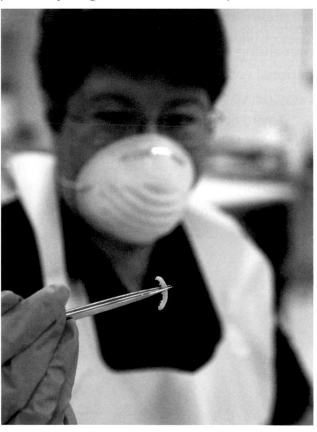

A CBP agriculture specialist discovers a pest potentially dangerous to American crops

of his patients. William set aside his mornings—prime earning hours for physicians—to conduct experiment after experiment in the small attic of his house in Hastings, Michigan. He rejected the standard method of making pills from paste; instead he created them from "starter particles." He added powdered drugs and moistening agents while he rotated the particles in a revolving pan. The result was a pill that held its contents, but was soft enough to dissolve easily when swallowed.

In 1885, William—Dr. William E. Upjohn—patented his "friable pill" and started the Upjohn Pill and Granule Company in a small brick building in nearby Kalamazoo. His first price list included 186 formulas for everything from quinine pills to iron pills. In the next six years, Upjohn sold millions of pills and generated the capital needed to enter the pharmaceutical market. In the next forty years, he marketed a superior product that sold widely throughout the United States and even the world. His business did not rely on any natural resources found in his state. He could have done his work anywhere. He stayed in Michigan because its economic system triggered his entrepreneurial energy and allowed him to keep the profits he made.

Let's look at another example that parallels the Upjohn story. One Sunday evening in 1927 in the town of Fremont, a young man named Dan waited impatiently for his wife Dorothy to feed their daughter, who was seven months old. They had a social engagement that evening, and Dan was ready to go. He paced back and forth, looking at his watch and waiting. Dorothy, meanwhile, was tediously straining vegetables into a bowl, piece by piece. Soon her fidgety husband stomped into the kitchen, pleading with his wife to hurry up. That's when Dorothy decided to teach him a lesson. "To press the point," Dorothy later recalled, "I dumped a whole container of peas into a strainer and bowl, placed them in Dan's lap, and asked him to see how he'd like to do that three times a day, seven days a week."

Dan got the message. The next day, when he went to work in his family-owned cannery, he had an idea for something new to put in the cans: strained baby food. During the next year, Dan Gerber would establish the baby food market and then dominate it for decades. He test-marketed strained carrots, peas, prunes, and spinach on babies in Fremont. Then he persuaded grocery stores around the country to carry his product. Thousands of mothers chose to pay to save time and energy; they bought 590,000 cans of Gerber's baby food at 15 cents per can in the first year.

Gerber baby food for sale (2016)

Gerber, like Upjohn, did not need his state's resources to flourish. But he needed Michigan's entrepreneurial spirit and freedom from heavy taxation and stifling regulation. In the late 1800s and early 1900s, of course, the whole United States had a small federal government, no income tax, and strong constitutional support for free enterprise. But Michigan, through its liberating state constitution, went out of the way to limit government and stake the state's future on what its entrepreneurs could accomplish.

Business was booming. Even blacks, who were subject to much discrimination, had opportunities in Michigan. A good example is the great inventor Elijah McCoy. McCoy was born in 1843 in Canada, where his parents had fled from Kentucky to escape slavery.

After the Civil War ended and blacks were legally free, McCoy settled in Ypsilanti, where he began work for the Michigan Central Railroad as a locomotive fireman.

He immediately applied his skills to a major problem: the dangerous overheating of locomotives. Trains had to stop regularly to oil engine parts to reduce friction. If they stopped infrequently, the overheating could damage parts or start fires. If they stopped too often, freight and passengers would be delayed. McCoy invented a lubricating cup that oiled engine parts as the train was moving. He secured a patent in 1872 and steadily improved the device.

Others tried to imitate his invention, but he kept ahead of them with superior engineering skills. The standard of quality was so high that to distinguish his product from cheaper imitations people began calling it "the real McCoy."

Elijah McCoy (1913)

McCoy showed remarkable creative energy during the next half-century. He received 51 more patents for inventions ranging from a forerunner of the ironing board to a special cup for administering medicine. Not even old age dimmed his creative light. When he was 77, he patented an improved air brake lubricator; when he was 80, he patented a vehicle tire.

McCoy was not an isolated example of black entrepreneurship. In 1887, Fred Pelham was president of his class at the University of Michigan. From there he became assistant civil engineer with the Michigan Central Railroad. His innovations in structure and design included the "skew arch" bridge. Some of the twenty bridges he built still stand in Michigan today.

Why, then, did so much of the building of the American empire take place in Michigan? To find out, we need to see why Michigan chose free enterprise over government direction. Then we need to study what some of the state's early residents accomplished. In a recent book on this subject, I examined seven of them:

John Jacob Astor, who began fur trading in the Michigan Territory in the early 1800s; Stevens T. Mason, a politician whose state-financed railroad scheme backfired, leading him to belatedly champion free enterprise; Henry Crapo, who helped Michigan become the top lumber-producing state in the union; Henry Ford and William Durant, who made the state the world center for automobile manufacturing, one of the greatest industries of the 20th century; Herbert Dow, who helped break forever European monopolies in chemicals; and Will Kellogg, who introduced flaked cereal, thus changing breakfast habits throughout the Western world.

Succeeding Through Serving Others

These men, with the exception of Mason, were indeed empire builders. The word *empire* comes from the Latin *imperium*, or dominion, and *imperare*, which means to command. The best entrepreneurs fulfill these terms. They dominate their industries and extend their command into new territories around the world. From a central location or capital, they expand their markets and control their industries—not by force but by service: selling products that customers want at competitive prices.

Several points are striking about Michigan's most successful entrepreneurs. First, they built their empires locally—in places like Flint, Midland, Battle Creek, and Dearborn— but expanded them to locations around the nation and then around the world. Many middle class families, whether in New York, Paris, or Buenos Aires, ate Cornflakes for breakfast, drove Chevys to work, used Dow's bleach on their clothes and his bromine for sedatives. Kellogg, Durant, Dow, and Ford, like Astor in an earlier generation, built empires that shaped the world long after their deaths.

Second, they were highly inventive and highly creative. They not only took risks and carved out markets but also introduced many of the key products needed to establish their empires of service. Dow heads the list with his 107 patents, but Kellogg and Ford

Kellogg's cereal for sale in Meppen, Germany (2014)

were in some ways even more impressive. Kellogg, with help from his brother, practically invented the whole flaked-cereal industry. His example inspired others, and, from Rice Krispies to All-Bran, Kellogg cereals set the standard. Henry Ford, among other things, invented the V-8 engine and assembled the team that made plate glass from a continuous ribbon with no hand work. More than this, his whole company was for years an experiment in creativity—from the assembly line to raising wages to cutting work hours.

A third point to remember about Michigan's entrepreneurs is that they wanted to build empires more than they wanted to make money. Of course, the two usually go together. But making such a distinction is critical to understanding the mind of Michigan's early entrepreneurs. Money, or capital, is valued not as an end but as a means to create an economic empire. In the same way, weapons are valued by an army not as an end but as a means to conquer people and territory. Capital is a tool for the entrepreneur in the same way that weapons are tools for the soldier. The big difference here is that an army creates and expands its empire by force; entrepreneurs create and expand their empires by service to others. A soldier controls by using weapons to threaten violence; an entrepreneur persuades by using capital to offer better products at lower prices.

The challenge to entrepreneurs in an undeveloped area like Michigan was raising capital. John Jacob Astor made his money in New York and plowed it into Michigan. Henry Crapo forged a complex network for wheedling capital from his cautious friends in New Bedford and Boston. Herbert Dow lobbied established businessmen in Cleveland. Will Kellogg sought help from a large investor in St. Louis. By the early 1900s, some Michigan cities were rich enough to support their own entrepreneurs. Henry Ford, with mixed success, solicited a variety of investors in Detroit. William Durant tapped the bankers of Flint—first to build carriages and later, Chevrolets.

With capital in hand, the next step was mobilizing workers behind tough and compelling goals. For Ford, the task was building a reliable car so cheaply that middle class Americans could afford it. For Dow, the issue was survival—how to make bleach, bromine, and dyes cheap enough to compete with European cartels. Kellogg and Durant started with high quality products, so the challenge was in marketing: how to get every American to eat a bowl of Cornflakes and to ride in a blue ribbon carriage.

Early Model T assembly line in Highland Park, Michigan

Workers, like soldiers, will usually follow if the leader knows how to lead. The prevailing theory of management said that employees must be controlled, directed, and closely supervised. Michigan's entrepreneurs, by contrast, tended to give their workers freedom to create, personal responsibility for hard tasks, and rewards and bonuses for jobs well done. Henry Ford wanted the best workers in Michigan, and he launched the "five dollar day" to get them. Will Kellogg liked to reward worthy employees with a handshake that contained a $20 bill. Herbert Dow might argue loudly with his chemists, but he trusted their abilities, paid them well, and turned them loose to invent and create.

Fourth, Michigan's empire builders all followed biblical principles, even though not all of them were practicing Christians. As George Gilder has observed, they truly believed in the commandments, "Do unto others as you would have them do unto you" and "Give and you will be given unto." He also notes that they suppressed their own desires to serve the desires of others, and they committed their work and wealth to bring to the world new goods that they knew might well be rejected.

The faith of these empire builders was continually tested. They all either went bankrupt or verged on it at some critical point in their lives. They did not experience the steady growth and predictable success that one might have expected from talented men with good and popular products to sell. They took leaps of faith, fell flat on their faces, then desperately changed their tactics and tried to raise new capital to stay afloat.

Herbert Dow, for example, failed in his first business venture; in his second, he was ousted from control. On his third try, he went into the bleach business, and he calculated his costs of production very carefully. Then came the unexpected. He was immediately challenged by a British cartel, which cut its price for bleach in half. Dow had to find ways to slash costs even more or he would fail a third time. When Will Kellogg finally broke loose from his old menial job, he calculated the cost of making Cornflakes. What he didn't count on was having his factory burn down and his main competitor buy up all the new equipment for making cereal. Henry Crapo floundered in the lumber business until he doubled his risks, bought some sawmills, and began to process and market his own timber. Only after years of cutting costs, improving products, and removing bottlenecks did these men make breakthroughs. Henry Ford refused to listen to the experts, who claimed that steam and electricity were the only practical options for automobiles; instead he developed the internal combustion engine. When Ford was losing sales to competitors, he was forced to adopt drastic measures, slashing the price of the Model T by 20 percent. Sales doubled, but who could have known his gamble would pay off? Only hindsight makes such accomplishments seem easy and inevitable.

Ford "Cycle of Production" display at the New York World's Fair (1939-1940)

The fifth trait of Michigan's empire builders was their fierce independence and their aversion to monopoly and to government solutions to problems. Even before statehood, John Jacob Astor displayed this independence with his American Fur Company when he challenged the government fur factories. The next two generations of Michigan entrepreneurs were among the most independent our nation has ever produced. When Henry Crapo served as governor, his defense of the Constitution of 1850 was intense. He sacrificed popularity, party loyalty, and even his health so that he could veto bill after bill that allowed Michigan cities to subsidize local railroads. Crapo was an expert in attracting outside capital, and he knew the dangers that subsidizing railroads posed to individual liberty and to the integrity and credit rating of his adopted state.

In 1919, fifty years after Crapo's death, his grandson, William Durant, was president of General Motors. In a speech that year, Durant sounded just like his grandfather:

> Competition is the life of trade. I stand for competition. I am opposed to monopoly or control on the principle that it destroys initiative, curtails freedom of action, and frequently leads to abuse of power.

Durant's chief competitor, Henry Ford, could not have agreed more. Ford, in fact, was one of the main reasons the auto industry was so free of monopoly and government control. The resulting pressure of competition improved the quality of cars dramatically — automatic starters, hydraulic brakes, and gas gauges became standard by 1930. With Ford and General Motors locked in combat, the American consumer was the winner. Vehicle sales soared from 181,000 in 1910 to over 5,000,000 in 1929. Trucks for moving freight were part of this rise because the railroad industry, with its price fixing and government controls, was too expensive and too cumbersome.

In the 1930s, Ford led the opposition to President Roosevelt's National Recovery Administration (NRA). Auto companies were pressured to join together to regulate wages, prices, and hours of work. Ford refused to join. Durant was out at General Motors, so he stood virtually alone. When the federal bureaucrats refused to accept his low bids on government contracts, Ford ignored them and survived on private sector business. The irony here is that Ford already led American industry in paying high wages. Why should

National Recovery Administration, Washington, D.C. (1935)

a government agency set minimum wages, Ford wondered, when he set the standard long before the 1930s? Referring to the NRA auto code, he said, "If we tried to live up to it, we would have to live down to it." Before the government could coerce him into joining the NRA's auto cartel, however, the Supreme Court stepped in and declared the NRA unconstitutional.

If possible, Herbert Dow opposed government activism even more strongly than Ford (except for protective tariffs). Dow actually built his chemical empire by challenging government-supported monopolies. In the 1890s, when Dow entered the chemical business, the British and the Germans had long dominated the chemical industry—and their governments encouraged them to form cartels and to control prices and production. American chemical companies not only lagged far behind Europe, they often faced predatory price cutting whenever they sold abroad. Some American companies, like DuPont, carved niches in special markets, such as gunpowder. But Dow was the first American to openly challenge the Europeans where they were already established—in areas like bleach, bromides, and indigo.

Dow Chemical Plant on Lake Michigan (1973)

In doing so, Dow gave the world a model demonstration in how to defeat predatory price cutting. Before Dow, many people could argue against monopolies and oligopolies this way: "If a corporation is big enough, it can cut prices below cost, drive out its small competitors, and then raise prices to whatever it wants to charge. Therefore, we need government regulation, antitrust laws perhaps, to control large greedy corporations." Dow showed how a small company could beat large firms. In the bromide industry, the Germans cut prices below cost with the specific intent of destroying Dow. In response, Dow secretly bought the cheap German bromides, repackaged them, and sold them at a profit in markets around the world! It was a brilliant strategy. During the early 1900s, Dow regularly expanded his chemical empire when the Germans tried to reap large profits from their cartels in indigo, magnesium, and other products.

New Empires

The 1920s was the last decade when an empire could be built without major interference from the federal government. With the Great Depression came the rapid expansion of federal powers. The Smoot-Hawley Tariff, passed in 1930, was the most restrictive tariff in U.S. history. The Reconstruction Finance Corporation had the government financing banks, railroads, and other industries. The Agricultural Adjustment Act regulated farm production; the National Industrial Recovery Act regulated most corporations—except for the Ford Motor Company. And later the Wagner Act shifted the balance of power from the entrepreneurs to the labor union bosses.

The tax revenues needed to pay for these and other new programs were astonishing. The top federal income tax rate in 1930 was 24 percent. In 1932, under President Hoover, the rate was hiked to 63 percent. Under President Roosevelt the rate was first raised to 79 percent and later jumped to over 90 percent. Large inheritance taxes scooped up what the income tax missed. During the 1930s, the empire builders were, in effect, asked to send their empires to Washington.

Herbert Dow died in 1930, before he could denounce such a request. William Durant lost his fortune on the stock market, before Washington could confiscate it. Ford and Kellogg chose to shelter their wealth from the swirling storms. With the Ford and Kellogg foundations quickly in place they preserved their empires, but they were no longer the commanders. The era of "laissez faire" was essentially over. A new breed of businessman began to emerge: the "political entrepreneur," who sought special concessions from government and empires built on political power instead of service. The old "market entrepreneur," who found success through creating better products at a lower cost, found it harder and harder to survive. . . .

Reprinted by permission from **Imprimis**, *the national speech digest of Hillsdale College, www.hillsdale.edu.*

Ford Advertisement (1937)

What Makes for Success?

Kemmons Wilson (1997)

Kemmons Wilson (1913-2003) quit high school during the Depression when his mother lost her job. He began making money by selling popcorn outside theaters. In 1952, he opened the first Holiday Inn in Memphis, Tennessee. Today, Holiday Inn properties make up one of the largest hotel chains in the world. Mr. Wilson has been called "the father of the modern innkeeping industry." In this speech, Mr. Wilson shares his principles for personal and economic success.

I am often asked, "What makes for success?" I know that most people regard success as the attainment of wealth. But I think that the most successful people are those who take pride in their work, pride in their family, and pride in their country. It is great to attain wealth, but money is really just one way—and hardly the best way—to keep score.

As parents, we all try to share with our children the knowledge we have gained through our own experiences, which usually include many successes and failures. As an entrepreneur, I have also tried to pass on to my children the importance of business and economics and how each relates to the world in which we live. I am a very fortunate man in that my three sons are partners in my work and they appear to have learned their lessons well. My only problem now is that I have to listen to *their* advice.

That was not the case back in 1951 when I took my wife and our five children on a vacation to Washington, D.C. Those were the good old days when the children still had to mind us and listen to our advice. A motel room only cost about $8.00 a night, but the proprietors inevitably charged $2.00 extra for each child. So the $8.00 charge soon ballooned into an $18.00 charge for my family. If we could get a room with two beds, our two daughters slept in one, and Dorothy and I slept in the other. Our three boys slept on the floor in sleeping bags. Sometimes there was a dollar deposit for the key and another dollar for the use of a television. This made my Scotch blood boil, and, after a few nights, I told my wife how unfair I thought all the extra charges were. They did not encourage couples to travel, especially with their children.

I was active in the construction business at the time, so I also told her that building a motel, or even a hotel, was no more difficult than building a home. I was seized by an idea: I could build a chain of affordable hotels, stretching from coast to coast. Families could travel cross-country and stay at one of my hotels every night. Most travel in 1951 was by automobile, but without the benefit of the interstate system we are so familiar with now, so this kind of service would be unique. Dorothy asked me how many hotels I thought it would take, and I threw out the number 400. She laughed and said it couldn't be done. Now, my mother, who raised me alone after my father died, had instilled in me the belief that I could do anything if I worked hard enough and wanted it badly enough. At that moment, I wanted it desperately just so my wife wouldn't laugh at me.

I learned a lot of things on that vacation. I measured the bedrooms and bathrooms in every motel in which we stayed, and by the time we returned home, I knew exactly what kind of hotels I wanted to build. I learned a few things from my kids, too. When you travel with five children all under the age of eight, you learn, for example, about the vital importance of a swimming pool. Have you ever stopped at a motel or hotel with your children when their first words weren't, "Make sure it has a swimming pool"? I also learned about the importance of having a doctor and a dentist on call. One of our children fell ill with a toothache and another one had a high fever. We had to use the telephone book and make a number of calls in order to track down professionals who were willing to help.

Features that we take for granted today were ones I determined would be standard in my hotels: free televisions, in-room telephones, ice machines, and restaurants. And, of course, children would stay free.

At home in Memphis, I showed a draftsman named Eddy Bluestein the lists and diagrams of what I wanted. Several days later, he brought me his rough sketches. On the first, he had sketched out in script the words, "Holiday Inn," a fictional name he had seen in a Bing Crosby movie the previous evening.

I heartily approved, and the first Holiday Inn opened in Memphis in 1952. Before it was finished, there were others under construction in the three remaining corners of the city. I wanted to make sure that motorists could not drive through Memphis without passing at least one Holiday Inn. By the end of 1953, all four hotels were open for business, but I had used up my savings and credit. That is when I started dreaming of franchising. I don't believe I knew the word at that time; I just thought that I had a great idea and that I could sell it along with my plans and specifications for a flat fee of $500 plus a royalty of 5 cents per room per night.

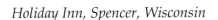

Holiday Inn, Spencer, Wisconsin

To find buyers, I went to see my friend, Wallace Johnson. He was also in the construction business and was active in the National Association of Homebuilders. I showed him my figures and explained that all we had to do was get one homebuilder in each major city in the United States to build a Holiday Inn and we would soon have a chain of 400 across the country. We invited 100 homebuilders to a meeting and 64 showed up. We sold 12 franchises, and with the great sum of $6,000 in additional capital, we thought we were off and running.

We were wrong.

Most of the homebuilders were too busy building homes to exercise their franchise option. Only three of them actually built one of our hotels. Worse yet, we discovered that there was no way we could sell the rights to build Holiday Inns as cheaply as we planned. After the first 15 franchises, the fee was raised to $2,000 and 5 cents per night or 3 percent of the gross room sales. We also decided that we needed to attract investors. Holiday Inn's first public offering was 120,000 shares at $9.75. Expenses only amounted to about 75 cents per share, so we ended up getting a check for a little more than $1 million. This time, we really were off and running.

The 50th Holiday Inn opened in Dyersburg, Tennessee in 1958, and the 100th opened in Tallahassee, Florida in 1959. The first Holiday Inn outside the United States opened in Montreal in 1960. In 1964, we opened the 500th hotel in Johnstown, Pennsylvania. This was the idea—this was my dream. When I retired 28 years later there were 1,759 Holiday Inns in 50 different countries. Today there are over 2,000.

Sometimes the first step is the hardest: coming up with an idea. Coming up with an idea should be like sitting on a pin—it should make you jump up and do something. I have had a great many ideas over the years. Some were good, some were great, and some I would prefer to forget about. The important thing is to take your best ideas and see them through. Not all of them are going to be winners, but just remember, a person who wins success may have been counted out many times before. He wins because he refuses to give up.

My own success was attended by quite a few failures along the way. But I refused to make the biggest mistake of all: worrying too much about making mistakes. A man who never makes mistakes is the man who never does anything. I have made as many or more mistakes than most people, but I always try to learn from them and to profit from my failures. It is stupid to make the same mistake twice, but I have done it many times. What has saved me from despair is the knowledge that, as the late Norman Vincent Peale once said, "Enthusiasm makes the difference." He was right. Enthusiasm is the most contagious disease in all the world, and it is a disease that cures instead of weakens the patient. Very little in this world has ever been achieved without enthusiasm.

I also believe that hard work has helped me to overcome my mistakes. The freedom to work is second only to the freedom to worship. Work is the master key that opens the door to all opportunities. If a person truly knows what he wants out of life and is willing to work hard enough for it, life will pay its richest rewards and greatest dividends. Work is not man's doom but man's blessing. A 40-hour week has no charm for me. I'm looking for a 40-hour day.

I have worked in boom times and in recessions, in the Great Depression and in time of war. Our government has been led by Republicans and Democrats, conservatives and liberals. Through all, I have seen our free enterprise system survive and provide the economic means to build the greatest society in the history of the world. I suppose such observations make me seem like a fellow with a lot of old-fashioned, corny ideas. Indeed, that is just the kind of fellow I am. I can prove it too, by quoting one of my favorite pieces of inspirational literature. I came across it years ago, and I still think it is the best way to sum up what makes for success:

For best results, this garden should be planted every day:

Five rows of "P"eas:	Five rows of lettuce:
Preparedness,	Let us love one another,
Promptness,	Let us be faithful,
Perseverance,	Let us be loyal,
Politeness,	Let us be unselfish,
Prayer.	Let us be truthful.
Three rows of squash:	Three rows of turnips:
Squash gossip,	Turn up for church,
Squash criticism,	Turn up with a new idea,
Squash indifference.	Turn up with the determination to do a better job tomorrow than you did today.

Reprinted by permission from Imprimis, *the national speech digest of Hillsdale College, www.hillsdale.edu.*

Lilian's Business Venture

Lucy Maud Montgomery (1900)

Lucy Maud Montgomery (1874-1942) was from Prince Edward Island, Canada. In addition to her "Anne of Green Gables" books, which made the island famous, she published many other novels, short stories, and poetry.

Lilian Mitchell turned into the dry-goods store on Randall Street, just as Esther Miller and Ella Taylor came out. They responded coldly to her greeting and exchanged significant glances as they walked away.

Lilian's pale face crimsoned. She was a tall, slender girl of about seventeen, and dressed in mourning. These girls had been her close friends once. But that was before the Mitchells had lost their money. Since then Lilian had been cut by many of her old chums and she felt it keenly.

The clerks in the store were busy and Lilian sat down to wait her turn. Near to her two ladies were also waiting and chatting.

"Helen wants me to let her have a birthday party," Mrs. Saunders was saying wearily. "She has been promised it so long and I hate to disappoint the child, but our girl left last week, and I cannot possibly make all the cakes and things myself. I haven't the time or strength, so Helen must do without her party."

"Talking of girls," said Mrs. Reeves impatiently, "I am almost discouraged. It is so hard to get a good all-round one. The last one I had was so saucy I had to discharge her, and the one I have now cannot make decent bread. I never had good luck with bread myself either."

"That is Mrs. Porter's great grievance too. It is no light task to bake bread for all those boarders. Have you made your jelly yet?"

"No. Maria cannot make it, she says, and I detest messing with jelly. But I really must see to it soon."

At this point a saleswoman came up to Lilian, who made her small purchases and went out.

"There goes Lilian Mitchell," said Mrs. Reeves in an undertone. "She looks very pale. They say they are dreadfully poor since Henry Mitchell died. His affairs were in a bad condition, I am told."

"I am sorry for Mrs. Mitchell," responded Mrs. Saunders. "She is such a sweet woman. Lilian will have to do something, I suppose, and there is so little chance for a girl here."

Lilian, walking down the street, was wearily turning over in her mind the problems of her young existence. Her father had died the preceding spring. He had been a supposedly prosperous merchant; the Mitchells had always lived well, and Lilian was a petted and only child. Then came the shock of Henry Mitchell's sudden death and of financial ruin. His affairs were found to be hopelessly involved; when all the debts were paid there was left only the merest pittance—barely enough for house-rent—for Lilian and her mother to live upon. They had moved into a tiny cottage in an unfashionable locality, and during the summer Lilian had tried hard to think of something to do. Mrs. Mitchell was a delicate woman, and the burden of their situation fell on Lilian's young shoulders.

There seemed to be no place for her. She could not teach and had no particular talent in any line. There was no opening for her in Willington, which was a rather sleepy little place, and Lilian was almost in despair.

"There really doesn't seem to be any real place in the world for me, Mother," she said rather dolefully at the supper table. "I've no talent at all; it is dreadful to have been born without one. And yet I must do something, and do it soon."

And Lilian, after she had washed up the tea dishes, went upstairs and had a good cry.

But the darkest hour, so the proverb goes, is just before the dawn, and after Lilian had had her cry out and was sitting at her window in the dusk, watching a thin new moon shining over the trees down the street, her inspiration came to her. A minute later she whirled into the tiny sitting-room where her mother was sewing.

"Mother, our fortune is made! I have an idea!"

"Don't lose it, then," said Mrs. Mitchell with a smile. "What is it, my dear?"

Lilian sobered herself, sat down by her mother's side, and proceeded to recount the conversation she had heard in the store that afternoon.

"Now, Mother, this is where my brilliant idea comes in. You have often told me I am a born cook and I always have good luck. Now, tomorrow morning I shall go to Mrs. Saunders and offer to furnish all the good things for Helen's birthday party, and then I'll ask Mrs. Reeves and Mrs. Porter if I may make their bread for them. That will do for a beginning, I like cooking, you know, and I believe that in time I can work up a good business."

"It seems to be a good idea," said Mrs. Mitchell thoughtfully, "and I am willing that you should try. But have you thought it all out carefully? There will be many difficulties."

"I know. I don't expect smooth sailing right along, and perhaps I'll fail altogether; but somehow I don't believe I will."

"A great many of your old friends will think—"

"Oh, yes; I know that too, but I am not going to mind it, Mother. I don't think there is any disgrace in working for my living. I'm going to do my best and not care what people say."

Early next morning Lilian started out. She had carefully thought over the details of her small venture, considered ways and means, and decided on the most advisable course. She would not attempt too much, and she felt sure of success.

To secure competent servants was one of the problems of Willington people. At Drayton, a large neighbouring town, were several factories, and into these all the working girls from Willington had crowded, leaving very few who were willing to go out to service. Many of those who did were poor cooks, and Lilian shrewdly suspected that many a harassed housekeeper in the village would be glad to avail herself of the new enterprise.

Lilian was, as she had said of herself, "a born cook." This was her capital, and she meant to make the most of it. Mrs. Saunders listened to her businesslike details with surprise and delight.

"It is the very thing," she said. "Helen is so eager for that party, but I could not undertake it myself. Her birthday is Friday. Can you have everything ready by then?"

"Yes, I think so," said Lilian briskly, producing her notebook. "Please give me the list of what you want and I will do my best."

From Mrs. Saunders she went to Mrs. Reeves and found a customer as soon as she had told the reason of her call. "I'll furnish all the bread and rolls you need," she said, "and they will be good, too. Now, about your jelly. I can make good jelly, and I'll be very glad to make yours."

When she left, Lilian had an order for two dozen glasses of apple jelly, as well as a standing one for bread and rolls. Mrs. Porter was next visited and grasped eagerly at the opportunity.

"I know your bread will be good," she said, "and you may count on me as a regular customer."

Lilian thought she had enough on hand for a first attempt and went home satisfied. On her way she called at the grocery store with an order that surprised Mr. Hooper. When she told him of her plan he opened his eyes.

"I must tell my wife about that. She isn't strong and she doesn't like cooking."

After dinner Lilian went to work, enveloped in a big apron, and whipped eggs, stoned raisins, stirred, concocted, and baked until dark. When bedtime came she was so tired that she could hardly crawl upstairs; but she felt happy too, for the day had been a successful one.

And so also were the days and weeks and months that followed. It was hard and constant work, but it brought its reward. Lilian had not promised more than she could perform, and her customers were satisfied. In a short time she found herself with a regular and growing business on her hands, for new customers were gradually added and always came to stay.

People who gave parties found it very convenient to follow Mrs. Saunders's example and order their supplies from Lilian. She had a very busy winter and, of course, it was not all plain sailing. She had many difficulties to contend with. Sometimes days came on which everything seemed to go wrong—when the stove smoked or the oven wouldn't heat properly, when cakes fell flat and bread was sour and pies behaved as only totally depraved pies can, when she burned her fingers and felt like giving up in despair.

Then, again, she found herself cut by several of her old acquaintances. But she was too sensible to worry much over this. The friends really worth having were still hers, her mother's face had lost its look of care, and her business was prospering. She was hopeful and wide awake, kept her wits about her and looked out for hints, and learned to laugh over her failures.

During the winter she and her mother had managed to do most of the work themselves, hiring little Mary Robinson next door on especially busy days, and now and then calling in the assistance of Jimmy Bowen and his hand sled to carry orders to customers. But when spring came Lilian prepared to open up her summer campaign on a much larger scale. Mary Robinson was hired for the season, and John Perkins was engaged to act as carrier with his express wagon. A summer kitchen was boarded in the backyard, and a new range bought; Lilian began operations with a striking advertisement in the Willington News and an attractive circular sent around to all her patrons. Picnics and summer weddings were frequent. In bread and rolls her trade was brisk and constant. She also took orders for pickles, preserves, and jellies, and this became such a flourishing branch that a second assistant had to be hired.

It was a cardinal rule with Lilian never to send out any article that was not up to her standard. She bore the loss of her failures, and sometimes stayed up half of the night to fill an order on time. "Prompt and perfect" was her motto.

The long hot summer days were very trying, and sometimes she got very tired of it all. But when on the anniversary of her first venture she made up her accounts she was well pleased. To be sure, she had not made a fortune; but she had paid all their expenses, had a hundred dollars clear, and had laid the solid foundations of a profitable business.

"Mother," she said jubilantly, as she wiped a dab of flour from her nose and proceeded to concoct the icing for Blanche Remington's wedding cake, "don't you think my business venture has been a decided success?"

Mrs. Mitchell surveyed her busy daughter with a motherly smile. "Yes, I think it has," she said.

Mind Amongst the Spindles

Harriet Martineau (1844)

The textile mills of Lowell, Massachusetts, were a major part of the early American industrial revolution. Many of the employees were young women. The Lowell Offering *was a monthly publication that featured poetry and fiction written by these workers. Subscribers from elsewhere in New England and around the United States received it. An English editor collected some of these selections in an 1845 publication called* Mind Amongst the Spindles. *The editor included the following letter by Harriet Martineau. Martineau (1802-1876) was an English social reformer and author who had visited the United States in 1834.*

Tynemouth, May 20, 1844.

My dear Friend,—Your interest in this Lowell book can scarcely equal mine; for I have seen the factory girls in their Lyceum, and have gone over the cotton-mills at Waltham, and made myself familiar on the spot with factory life in New England; so that in reading the "Offering," I saw again in my memory the street of houses built by the earnings of the girls, the church which is their property, and the girls themselves trooping to the mill, with their healthy countenances, and their neat dress and quiet manners, resembling those of the tradesman class of our country.

Boott Cotton Mills in Lowell, Massachusetts

My visit to Lowell was merely for one day, in company with Mr. Emerson's party,—he (the pride and boast of New England as an author and philosopher) being engaged by the Lowell factory people to lecture to them, in a winter course of historical biography. Of course the lectures were delivered in the evening, after the mills were closed. The girls were then working seventy hours a week, yet, as I looked at the large audience (and I attended more to them than to the lecture) I saw no sign of weariness among any of them. There they sat, row behind row, in their own Lyceum—a large hall, wainscoted with mahogany, the platform carpeted, well lighted, provided with a handsome table, desk, and seat, and adorned with portraits of a few worthies, and as they thus sat listening to their lecturer, all wakeful and interested, all

Skywalks between buildings in the Boott Cotton Mills complex, Lowell, Massachusetts

well-dressed and lady-like, I could not but feel my heart swell at the thought, of what such a sight would be with us.

The difference is not in rank, for these young people were all daughters of parents who earn their bread with their own hands. It is not in the amount of wages, however usual that supposition is, for they were then earning from one to three dollars a-week, besides their food; the children one dollar, the second rate workers two dollars, and the best three: the cost of their dress and necessary comforts being much above what the same class expend in this country. It is not in the amount of toil; for, as I have said, they worked seventy clear hours per week. The difference was in their superior culture. Their minds are kept fresh, and strong, and free by knowledge and power of thought; and this is the reason why they are not worn and depressed under their labors. They begin with a poorer chance for health than our people; for the health of the New England women generally is not good, owing to circumstances of climate and other influences; but among the 3800 women and girls in the Lowell mills when I was there, the average of health was not lower than elsewhere; and the disease which was most mischievous was the same that proves most fatal over the whole country—consumption; while there were no complaints peculiar to mill life.

At Waltham, where I saw the mills, and conversed with the people, I had an opportunity of observing the invigorating effects of mind in a life of labor. Twice the wages and half the toil would not have made the girls I saw happy and healthy, without that cultivation of mind which afforded them perpetual support, entertainment, and motive for activity. They were not highly educated, but they had pleasure in books and lectures, in correspondence with home; and had their minds so open to fresh ideas, as to be drawn off from thoughts of themselves and their own concerns. When at work they were amused with thinking over the last book they had read, or with planning the account they should write home of the last Sunday's sermon, or with singing over to themselves the song they meant to practise in the evening; and when evening came, nothing was heard of tired limbs and eagerness for bed, but, if it was summer, they sallied out, the moment tea was over, for a walk, and if it was winter, to the lecture-room or to the ball-room for a dance, or they got an hour's practice at the piano, or wrote home, or shut themselves up with a new book. It was during the hours of work in the mill that the papers in the "Offering" were meditated, and it was after work in the evenings that they were penned.

There is, however, in the case of these girls, a stronger support, a more elastic spring of vigor and cheerfulness than even an active and cultivated understanding. The institution of factory labor has brought ease of heart to many; and to many occasion for noble and generous deeds. The ease of heart is given to those who were before suffering in silent poverty, from the deficiency of profitable employment for women, which is even greater in America than with us. It used to be understood there that all women were maintained by the men of their families; but the young men of New England are apt to troop off into the West, to settle in new lands, leaving sisters at home. Some few return to fetch a wife, but the greater number do not, and thus a vast over proportion of young women remains; and to a multitude of these the opening of factories was a most welcome event, affording means of honorable maintenance, in exchange for pining poverty at home.

As for the noble deeds, it makes one's heart glow to stand in these mills, and hear of the domestic history of some who are working before one's eyes, unconscious of being observed or of being the object of any admiration. If one of the sons of a New England farmer shows a love for books and thought, the ambition of an affectionate sister is roused, and she thinks of the glory and honor to the whole family, and the blessing to him, if he could have a college education. She ponders this till she tells her parents, some day, of her wish to go to Lowell, and earn the means of sending her brother to college. The desire is yet more urgent if the brother has a pious mind, and a wish to enter the ministry. Many a clergyman in America has been prepared for his function by the devoted industry of sisters; and many a scholar and professional man dates his elevation in social rank and usefulness from his sister's, or even some affectionate aunt's entrance upon mill life, for his sake. Many girls, perceiving anxiety in their fathers' faces, on account of the farm being incumbered, and age coming on without release from the debt, have gone to Lowell, and worked till the mortgage was paid off, and the little family property free. Such motives may well lighten and sweeten labor; and to such girls labor is light and sweet.

Some, who have no such calls, unite the surplus of their earnings to build dwellings for their own residence, six, eight, or twelve living together with the widowed mother or elderly aunt of one of them to keep house for, and give countenance to the party. I saw a whole street of houses so built and owned, at Waltham; pretty frame houses, with the broad piazza, and the green Venetian blinds, that give such an air of coolness and pleasantness to American village and country abodes. There is the large airy eating-room, with a few prints hung up, the piano at one end, and the united libraries of the girls, forming a good-looking array of books, the rocking chairs universal in America, the stove adorned in summer with flowers, and the long dining-table in the middle. The chambers do not answer to our English ideas of comfort. There is a strange absence of the wish for privacy; and more girls are accommodated in one room than we should see any reason for in such comfortable and pretty houses.

In the mills the girls have quite the appearance of ladies. They sally forth in the morning with their umbrellas in threatening weather, their calashes to keep their hair neat, gowns of print or gingham, with a perfect fit, worked collars or pelerines, and waistbands of ribbon. For Sundays and social evenings they have their silk gowns, and neat gloves and shoes. Yet through proper economy,—the economy of educated and thoughtful people,— they are able to lay by for such purposes as I have mentioned above. The deposits in the Lowell Savings' Bank were, in 1834, upwards of 114,000 dollars, the number of operatives being 5000, of whom 3800 were women and girls.

I thank you for calling my attention back to this subject. It is one I have pleasure in recurring to. There is nothing in America which necessitates the prosperity of manufactures as of agriculture, and there is nothing of good in their factory system that may not be emulated elsewhere—equalled elsewhere, when the people employed are so educated as to have the command of themselves and of their lot in life, which is always and everywhere controlled by mind, far more than by outward circumstances.

I am very truly yours,
H. Martineau.

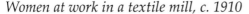

Women at work in a textile mill, c. 1910

Labor Unions in a Free Market

Ernest van den Haag (1979)

Dr. Ernest van den Haag (1914-2002) was a writer, a professor, and a psychoanalyst. An immigrant to the United States, he received his Ph.D. from New York University. In this presentation he deals with important issues related to labor unions. The footnotes are part of the original text.

I shall try to deal with four topics: I. Why do labor unions exist? What do they do? II. What are the effects of their activities? III. Strikes and restrictive practices. IV. How could the law control labor unions and their activities in the public interest?

I. Why do labor unions exist? What do they do?

G. F. W. Hegel once said, "Everything that is, is rational." Surely that is not true if rational means "desirable." But it is true, if rational means explainable as the effect of causes. For, actions are undertaken, and associations continue, only as long as they foster the interests—material or psychological—of at least some persons. That goes for the Mafia, and for the police department, for Hillsdale College—and for labor unions.

Unions yield power, prestige, and income to their officers; but they would not be supported by the members if their interests were not served too. They are: unions often succeed in raising wages and other benefits. Because they can obtain these advantages, unions are supported by many employees. In the U.S. one-fourth of the labor force is unionized; in other countries the proportion is even higher.

Unions also give workers a feeling, so often lacking in our life, of participation, of solidarity with fellow employees and of community. This feeling is not generated by simply working with others. It is created when unions succeed in providing fringe benefits (e.g., health services, or pensions, or life insurance) tied to the job and common leisure activities (outings, vacations, etc.) for their members. These things could be provided by employers, too (they are in Japan) regardless of unions. But in the U.S. employers have acted in this area only for executives. This failure has helped unions to give workers a proprietary stake in their jobs while fostering solidarity among members and antagonism to employers. Unions have been able to create solidarity among members by helping them to perceive one another as brothers standing together against a hostile and exploitative father figure on whom they depend: the boss. Few things strengthen solidarity more than a common enemy. To be sure, economic life actually rests on cooperation. Without employers there can be no employees. Yet there is ambivalence and occasional conflict about how the products of the common work of employees and management, of labor and capital, are to be shared, and about who is to make decisions. Unions capitalize on

106

the feelings of members that they ought to get more power and money and promise to get both for them.

Unions do not always benefit members. Some workers feel they are better off on their own. Others resent specific union practices or policies, or the cost of membership. Wherefore quite a number of workers resist unionization; they are often pressured and sometimes legally compelled to join unions if they want to keep their jobs. Despite these practices, union members are now a smaller proportion of all employees than they were in the past. Unions retain high membership mainly where there is a strong union tradition, or where workers

Union and labor activists gather to urge the New York Wage Board to implement a $15 per hour minimum wage (2015)

are compelled to join. They have gained new members chiefly among government workers: the employer—the government—has been politically unwilling or unable to resist them. Public, unlike private, employers have a nearly bottomless purse, fed by the printing press, or by taxation. Thus, New York City, as employer, hovers near bankruptcy because of too many overpaid employees. The unions prevent the necessary firings and wage and pension decreases.

II. What are the effects of their activities?

When unions benefit their members by obtaining higher wages, the money cannot come out of the profits of employers, although members are encouraged to believe that it does. All the employer's yearly profit hardly ever suffices to pay for a single hefty pay raise. (If he were deprived of all profit, the employer would have no reason to stay in business.) On the average, employers make a profit of roughly .05 per dollar of sales. Labor costs usually make up more than half of the sales dollar. Hence an increase cannot come out of profits. Thus the money for raises must come:

1. Out of higher productivity—more value produced per unit of input. But productivity increases only 3% a year on the average (less in the last few years). Unions attempt to raise wage rates far beyond that.

2. From higher prices for whatever is produced by the workers whose wage rate has risen. But when prices rise, less is being sold than would be sold at a lower price—else sellers would have charged more to begin with. When less is sold, less is produced and fewer workers are employed in the industries that had to raise prices. Or, sometimes,

prices do not rise despite higher wage costs. The market may not permit price hikes without excessive sales losses. In that case the least efficient producers lose money and drop out. Once more, less is produced and fewer workers are employed.

Labor union supporters gather at the California State Capitol in Sacramento for the "Save the American Dream Rally" (2011)

Either way, union members get higher wages only at the expense of workers who do not get, or do not keep, jobs because of lower sales and less production. These workers remain unemployed or have to go into lower paying non-unionized jobs. (Recently some of the losses have been shifted to taxpayers. Those who become unemployed, because of the higher wage rates union demand, receive unemployment and other benefits. As a result they may not be willing to work in low paying occupations.)

3. If real wages for all workers—their actual purchasing power—could be increased by union activity (or by government decree), Italian or English wages, or Soviet wages, would be higher than ours. They are not. Or, our government could double all wages by law and get itself reelected forever. This sort of thing often has been tried (minimum wage laws are a remnant of such attempts) but it does not work.* Actually, if all wages are increased—by concerted union action or by governments—one of two things happens:

(a) If the government does not allow the volume of monetary circulation to increase, inflation is prevented: prices cannot rise as wages do. When wages increase and prices (or productivity) do not (or not as much), profits decline and become losses for some; many firms stop, or reduce production, and hardly any expand. There is unemployment, and the real income of the population as a whole is reduced, although the workers who keep their jobs do well. They are not likely to enjoy it though. They lose overtime. Also they may fear for their jobs as others are fired and production is reduced. And among the fired, they may have relatives and friends.

---

* *Minimum wage laws, where the government rather than unions raises the wage, result in high unemployment among the least productive workers—mainly black adolescents. Employers do not hire those to whom they have to pay more than the market value of their contribution to production. Many of those unemployed because of minimum wage laws turn to crime—an uncovered occupation. Hence the crime rate among black adolescents is particularly high. They have been excluded from legitimate occupations owing to the efforts, presumably on their behalf, of their liberal and union friends.*

(b) If the government allows the volume of monetary circulation to increase as wages do, there is inflation. Prices rise, and real wages (purchasing power) do not go up. Workers get more and have to pay more. People on fixed incomes suffer, and so do creditors who get the money due them but can buy less for it. All kinds of undesirable things happen, and there either is hyperinflation—rapid devaluation of the currency (rapid price level increases) and a return to barter—or the government deflates after all, i.e., it finally reduces the volume of monetary circulation. The government can do so by reducing its own expenditure financed by creating money, by increasing interest rates, and by other means which shrink the volume of money in circulation. In a major deflation prices fall and so do profits, employment and production. This is what Chile had to do after President Allende decreed wage increases financed by inflation, and to some extent we are doing so now [in 1978 and 1979]. In a minor deflation, such as we are bringing about, prices merely stop rising, or rise at a lower rate.

That much if all wages rise. The rise does not help workers, whether they have unions or not, because the real wage level (the wages of workers as a group, as distinguished from the wages of groups of workers) does not depend on unions, or laws, but on productivity. However, as indicated, unions can benefit their members by increasing not the wage level but the wages of groups of members, or of unionized industries and firms, at the expense of causing unemployment and an oversupply of workers, or depressed wages, in non-unionized industries.

Thus, unions do not foster the interest of the working class as a whole—but members may find that unions can increase their own wages and benefits. Even if inflation occurs, union members usually do not understand the role of unions in causing it: greedy speculators and businessmen are blamed by union leaders. The members are led to feel that the union continues to serve their interests and to protect them from the effects of the inflation for which "speculators" or "business" are blamed.

III. Strikes and restrictive practices.

With or without unions, wage rates are determined by the demand for, and the supply of, different kinds of labor. But with unions the market is not free. The function of unions is to attempt to monopolize and restrict the supply of labor—at least of labor in specific places and of specific kinds—and to obtain a monopoly price for it, higher than the free market price would be.* This is done in two ways:

1. By restricting union membership while compelling employers to hire only union members. This is how craft unions prevent employers from availing themselves of the

---

* *Unions are legally exempted from anti-monopoly legislation.*

Verizon Wireless workers on strike in New York City (2016)

full labor pool. Thus, the drivers of newspaper delivery trucks in New York get high wages. They allow very few people to join the union and prevent the newspapers from hiring non-union members. They can bargain from the monopoly position they create because New York law, and the practices of the New York police department, would make it impossible for the newspapers to hire non-union drivers: they might be killed, and their trucks would be sabotaged.

2. By threatening to strike, unions may be able to compel employers to confine their hiring to union members and to pay them higher than free market wages. Even when industrial (as distinguished from craft) unions permit employers to hire non-union members, or allow anyone to join, the strike threat can be used to raise wages whenever enough employees can be persuaded or intimidated into refraining from work in a concerted effort to support union demands.

To strike is to refrain from working while keeping one's job and discouraging, or preventing, others from doing it.* In economic terms, to strike is to withhold the supply of labor, to prevent its being replaced, and to attempt to compel employers to pay the price the union wishes to charge. Unless the employer can break the strike, by hiring non-strikers, or by getting strikers to return, he has to accept the union's terms. He has to pay a wage higher than the free market wage—the wage just high enough to attract the workers he needs.

Strikes—and all union-imposed monopoly prices for labor—are contrary to the public interest. If lost by the union, strikes leave the status quo ante in force—after a loss of production and income by employers and employees and, often, considerable losses to third parties. If won by the union, strikes, in addition to losses of income and production, lead to a redistribution of income from non-union to union members; this increases the inequality of incomes while not increasing the income of workers as a whole. Finally, if

---

* *A "lock-out"—an attempt by an employer to pressure workers to accept his wages and working conditions by refusing to employ them otherwise and dismissing those who are employed—apart from occurring quite rarely, is not parallel to a strike: employers do not attempt, by pickets or otherwise, to prevent their employees from finding other jobs.*

they lead to general wage increases, strikes generate inflation. Strikes cannot redistribute income from employers to employees.

Nonetheless, it would be a mistake to blame unions for all strikes. Strikes can happen without unions, as history shows, and against unions, as "wild cat" strikes show. Indeed, unionization may prevent strikes as well as bring them about. As much may be said about most other union activity. It is true that much union activity is harmful to the public interest. Feather-bedding is; so are work rules which require employment of unproductive workers; and jurisdictional disputes: all of these reduce productivity. But the free market, though efficient, is also uncomfortable. Groups always have tried to protect themselves against some of the most uncomfortable effects of the free market, such as loss of jobs in any industry because of technological change, or competition. (Employment elsewhere may be available, but the transition is difficult.) Groups of employers have tried to protect themselves by tariffs, or laws, or licensing requirements. Groups of workers, too, will protect themselves spontaneously, and it is futile merely to point out that their actions are against the public interest. People tend to protect their own. At best we can minimize the harmful effects of special interest actions, including those of unions. To this I shall turn now.

IV. How could the law control labor unions and their activities in the public interest?

In the U.S., unions and their relations with employers and with the community at large are to a great extent regulated by law. This regulation is a mixed blessing. But other countries, such as England, with much less legal regulation, are not better off. Thus the issue is how much and what kind of regulation is needed, and how it can be made effective in the public interest. In the U.S. a deliberate attempt has been made to legally protect unions against what was thought of as the overwhelming power of employers. But the power distribution has changed, partly as a result of these laws, and today employers, individuals, and the public, do need protection from unions more than unions need protection from employers. Nonetheless, present law still attempts

1. to protect and foster union activities;

2. to compel employers to bargain;

3. to compel employers not to replace strikers;

4. to give unions a monopoly in representing workers to employers, in fixing the price of labor and the conditions of employment;

5. to compel the government to pay union wages (in practice more than union wages) to all its employees and to force government contractors to do so (the Davis-Bacon Act).

6. Very little regulation restricts the power of unions to interfere with the processes of production, to determine how many people and who will do a particular job, to strike at will, and to deprive society of needed services.

As long as employers have a chance to resist strikes by replacing workers or by moving away, union demands can be restrained. But there is little chance of doing so. Usually employers have to yield or give up their businesses. The latter possibility, which would deprive union members of employment, may or may not restrain union demands. It seldom does, for union leaders depend on the votes of their members. They cannot easily moderate their demands on employers, for other more militant leaders may be elected in their stead. Hence, when unions have enough power to use the strike threat effectively, the wages of members tend to rise, making unemployment of non-members, or inflation, hard to avoid.

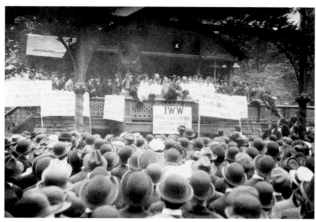

Crowd listens to a labor leader speak during the Brooklyn barbers' strike of 1913 in Union Square, New York City

A union must be bargained with by law, if the majority of employees join. The union then will bargain for non-members as well—whether or not they like it; usually it can compel the minority to join as a condition of continued employment. Employers must bargain not only for wages, but also for working conditions, promotions, seniority, manning, hiring and firing, the use of technology, the amount of production per worker, and fringe benefits.* Unions are allowed to picket to advertise disputes. And although pickets legally are not allowed to intimidate or to prevent workers or others who wish to work, or to enter the plant, from doing so, in practice pickets can prevent non-strikers from working. Unions also are allowed to boycott products and producers and to harass customers and third parties not involved in a labor conflict so as to get indirectly at their employers.

One peculiar result is that unions have driven the price of labor so high in some industries (e.g., maritime and housing) that government subsidies become necessary if the industry is to continue. Unions have used political means to get these subsidies. Thus, in effect, the higher wages are paid by taxpayers who pay subsidies for housing and maritime activity.

---

* To bargain is defined as yielding on some of one's initial positions.

What could regulation do to protect the public interest while being fair to all parties involved? It will be convenient to deal with occupations and industries according to the degree of interest the public has in avoiding strikes.

1. Strikes should not be permitted in public service industries or by public employees—e.g., police and firemen, garbage men, teachers, hospital or nursing home personnel, and workers in major utilities, such as electricity producers or mass transportation facilities, whether publicly or privately owned.

Here strikes should be altogether prohibited because quite obviously the harm they cause to innocent bystanders—electricity consumers, hospital patients, school children—is far greater than any conceivable benefit to the parties in conflict could be. Workers volunteer to work in the public service industries. In accepting employment they should be notified that strikes are prohibited by law. Indeed there are such prohibitions in many states. But they are not enforceable because the penalties have been kept so mild as not to deter strikes. Appropriate penalties would have to include:

(a) Fines of sufficient size levied on the union: e.g., for the first day of strike (or slowdown) an amount equal to one year's dues for each member; for the second and third an amount equal to two years' dues, etc.

(b) Each striking union member would lose three years' seniority for each day of striking.

(c) Each striker would lose a part of his pension benefits for each day of striking so that on the fifth day all his pension benefits would be lost (except for any amount he himself paid in).

(d) A similar reduction in other accumulated benefits.[*]

All of the above should be mandatory: neither courts, nor employers, nor public authorities, should be allowed to reduce these penalties once the existence of an illegal strike and the participation of the union and of the individual strikers involved has been established.

It is most unlikely that under these conditions strikes would take place—they would be suicidal for the unions and for their members. This is the point. To repeat, strikes in public service industries do harm to innocent bystanders far in excess of any benefit the strikers can hope to receive.

In the absence of effective strike threats, what would prevent employers, public or private, from driving down the wages of employees? If these wages (including fringe benefits) were to fall below what employees can earn in other occupations, a shortage

---

* *Jailing of strikers or strike leaders has been shown to be wholly ineffective. So are fines, unless massive size is mandated.*

of labor would develop. The industry that pays low wages would be compelled to raise them to get the workers it needs. On the other hand, as long as there are more eligible people who want to be teachers, or policemen, than there are jobs for them, teachers and policemen are not underpaid. If the supply greatly exceeds the demand, they are overpaid, if we use not moral but market standards. (The medieval moral notion of a "fair wage"—*pretium justum*—ignores market forces and makes no economic sense.)

There remain a host of questions about which employees may wish to bargain through a union. They can do so without strike threats. Grievance and obligatory arbitration procedures may be set up and even binding arbitration may be required. However, wages should not be subject to arbitration—for they will be regulated satisfactorily by the market in the absence of arbitration. And arbitrators could do no more than guess what the market wage is likely to be. (Moreover they have a tendency to be generous with other people's money.)

2. What about strikes in privately owned industries less directly affecting the public interest—e.g., newspapers, steel mills, coal mines, textile firms . . . ? There are gradations. Present law gives considerable power to the President to take action to prevent or delay strikes if he finds there is a national emergency. Such strikes may be a menace even when they do not paralyze essential services. A steel strike may harm automobile workers who are not involved and even make them unemployed if it lasts long enough. However, except in time of war, such a strike need not create an emergency.

I suggest the following:

(a) Strikes should be legal only if not contrary to contracts.

(b) Union members should vote on authorizing strikes only after governmental mediation and non-binding arbitration have failed.

(c) Strikers, who, after all, voluntarily refrain from working and earning, should not be entitled to receive unemployment or welfare benefits.

(d) Nor should strikers be allowed to intimidate others or to prevent them from working.

(e) Employers should be free to keep employees hired during a strike and to fire strikers for being strikers. (Thus employers will have a chance to win as well as lose. Strikes will become more risky for unions.)

(f) While unions should be free to bargain on working conditions, wages and benefits, they should not be allowed to compel employers to hire or keep workers they feel are not needed. Featherbedding should be outlawed, and manning should not be subject to bargaining. Featherbedding increases the cost of production (which ultimately has to be paid for by the public) and keeps workers paid for something unproductive, preventing them from doing something productive. (Featherbedding has greatly contributed to ruining our railroads.)

(g) Unions should be able to bargain on pensions (and on severance pay). But, by law, pensions should never be permitted to exceed two-thirds of the pay received by employees while on the job. Else, the employer might have to pay the same whether a worker is working or not—which would lead to a reduction in social productivity. (These rules must be enforced by effective penalties. Hefty mandatory fines for violators might be enough—unions don't like to lose their treasure.)

The proposed restrictions on union activity may appear one-sided and, therefore, unfair. Actually they restore the balance that has been tilted in favor of unions by legislation. Moreover, employer-employee relations are not like a football match in which both teams should have an equal chance under fair conditions.

Strikes harm third persons, not just employers and employees. Unions and employers fight, win or lose, at the expense of the public interest. The public loses more, in all major strikes, than either party can hope to win. And if the union wins and compels the employer to pay wages in excess of those that demand and supply in a free market would have brought about, union members benefit at the expense of other workers and of the public at large. Thus the problem is not of arranging a fair fight between unions and employers, but rather of avoiding a fight altogether, and of limiting the results of union victories in the interest of other workers and of the public at large. The very existence of unions and of strikes, however unavoidable, tilts the mechanism of the free market in an unfair manner in favor of the union members and against other workers and the public. Legal restrictions on union power, far from being unfair, merely reduce the invasion of the labor market by monopoly power.

Reprinted by permission from Imprimis, *the national speech digest of Hillsdale College, www.hillsdale.edu.*

Members of a sheet metal workers union protest at the California State Capitol in Sacramento (2011)

My Life and Work

Henry Ford (1922)

Henry Ford (1863-1947) was founder of the Ford Motor Company. He wrote his autobiography in collaboration with journalist Samuel Crowther. This excerpt is from the chapter on wages.

Austrian postage stamp showing Henry Ford (2003)

There is nothing to running a business by custom—to saying: "I pay the going rate of wages." The same man would not so easily say: "I have nothing better or cheaper to sell than any one has." No manufacturer in his right mind would contend that buying only the cheapest materials is the way to make certain of manufacturing the best article. Then why do we hear so much talk about the "liquidation of labour" and the benefits that will flow to the country from cutting wages—which means only the cutting of buying power and the curtailing of the home market? What good is industry if it be so unskillfully managed as not to return a living to everyone concerned? No question is more important than that of wages—most of the people of the country live on wages. The scale of their living—the rate of their wages—determines the prosperity of the country.

Throughout all the Ford industries we now have a minimum wage of six dollars a day; we used to have a minimum of five dollars; before that we paid whatever it was necessary to pay. It would be bad morals to go back to the old market rate of paying—but also it would be the worst sort of bad business.

First get at the relationships. It is not usual to speak of an employee as a partner, and yet what else is he? Whenever a man finds the management of a business too much for his own time or strength, he calls in assistants to share the management with him. Why, then, if a man finds the production part of a business too much for his own two hands should he deny the title of "partner" to those who come in and help him produce? Every business that employs more than one man is a kind of partnership. The moment a man calls for assistance in his business—even though the assistant be but a boy—that moment he has taken a partner. He may himself be sole owner of the resources of the business and sole director of its operations, but only while he remains sole manager and sole producer can he claim complete independence. No man is independent as long as he has to depend on another man to help him. It is a reciprocal relation—the boss is the partner of his worker, the worker is partner of his boss. And such being the case, it is useless for one group or the other to assume that it is the one indispensable unit. Both are indispensable. The one can become unduly assertive only at the expense of the other—and eventually at its own expense as well. It is utterly foolish for Capital or for Labour to think of themselves as groups. They are partners. When they pull and haul against each other—they simply injure the organization in which they are partners and from which both draw support.

It ought to be the employer's ambition, as leader, to pay better wages than any similar line of business, and it ought to be the workman's ambition to make this possible. Of course there are men in all shops who seem to believe that if they do their best, it will be only for the employer's benefit—and not at all for their own. It is a pity that such a feeling should exist. But it does exist and perhaps it has some justification. If an employer urges men to do their best, and the men learn after a while that their best does not bring any reward, then they naturally drop back into "getting by." But if they see the fruits of hard work in their pay envelope—proof that harder work means higher pay—then also they begin to learn that they are a part of the business, and that its success depends on them and their success depends on it.

"What ought the employer to pay?"—"What ought the employee to receive?" These are but minor questions. The basic question is "What can the business stand?" Certainly no business can stand outgo that exceeds its income. When you pump water out of a well at a faster rate than the water flows in, the well goes dry. And when the well runs dry, those who depend on it go thirsty. And if, perchance, they imagine they can pump one well dry and then jump to some other well, it is only a matter of time when all the wells will be dry. There is now a widespread demand for more justly divided rewards, but it must be recognized that there are limits to rewards. The business itself sets the limits. You cannot distribute $150,000 out of a business that brings in only $100,000. The business limits the wages, but does anything limit the business? The business limits itself by following bad precedents.

If men, instead of saying "the employer ought to do thus-and-so," would say, "the business ought to be so stimulated and managed that it can do thus-and-so," they would get somewhere. Because only the business can pay wages. Certainly the employer cannot, unless the business warrants. But if that business does warrant higher wages and the employer refuses, what is to be done? As a rule a business

Henry Ford is greeted by newspaper reporters as he leaves the White House after meeting with President Franklin Roosevelt. (1938)

means the livelihood of too many men, to be tampered with. It is criminal to assassinate a business to which large numbers of men have given their labours and to which they have learned to look as their field of usefulness and their source of livelihood. Killing the business by a strike or a lockout does not help. The employer can gain nothing by looking over the employees and asking himself, "How little can I get them to take?" Nor the employee by glaring back and asking, "How much can I force him to give?" Eventually both will have to turn to the business and ask, "How can this industry be made safe and profitable, so that it will be able to provide a sure and comfortable living for all of us?"

But by no means all employers or all employees will think straight. The habit of acting shortsightedly is a hard one to break. What can be done? Nothing. No rules or laws will effect the changes. But enlightened self-interest will. It takes a little while for enlightenment to spread. But spread it must, for the concern in which both employer and employees work to the same end of service is bound to forge ahead in business.

What do we mean by high wages, anyway?

We mean a higher wage than was paid ten months or ten years ago. We do not mean a higher wage than ought to be paid. Our high wages of to-day may be low wages ten years from now.

If it is right for the manager of a business to try to make it pay larger dividends, it is quite as right that he should try to make it pay higher wages. But it is not the manager of the business who pays the high wages. Of course, if he can and will not, then the blame is on him. But he alone can never make high wages possible. High wages cannot be paid unless the workmen earn them. Their labour is the productive factor. It is not the only productive factor—poor management can waste labour and material and nullify the efforts of labour. Labour can nullify the results of good management. But in a partnership of skilled management and honest labour, it is the workman who makes high wages possible. He invests his energy and skill, and if he makes an honest, wholehearted investment, high wages ought to be his reward. Not only has he earned them, but he has had a big part in creating them.

It ought to be clear, however, that the high wage begins down in the shop. If it is not created there it cannot get into pay envelopes. There will never be a system invented which will do away with the necessity of work. Nature has seen to that. Idle hands and minds were never intended for any one of us. Work is our sanity, our self-respect, our salvation. So far from being a curse, work is the greatest blessing. Exact social justice flows only out of honest work. The man who contributes much should take away much. Therefore no element of charity is present in the paying of wages. The kind of workman who gives the business the best that is in him is the best kind of workman a business can have. And he cannot be expected to do this indefinitely without proper recognition of his contribution. The man who comes to the day's job feeling that no matter how much he may give, it will not yield him enough of a return to keep him beyond want, is not in shape to do his day's work. He is anxious and worried, and it all reacts to the detriment of his work.

But if a man feels that his day's work is not only supplying his basic need, but is also giving him a margin of comfort and enabling him to give his boys and girls their opportunity and his wife some pleasure in life, then his job looks good to him and he is free to give it of his best. This is a good thing for him and a good thing for the business. The man who does not get a certain satisfaction out of his day's work is losing the best part of his pay.

Ford Motor Company Headquarters in Dearborn, Michigan (2015)

For the day's work is a great thing—a very great thing! It is at the very foundation of the world; it is the basis of our self-respect. And the employer ought constantly to put in a harder day's work than any of his men. The employer who is seriously trying to do his duty in the world must be a hard worker. He cannot say, "I have so many thousand men working for me." The fact of the matter is that so many thousand men have him working for them—and the better they work the busier they keep him disposing of their products. Wages and salaries are in fixed amounts, and this must be so, in order to have a basis to figure on. Wages and salaries are a sort of profit-sharing fixed in advance, but it often happens that when the business of the year is closed, it is discovered that more can be paid. And then more ought to be paid. When we are all in the business working together, we all ought to have some share in the profits—by way of a good wage, or salary, or added compensation. And that is beginning now quite generally to be recognized.

There is now a definite demand that the human side of business be elevated to a position of equal importance with the material side. And that is going to come about. It is just a question whether it is going to be brought about wisely—in a way that will conserve the material side which now sustains us, or unwisely and in such a way as shall take from us all the benefit of the work of the past years. Business represents our national livelihood, it reflects our economic progress, and gives us our place among other nations. We do not want to jeopardize that. What we want is a better recognition of the human element in business. And surely it can be achieved without dislocation, without loss to any one, indeed with an increase of benefit to every human being. And the secret of it all is in a recognition of human partnership. Until each man is absolutely sufficient unto himself, needing the services of no other human being in any capacity whatever, we shall never get beyond the need of partnership.

Such are the fundamental truths of wages. They are partnership distributions.

Random Reminiscences of Men and Events
John D. Rockefeller (1909)

John D. Rockefeller (1839-1937) was one of the founders of Standard Oil in 1870 and served as its chairman until 1897. Rockefeller became the wealthiest person in the United States and used his fortune to support various charities and scientific research. This excerpt from a short memoir is from chapter six on "The Difficult Art of Giving."

It is, no doubt, easy to write platitudes and generalities about the joys of giving, and the duty that one owes to one's fellow men, and to put together again all the familiar phrases that have served for generations whenever the subject has been taken up.

I can hardly hope to succeed in starting any new interest in this great subject when gifted writers have so often failed. Yet I confess I find much more interest in it at this time than in rambling on, as I have been doing, about the affairs of business and trade. It is most difficult, however, to dwell upon a very practical and business-like side of benefactions generally, without seeming to ignore, or at least to fail to appreciate fully, the spirit of giving which has its source in the heart, and which, of course, makes it all worth while.

In this country we have come to the period when we can well afford to ask the ablest men to devote more of their time, thought, and money to the public well-being. I am not so presumptuous as to attempt to define exactly what this betterment work should consist of. Every man will do that for himself, and his own conclusion will be final for himself. It is well, I think, that no narrow or preconceived plan should be set down as the best.

I am sure it is a mistake to assume that the possession of money in great abundance necessarily brings happiness. The very rich are just like all the rest of us; and if they get pleasure from the possession of money, it comes from their ability to do things which give satisfaction to someone besides themselves.

Limitations of the Rich

The mere expenditure of money for things, so I am told by those who profess to know, soon palls upon one. The novelty of being able to purchase anything one wants soon passes, because what people most seek cannot be bought with money. These rich men we read about in the newspapers cannot get personal returns beyond a well-defined limit for their expenditure. They cannot gratify the pleasures of the palate beyond very moderate bounds, since they cannot purchase a good digestion; they cannot lavish very much money on fine raiment for themselves or their families without suffering from public ridicule; and in their homes they cannot go much beyond the comforts of the less wealthy without involving them in more pain than pleasure. As I study wealthy men, I can see but one way in which they can secure a real equivalent for money spent, and that is to cultivate a taste for giving where the money may produce an effect which will be a lasting gratification.

A man of business may often most properly consider that he does his share in building up a property which gives steady work for few or many people; and his contribution consists in giving to his employees good working conditions, new opportunities, and a strong stimulus to good work. Just so long as he has the welfare of his employees in his mind and follows his convictions, no one can help honouring such a man. It would be the narrowest sort of view to take, and I think the meanest, to consider that good works consist chiefly in the outright giving of money.

The Best Philanthropy

The best philanthropy, the help that does the most good and the least harm,

John D. Rockefeller (right) gives Harvey Firestone a dime on the golf course to reward Firestone for his "splendid long putt." (1930)

the help that nourishes civilization at its very root, that most widely disseminates health, righteousness, and happiness, is not what is usually called charity. It is, in my judgment, the investment of effort or time or money, carefully considered with relation to the power of employing people at a remunerative wage, to expand and develop the resources at hand, and to give opportunity for progress and healthful labour where it did not exist before. No mere money-giving is comparable to this in its lasting and beneficial results.

If, as I am accustomed to think, this statement is a correct one, how vast indeed is the philanthropic field! It may be urged that the daily vocation of life is one thing, and the work of philanthropy quite another. I have no sympathy with this notion. The man who plans to do all his giving on Sunday is a poor prop for the institutions of the country.

The excuse for referring so often to the busy man of affairs is that his help is most needed. I know of men who have followed out this large plan of developing work, not as a temporary matter, but as a permanent principle. These men have taken up doubtful enterprises and carried them through to success often at great risk, and in the face of great scepticism, not as a matter only of personal profit, but in the larger spirit of general uplift.

Disinterested Service the Road to Success

If I were to give advice to a young man starting out in life, I should say to him: If you aim for a large, broad-gauged success, do not begin your business career, whether you sell your labour or are an independent producer, with the idea of getting from the world by hook or crook all you can. In the choice of your profession or your business employment, let your first thought be: Where can I fit in so that I may be most effective in the work of the world? Where can I lend a hand in a way most effectively to advance the general interests? Enter life in such a spirit, choose your vocation in that way, and you have taken the first step on the highest road to a large success. Investigation will show that the great fortunes which have been made in this country, and the same is probably true of other lands, have come to men who have performed great and far-reaching economic services—men who, with great faith in the future of their country, have done most for the development of its resources. The man will be most successful who confers the greatest service on the world. Commercial enterprises that are needed by the public will pay. Commercial enterprises that are not needed fail, and ought to fail.

On the other hand, the one thing which such a business philosopher would be most careful to avoid in his investments of time and effort or money, is the unnecessary duplication of existing industries. He would regard all money spent in increasing needless competition as wasted, and worse. The man who puts up a second factory when the factory in existence will supply the public demand adequately and cheaply is wasting the national wealth and destroying the national prosperity, taking the bread from the labourer and unnecessarily introducing heartache and misery into the world.

Rockefeller with bicycle (1913)

Probably the greatest single obstacle to the progress and happiness of the American people lies in the willingness of so many men to invest their time and money in multiplying competitive industries instead of opening up new fields, and putting their money into lines of industry and development that are needed. It requires a better type of mind to seek out and to support or to create the new than to follow the worn paths of accepted success; but here is the great chance in our still rapidly developing country.

Program for Economic Recovery

Ronald Reagan (1981)

Shortly after he became president, Ronald Reagan delivered this address before a joint session of Congress outlining his economic proposals.

Mr. Speaker, Mr. President [of the Senate], distinguished Members of Congress, honored guests, and fellow citizens:

Only a month ago I was your guest in this historic building, and I pledged to you my cooperation in doing what is right for this Nation that we all love so much. I'm here tonight to reaffirm that pledge and to ask that we share in restoring the promise that is offered to every citizen by this, the last, best hope of man on Earth.

All of us are aware of the punishing inflation which has for the first time in 60 years held to double-digit figures for 2 years in a row. Interest rates have reached absurd levels of more that 20 percent and over 15 percent for those who would borrow to buy a home. All across this land one can see newly built homes standing vacant, unsold because of mortgage interest rates.

President Ronald Reagan

Almost 8 million Americans are out of work. These are people who want to be productive. But as the months go by, despair dominates their lives. The threats of layoff and unemployment hang over other millions, and all who work are frustrated by their inability to keep up with inflation.

One worker in a Midwest city put it to me this way: He said, "I'm bringing home more dollars than I ever believed I could possibly earn, but I seem to be getting worse off." And he is. Not only have hourly earnings of the American worker, after adjusting for inflation, declined 5 percent over the past 5 years, but in these 5 years, Federal personal taxes for the average family have increased 67 percent. We can no longer procrastinate and hope that things will get better. They will not. Unless we act forcefully—and now—the economy will get worse.

Can we, who man the ship of state, deny it is somewhat out of control? Our national debt is approaching $1 trillion. A few weeks ago I called such a figure, a trillion dollars, incomprehensible, and I've been trying ever since to think of a way to illustrate how big a trillion really is. And the best I could come up with is that if you had a stack of thousand-dollar bills in your hand only 4 inches high, you'd be a millionaire. A trillion dollars would be a stack of thousand-dollar bills 67 miles high. The interest on the public debt this year we know will be over $90 billion, and unless we change the proposed spending for the fiscal year beginning October 1st, we'll add another almost $80 billion to the debt.

Adding to our troubles is a mass of regulations imposed on the shopkeeper, the farmer, the craftsman, professionals, and major industry that is estimated to add $100 billion to the price of the things we buy, and it reduces our ability to produce. The rate of increase in American productivity, once one of the highest in the world, is among the lowest of all major industrial nations. Indeed, it has actually declined in the last 3 years.

Now, I've painted a pretty grim picture, but I think I've painted it accurately. It is within our power to change this picture, and we can act with hope. There's nothing wrong with our internal strengths. There has been no breakdown of the human, technological, and natural resources upon which the economy is built.

Based on this confidence in a system which has never failed us, but which we have failed through a lack of confidence and sometimes through a belief that we could fine-tune the economy and get it tuned to our liking, I am proposing a comprehensive four-point program. Now, let me outline in detail some of the principal parts of this program. You'll each be provided with a completely detailed copy of the entire program.

This plan is aimed at reducing the growth in government spending and taxing, reforming and eliminating regulations which are unnecessary and unproductive or counterproductive, and encouraging a consistent monetary policy aimed at maintaining the value of the currency. If enacted in full, this program can help America create 13 million new jobs, nearly 3 million more than we would have without these measures. It will also help us to gain control of inflation.

It's important to note that we're only reducing the rate of increase in taxing and spending. We're not attempting to cut either spending or taxing levels below that which we presently have. This plan will get our economy moving again, [create] productivity growth, and thus create the jobs that our people must have.

And I'm asking that you join me in reducing direct Federal spending by $41.4 billion in fiscal year 1982, and this goes along with another $7.7 billion in user fees and off-budget savings for a total of $49.1 billion. And this will still allow an increase of $40.8 billion over 1981 spending.

Now, I know that exaggerated and inaccurate stories about these cuts have disturbed many people, particularly those dependent on grant and benefit programs for their basic needs. Some of you have heard from constituents, I know, afraid that social security checks, for example, were going to be taken away from them. Well, I regret the fear that these unfounded stories have caused, and I welcome this opportunity to set things straight.

We will continue to fulfill the obligations that spring from our national conscience. Those who, through no fault of their own, must depend on the rest of us—the poverty stricken, the disabled, the elderly, all those with true need—can rest assured that the social safety net of programs they depend on are exempt from any cuts.

The full retirement benefits of the more than 31 million social security recipients will be continued, along with an annual cost-of-living increase. Medicare will not be cut, nor will supplemental income for the blind, the aged, and the disabled. And funding will continue for veterans pensions. School breakfasts and lunches for the children of low-income families will continue, as will nutrition and other special services for the aging. There will be no cut in Project Head Start or summer youth jobs.

All in all, nearly $216 billion worth of programs providing help for tens of millions of Americans will be fully funded. But government will not continue to subsidize individuals or particular business interests where real need cannot be demonstrated. And while we will reduce some subsidies to regional and local governments, we will at the same time convert a number of categorical grant programs into block grants to reduce wasteful administrative overhead and to give local governments and States more flexibility and control. We call for an end in duplication to Federal programs and reform of those which are not cost-effective.

Now, already some have protested that there must be no reduction in aid to schools. Well, let me point out that Federal aid to education amounts to only 8 percent of the total educational funding, and for this 8 percent, the Federal Government has insisted on a tremendously disproportionate share of control over our schools. Whatever reductions we've proposed in that 8 percent will amount to very little in the total cost of education. They will, however, restore more authority to States and local school districts.

Historically, the American people have supported by voluntary contributions more artistic and cultural activities than all the other countries in the world put together. I wholeheartedly support this approach and believe that Americans will continue their generosity. Therefore, I'm proposing a savings of $85 million in the Federal subsidies now going to the arts and humanities.

There are a number of subsidies to business and industry that I believe are unnecessary, not because the activities being subsidized aren't of value, but because the marketplace contains incentives enough to warrant continuing these activities without a government subsidy. One such subsidy is the Department of Energy's synthetic fuels program. We will continue support of research leading to development of new technologies and more independence from foreign oil, but we can save at least $3.2 billion by leaving to private industry the building of plants to make liquid or gas fuels from coal.

We're asking that another major industry—business subsidy I should say, the Export-Import Bank loan authority, be reduced by one-third in 1982. We're doing this because the primary beneficiaries of taxpayer funds in this case are the exporting companies themselves—most of them profitable corporations.

This brings me to a number of other lending programs in which government makes low-interest loans, some of them at an interest rate as low as 2 percent. What has not been very well understood is that the Treasury Department has no money of its own to lend; it has to go into the private capital market and borrow the money. So, in this time of excessive interest rates, the government finds itself borrowing at an interest rate several times as high as the interest it gets back from those it lends the money to. And this difference, of course, is paid by your constituents—the taxpayers. They get hit again if they try to borrow, because government borrowing contributes to raising all interest rates.

By terminating the Economic Development Administration, we can save hundreds of millions of dollars in 1982 and billions more over the next few years. There's a lack of consistent and convincing evidence that EDA and its Regional Commissions have been effective in creating new jobs. They have been effective in creating an array of planners, grantsmen, and professional middlemen. We believe we can do better just by the expansion of the economy and the job creation which will come from our economic program.

The Food Stamp program will be restored to its original purpose, to assist those without resources to purchase sufficient nutritional food. We will, however, save $1.8 billion in fiscal year 1982 by removing from eligibility those who are not in real need or who are abusing the program. But even with this reduction, the program will be budgeted for more than $10 billion.

We will tighten welfare and give more attention to outside sources of income when determining the amount of welfare that an individual is allowed. This, plus strong and effective work requirements, will save $520 million in the next year.

I stated a moment ago our intention to keep the school breakfast and lunch programs for those in true need. But by cutting back on meals for children of families who can afford to pay, the savings will be $1.6 billion in the fiscal year 1982.

Now, let me just touch on a few other areas which are typical of the kind of reductions we've included in this economic package. The Trade Adjustment Assistance program provides benefits for workers who are unemployed when foreign imports reduce the market for various American products, causing shutdown of plants and layoff of workers.

This Fisher Body Works factory in Detroit, Michigan, ended its automotive production in 1984. (2015)

The purpose is to help these workers find jobs in growing sectors of our economy. There's nothing wrong with that, but because these benefits are paid out on top of normal unemployment benefits, we wind up paying greater benefits to those who lose their jobs because of foreign competition than we do to their friends and neighbors who are laid off due to domestic competition. Anyone must agree that this is unfair. Putting these two programs on the same footing will save $1.15 billion in just 1 year.

Earlier I made mention of changing categorical grants to States and local governments into block grants. Now, we know of course that the categorical grant programs burden local and State governments with a mass of Federal regulations and Federal paperwork. Ineffective targeting, wasteful administrative overhead—all can be eliminated by shifting the resources and decision-making authority to local and State government. This will also consolidate programs which are scattered throughout the Federal bureaucracy, bringing government closer to the people and saving $23.9 billion over the next 5 years.

Our program for economic renewal deals with a number of programs which at present are not cost-effective. An example is Medicaid. Right now Washington provides the States with unlimited matching payments for their expenditures; at the same time, we here in Washington pretty much dictate how the States are going to manage those programs. We want to put a cap on how much the Federal Government will contribute, but at the same time allow the States much more flexibility in managing and structuring the programs. I know from our experience in California that such flexibility could have led to far more cost-effective reforms. Now, this will bring a savings of $1 billion next year.

The space program has been and is important to America, and we plan to continue it. We believe, however, that a reordering of priorities to focus on the most important and cost-effective NASA programs can result in a savings of a quarter of a million dollars.

Now, coming down from space to the mailbox, the Postal Service has been consistently unable to live within its operating budget. It is still dependent on large Federal subsidies.

We propose reducing those subsidies by $632 million in 1982 to press the Postal Service into becoming more effective, and in subsequent years the savings will continue to add up.

The Economic Regulatory Administration in the Department of Energy has programs to force companies to convert to specific fuels. It has the authority to administer a gas rationing plan, and prior to decontrol it ran the oil price control program. With these and other regulations gone we can save several hundreds of millions of dollars over the next few years.

NASA's Kennedy Space Center in Titusville, Florida

I'm sure there's one department you've been waiting for me to mention, the Department of Defense. It's the only department in our entire program that will actually be increased over the present budgeted figure. But even here there was no exemption. The Department of Defense came up with a number of cuts which reduce the budget increase needed to restore our military balance. These measures will save $2.9 billion in 1982 outlays, and by 1986 a total of $28.2 billion will have been saved—or perhaps I should say, will have been made available for the necessary things that we must do. The aim will be to provide the most effective defense for the lowest possible cost.

I believe that my duty as President requires that I recommend increases in defense spending over the coming years. I know that you're all aware—but I think it bears saying again—that since 1970 the Soviet Union has invested $300 billion more in its military forces than we have. As a result of its massive military buildup, the Soviets have made a significant numerical advantage in strategic nuclear delivery systems, tactical aircraft, submarines, artillery, and anti-aircraft defense. To allow this imbalance to continue is a threat to our national security. Notwithstanding our economic straits, making the financial changes beginning now is far less costly than waiting and having to attempt a crash program several years from now.

We remain committed to the goal of arms limitation through negotiation. I hope we can persuade our adversaries to come to realistic balanced and verifiable agreements. But, as we negotiate, our security must be fully protected by a balanced and realistic defense program.

Now, let me say a word here about the general problem of waste and fraud in the Federal Government. One government estimate indicated that fraud alone may account for anywhere from 1 to 10 percent—as much as $25 billion of Federal expenditures for social programs. If the tax dollars that are wasted or mismanaged are added to this fraud total, the staggering dimensions of this problem begin to emerge.

The Office of Management and Budget is now putting together an interagency task force to attack waste and fraud. We're also planning to appoint as Inspectors General highly trained professionals who will spare no effort to do this job. No administration can promise to immediately stop a trend that has grown in recent years as quickly as government expenditures themselves, but let me say this: Waste and fraud in the Federal Government is exactly what I've called it before—an unrelenting national scandal, a scandal we're bound and determined to do something about.

Marching in lockstep with the whole program of reductions in spending is the equally important program of reduced tax rates. Both are essential if we're to have economic recovery. It's time to create new jobs, to build and rebuild industry, and to give the American people room to do what they do best. And that can only be done with a tax program which provides incentive to increase productivity for both workers and industry.

Our proposal is for a 10-percent across-the-board cut every year for 3 years in the tax rates for all individual income taxpayers, making a total cut in the tax-cut rates of 30 percent. This 3-year reduction will also apply to the tax on unearned income, leading toward an eventual elimination of the present differential between the tax on earned and unearned income.

Now, I would have hoped that we could be retroactive with this. But as it stands, the effective starting date for these 10-percent personal income tax rate reductions will call for as of July 1st of this year.

Again, let me remind you that while this 30-percent reduction will leave the taxpayers with $500 billion more in their pockets over the next 5 years, it's actually only a reduction in the tax increase already built into the system. Unlike some past ``tax reforms,'' this is not merely a shift of wealth between different sets of taxpayers. This proposal for an equal reduction in everyone's tax rates will expand our national prosperity, enlarge national incomes, and increase opportunities for all Americans.

Some will argue, I know, that reducing tax rates now will be inflationary. A solid body of economic experts does not agree. And tax cuts adopted over the past three-fourths of a century indicate these economic experts are right. They will not be inflationary. I've had advice that in 1985 our real production in goods and services will grow by 20 percent and be $300 billion higher than it is today. The average worker's wage will rise in real purchasing power 8 percent, and this is in after-tax dollars. And this, of course, is predicated on a complete program of tax cuts and spending reductions being implemented.

The other part of the tax package is aimed directly at providing business and industry with the capital needed to modernize and engage in more research and development. This will involve an increase in depreciation allowances, and this part of our tax proposal will be retroactive to January 1st.

The present depreciation system is obsolete, needlessly complex, and economically counterproductive. Very simply, it bases the depreciation of plant machinery and vehicles and tools on their original cost, with no recognition of how inflation has increased their replacement cost. We're proposing a much shorter write-off time than is presently allowed—a 5-year-write-off for machinery, 3 years for vehicles and trucks, and a 10-year write-off for plant. In fiscal year 1982 under this plan, business would acquire nearly $10 billion for investment; by 1985, the figure would be nearly 45 billion.

These changes are essential to provide the new investment which is needed to create millions of new jobs between now and 1985 [1986], and to make America competitive once again in the world market. These won't be make-work jobs. They are productive jobs, jobs with a future.

I'm well aware that there are many other desirable and needed tax changes, such as indexing the income tax brackets to protect taxpayers against inflation; the unjust discrimination against married couples if both are working and earning; tuition tax credits; the unfairness of the inheritance tax, especially to the family-owned farm and the family-owned business; and a number of others. But our program for economic recovery is so urgently needed to begin to bring down inflation that I'm asking you to act on this plan first and with great urgency. And then, I pledge I will join with you in seeking these additional tax changes at the earliest date possible.

American society experienced a virtual explosion in government regulation during the past decade. Between 1970 and 1979, expenditures for the major regulatory agencies quadrupled. The number of pages published annually in the Federal Register nearly tripled, and the number of pages in the Code of Federal Regulations increased by nearly two-thirds. The result has been higher prices, higher unemployment, and lower productivity growth. Overregulation causes small and independent business men and women, as well as large businesses to defer or terminate plans for expansion. And since they're responsible for most of the new jobs, those new jobs just aren't created.

Now, we have no intention of dismantling the regulatory agencies, especially those necessary to protect environment and assure the public health and safety. However, we must come to grips with inefficient and burdensome regulations, eliminate those we can and reform the others.

I have asked Vice President Bush to head a Cabinet-level Task Force on Regulatory Relief. Second, I asked each member of my Cabinet to postpone the effective dates of the hundreds of new regulations which have not yet been implemented. Third, in coordination with the Task Force, many of the agency heads have already taken prompt action to review and rescind existing burdensome regulations. And finally, just yesterday I signed an Executive order that for the first time provides for effective and coordinated management of the regulatory process.

Much has been accomplished, but it's only a beginning. We will eliminate those regulations that are unproductive and unnecessary by Executive order where possible and cooperate fully with you on those that require legislation.

The final aspect of our plan requires a national monetary policy which does not allow money growth to increase consistently faster than the growth of goods and services. In order to curb inflation we need to slow the growth in our money supply.

Now, we fully recognize the independence of the Federal Reserve System and will do nothing to interfere with or undermine that independence. We will consult regularly with the Federal Reserve Board on all aspects of our economic program and will vigorously pursue budget policies that'll make their job easier in reducing monetary growth. A successful program to achieve stable and moderate growth patterns in the money supply will keep both inflation and interest rates down and restore vigor to our financial institutions and markets.

Ronald Reagan statue in Warsaw, Poland

This, then, is our proposal—America's new beginning: a program for economic recovery. I don't want it to be simply the plan of my administration. I'm here tonight to ask you to join me in making it our plan. Together we can embark on this road— [applause].

Thank you very much. I should have arranged to quit right here. [Laughter]

Well, together we can embark on this road, not to make things easy, but to make things better. Our social, political, and cultural, as well as our economic institutions, can no longer absorb the repeated shocks that have been dealt them over the past decades. Can we do the job? The answer is yes. But we must begin now.

We're in control here. There's nothing wrong with America that together we can't fix. I'm sure there'll be some who raise the old familiar cry, ``Don't touch my program; cut somewhere else.'' I hope I've made it plain that our approach has been evenhanded, that only the programs for the truly deserving needy remain untouched. The question is, are we simply going to go down the same path we've gone down before, carving out one special program here, another special program there? I don't think that's what the American people expect of us. More important, I don't think that's what they want. They're ready to return to the source of our strength.

The substance and prosperity of our nation is built by wages brought home from the factories and the mills, the farms, and the shops. They are the services provided in 10,000 corners of America; the interest on the thrift of our people and the returns for their risk-taking. The production of America is the possession of those who build, serve, create, and produce.

For too long now, we've removed from our people the decisions on how to dispose of what they created. We've strayed from first principles. We must alter our course.

The taxing power of government must be used to provide revenues for legitimate government purposes. It must not be used to regulate the economy or bring about social change. We've tried that, and surely we must be able to see it doesn't work.

Spending by government must be limited to those functions which are the proper province of government. We can no longer afford things simply because we think of them. Next year we can reduce the budget by $41.4 billion, without harm to government's legitimate purposes or to our responsibility to all who need our benevolence. This, plus the reduction in tax rates, will help bring an end to inflation.

In the health and social services area alone, the plan we're proposing will substantially reduce the need for 465 pages of law, 1,400 pages of regulations, 5,000 Federal employees who presently administer 7,600 separate grants in about 25,000 separate locations. Over 7 million man and woman hours of work by State and local officials are required to fill out government forms.

I would direct a question to those who have indicated already an unwillingness to accept such a plan: Have they an alternative which offers a greater chance of balancing the budget, reducing and eliminating inflation, stimulating the creation of jobs, and reducing the tax burden? And, if they haven't, are they suggesting we can continue on the present course without coming to a day of reckoning? If we don't do this, inflation and the growing tax burden will put an end to everything we believe in and our dreams for the future.

We don't have an option of living with inflation and its attendant tragedy, millions of productive people willing and able to work but unable to find a buyer for their work in the job market. We have an alternative, and that is the program for economic recovery.

True, it'll take time for the favorable effects of our proposal to be felt. So, we must begin now. The people are watching and waiting. They don't demand miracles. They do expect us to act. Let us act together.

Thank you, and good night.

The Legitimate Role of Government in a Free Society

Walter E. Williams (2000)

Walter Williams (b. 1936) is the John M. Olin Distinguished Professor of Economics at George Mason University in Virginia. He holds a Ph.D. in economics from UCLA. Dr. Williams has published several books and dozens of articles. He appears often on radio and television discussing economic issues. In this speech Dr. Williams discusses a vital but often overlooked topic.

What did the founders of the United States see as the legitimate role of government? To answer that question we should turn to the rule book they gave us: the United States Constitution. Most of what they considered legitimate functions of the federal government are found in Article I, Section 8 of our Constitution, which says, in part: "The Congress shall have Power To lay and collect Taxes, Duties, Imposts and Excises, to pay the Debts and provide for the common Defense and general Welfare of the United States . . . To borrow Money on the credit of the United States . . . To regulate Commerce with foreign Nations, and among the several States, and with the Indian tribes . . . To coin money . . . To establish Post Offices and post Roads . . . To raise and support Armies." The framers granted Congress taxing and spending powers for a few other activities, but nowhere in the Constitution do we find authority for up to three-quarters of what Congress taxes and spends for today. There is no constitutional authorization for farm subsidies, bank bailouts, or food stamps—not to mention midnight basketball. We have made a significant departure from the constitutional principles of individual freedom and limited government that made us a rich nation in the first place.

These principles of freedom were embodied in our nation through the combined institutions of private ownership of property and free enterprise, both of which have suffered devastating attacks and are mere skeletons of what they were in the past.

The Social Value of Private Property and Free Enterprise

Private property performs at least two important social functions: it encourages people to do voluntarily what is in the social interest, and it minimizes the coercive power that one man or the state can have over another. And it performs these functions without appeals to beneficence.

I do not care much about future generations. After all, what has a child born in 2050 A.D. ever done for me? My actions, however, do not reflect this personal sentiment. Several years ago I planted young trees on my property and made other improvements. I will be dead by the time the trees mature. A child born in 2050 A.D. will enjoy the fruits of my sacrifices. I could just as easily have spent the money for [things] which I would have fully enjoyed all to myself. Why did I make these improvements to my property? At least part of the reason is that I will get a higher price when I sell the property if its quality is higher and it can be expected to provide housing services for a longer period of time. By pursuing my own interest, I made it possible for future generations to have a nice house. Would I have had the same strong incentive if the government owned my house? Obviously not.

Look around the world: you will see that what receives the least care tends to be commonly owned; that which receives the best care tends to be privately owned. In free markets, one's personal wealth is held hostage to socially responsible behavior. To take

another example, the citizens of New York derive their daily meals not from the benevolence of the Missouri farmer (who may in fact hate New Yorkers) but because it is in his own private self-interest to supply them. Most things get done because of self-interest and private property rights.

The Founders understood that relatively free markets are the most effective form of social organization for promoting individual freedom. Indeed, capitalism is defined as a system wherein individuals are free to pursue their own interests, make voluntary exchanges, and hold private property rights in goods and services. Much of the original intent of the United States Constitution, as seen in the document itself and in the Federalist Papers that advocated its ratification, was to bring about a climate in which this kind of social organization could occur. In a free society, most relationships should be voluntary, and involuntary exchange should be minimized.

Widespread private control and ownership of property is consistent with this objective. Despite the size and alleged power of industrial giants like IBM, AT&T, and General Motors, in a free market they cannot get a dollar from me unless I volunteer to give it to them. Widespread government ownership and/or control of property is the antithesis of voluntary exchange. Government is the major source of forced exchanges, the most prominent of which is taxation.

IBM logo on the IBM building in New York City

A Totalitarian Future?

Anything that weakens the institution of private property interferes with the attainment of the socially desirable outcomes just described. Taxes represent government claims on private property. As taxes rise, you own less and less of what you earn. If the tax rate were ever to reach 100 percent, the government would have destroyed private property, and you would own none of what you had earned. Keep in mind that a working definition of slavery is that you work but do not have any rights to the fruit of your labor.

Taxation and regulation constitute the confiscation of some or all of the freedom to own and use property. This confiscation has reached unprecedented proportions. In 1902 expenditures at all levels of government totaled $1.7 billion, and the average taxpayer paid only $60 a year in taxes. In fact, from 1787 to 1920, federal expenditures never exceeded 4 percent of the Gross National Product (GNP), except in wartime. Today federal expenditures alone are $1.8 trillion—almost 30 percent of GNP—and state and local governments spend over a trillion more. The average taxpayer now pays more than $8,000 a year, working from January 1 to May 8 to pay federal, state, and local taxes. In addition to the out-of-pocket cost, Americans spend 5.4 billion hours each year complying with the federal tax code—roughly the equivalent of 3 million people working full time. If it were employed in productive activity, the labor now devoted to tax compliance would be worth $232 billion annually. The federal cost of hiring 93,000 IRS employees is $6 billion. If these Americans weren't fooling around with the tax code, they could produce the entire annual output of the aircraft, trucking, auto, and food-processing industries combined.

In spite of the tax burden, capitalism has been so successful in eliminating disease, pestilence, hunger, and gross poverty that other human problems now appear both unbearable and inexcusable. Free enterprise thus is threatened today not because of its failure but, somewhat ironically, because of its success. Although the rise of capitalism brought better treatment to women, racial minorities, the handicapped, criminals, and the insane, social reformers assert that "it doesn't work" and "is dehumanizing." In the name of ideals such as income equality, sex and race balance, affordable housing and medical care, orderly markets, consumer protection, and energy conservation, to name just a few, we have imposed widespread government controls that have subordinated us to a point at which considerations of personal freedom are but secondary or tertiary matters. If you take tiny steps toward a goal, one day you will get there, and the ultimate end of this process is totalitarianism, which is no more than a reduced form of servitude. As David Hume said, "It is seldom that liberty of any kind is lost all at once."

In the vanguard of this totalitarian movement are defenders of the "new human rights," the chief advocates of curtailing rights to property and profits. They are anti-competition and pro-monopoly. They support control and coercion by the state. They believe that they have more intelligence and wisdom than the masses and that they are ordained to impose that wisdom forcibly on the rest of us. They want to replace the market with economic planning, which is nothing more than the forcible superseding of other people's plans by a powerful elite. Of course they have what they call good reasons, but every tyrant has what he calls a good reason for restricting the freedom of others.

The elites' assault on the principles of freedom would have been less devastating had not Americans from all walks of life, whether they realized it or not, demonstrated a deep and abiding contempt for private property rights and economic freedom that stemmed primarily from their desire for government to do good. They decided that government should care for the poor, the disadvantaged, the elderly, failing businesses, college students, and many other "deserving" segments of our society. It's nice to do those things, but we have to recognize that government has no resources of its own. Congressmen and senators are not spending their own money for these programs.

Furthermore, there is no Tooth Fairy or Santa Claus who gives them the resources. The only way the government can give one American one dollar is to confiscate it first, under intimidation, threats, and coercion, from another American. In other words, for government to do good, it must first do evil. If a private person were to do the things that government does, he would be condemned as a common thief. The only difference is legality, and legality alone is no talisman for moral people. This reasoning explains why socialism is evil. It uses bad means (coercion) to achieve what are seen as good ends (helping people).

From Good Intentions to Corruption

Government was not long in the business of doing good before Americans found they could use government to live at the expense of other Americans, both through the tax code and through "privilege granting," a government activity that dates back to medieval times in Europe, where guilds and mercantile associations controlled trade in their particular areas. With a payment to the king or a reigning lord they were granted monopoly privileges. In modern times, we have the equivalent; we just call them political contributions.

Almost every group in the nation has come to feel that the government owes it a special privilege or favor. Manufacturers feel that the government owes them protective tariffs. Farmers feel that the government owes them crop subsidies. Unions feel that the government should keep their jobs protected from non-union competition. Residents of coastal areas feel that the government should give them funds for rivers and harbors. Intellectuals feel that the government should give them funds for research. The unemployed and the unemployable feel that the government owes them a living. Big business feels that the government should protect them from the rigors of market competition. Members of almost every occupation, profession, or trade feel that the government should use licensing requirements and other forms of regulation to protect their incomes from competition that would be caused by others entering the trade.

Conservatives are by no means exempt from this practice. They rail against food stamps, legal aid, and Aid to Families with Dependent Children, but they come out in favor of aid to dependent farmers, aid to dependent banks, and aid to dependent motorcycle companies. They don't have a moral leg to stand on. They merely prove to the nation that it is just a matter of whose ox is being gored. Conservatives as well as liberals validate H. L. Mencken's definition of an election: "—government is a broker in pillage, and every election is a sort of advance auction sale of stolen goods." To the extent he was right, we must acknowledge that we, not the politicians, are the problem.

This cartoon from 1901 is called "The 'Fake' Beggars." It depicts J. P. Morgan and Mark Hanna, two successful businessmen of the time, asking Uncle Sam for subsidies.

The Way Back

Our government has become destructive of the ends it was created to serve. John Stuart Mill, who wrote the classic text *On Liberty*, said, in discussing the limits of government power, "[T]he only purpose for which power can be rightfully exercised over any member of a civilized society, against his will, is to prevent harm to others. His own good, either physical or moral, is not sufficient warrant." Mill added, "He cannot rightfully

John Stuart Mill

be compelled because it would be better for him to do so . . . because it will make him happier" or because, in the opinion of others, "to do so would be wise, or even right." Finally, Mill said, "These are good reasons for remonstrating him, or persuading him, but not for compelling him, or visiting him with an evil in the case he do otherwise."

We have gone much further than what Mill and John Locke argued are the limits to coercion in a free society. Part of the problem is that the Constitution contains little language explicitly protecting economic rights. We must find a way to set a limit on what Congress can take from us. It should take the form of a constitutional amendment limiting peacetime federal spending to a specific, lower percentage of the Gross Domestic Product. If we can't get Congress to pass such an amendment, we should reconvene the constitutional convention for the narrow purpose of a spending-limitation amendment. . . .

If the Founders were to come back to today's America, I think they would be very disappointed in our choice to accept what we see as safety in exchange for liberty. But I would also say that it is not too late for us to wake up and respond to the erosion of our liberties. Americans have never done wrong things for a long while. But we must get about the task of putting government back where our Founders intended while we have the liberty to do so.

Reprinted by permission from Imprimis, *the national speech digest of Hillsdale College, www.hillsdale.edu.*

US Foods IPO

Intercontinental Exchange (2016)

A private company that wishes to raise capital may choose to become a public company through an initial public offering (IPO). In an IPO, the company allows investors to purchase shares of stock in the company. US Foods, Inc. is a foodservice distributor headquartered in Rosemont, Illinois. The company employs approximately 25,000 people in more than sixty locations around the country.

NEW YORK—(BUSINESS WIRE)—US Foods Holding Corp. (US Foods), a leading foodservice distributor in the United States, began trading today on the New York Stock Exchange (NYSE) under the ticker symbol "USFD," after its initial public offering. US Foods raised $1.02 billion in gross proceeds and is the second U.S. IPO in 2016 to raise over $1 billion in proceeds, following MGM Growth Properties (NYSE: MGP), which listed in April. GTS is the NYSE Designated Market Maker (DMM) for the company's shares.

To mark US Foods' public debut, President and CEO Pietro Satriano, accompanied by members of US Foods' management committee, rang The Opening Bell® and visited the company's DMM on the NYSE trading floor to observe the opening of USFD.

The celebration continued outside the NYSE in "Experience Square" with the recreation of a restaurant kitchen beneath the NYSE façade. The nearly 50 foot line was designed to underscore the company's focus on bringing great food and an easy customer experience to foodservice operators and shine a spotlight on independent restaurants.

US Foods sign on the New York Stock Exchange during the company's IPO (2016)

"Our strategy of Great Food. Made Easy. is all about addressing and exceeding the needs and expectations of the independent restaurant customer and helping them to grow their business," said Marshall Warkentin, senior vice president, Marketing, US Foods. "From delivering new, innovative products to offering game-changing technology, US Foods is committed to helping restaurant owners, chefs and foodservice professionals make it in this tough industry."

Five US Foods independent restaurant customers from different corners of the country were present to serve their signature bite from this one of a kind kitchen. The chefs represented different regions of the country and each cooked up the dish that best represents their restaurant.

The chefs include:

- Cristy Nolton – culinary director, Yeah Burger, Atlanta, GA
- Donna Lee – owner, Brown Bag Seafood, Chicago, IL
- Brian Ellis – executive chef, The Smith, New York, NY
- Taion McElveen – chef, Eschelon Experiences, Raleigh, NC
- Kenneth Danko – chef/owner, Devilicious, Temecula, CA

"We couldn't imagine celebrating the listing of our company on the NYSE without sharing the spotlight with some of the most passionate restaurant owners and chefs who work tirelessly to deliver amazing dishes to America's tables," Warkentin said.

"We're delighted to welcome US Foods Holding Corp. to the NYSE's community of esteemed companies," said Tom Farley, NYSE Group President. "US Foods is a distinguished leader in food distribution, inspiring and empowering its partners to deliver best-in-class dining experiences, as well as offering an array of innovative products including technology and business solutions. We congratulate the US Foods team on its IPO, and we are proud to mark this exciting new chapter for the company and its shareholders."

Poverty and Wealth

Ella Wheeler Wilcox (c. 1883)

Ella Wheeler (1850-1919) was born in Wisconsin and began writing poetry as a child. After her marriage to Robert Wilcox, the couple lived in New York and Connecticut. Their one son died in infancy.

The stork flew over a town one day,
And back of each wing an infant lay;
One to a rich man's home he brought,
And one he left at a labourer's cot.
The rich man said, 'My son shall be
A lordly ruler o'er land and sea.'
The labourer sighed, ''Tis the good God's will
That I have another mouth to fill.'
The rich man's son grew strong and fair,
And proud with the pride of a millionaire.
His motto in life was, 'Live while you may, '
And he crowded years in a single day.
He bought position and name and place,
And he bought him a wife with a handsome face.
He journeyed over the whole wide world,
But discontent his heart lay curled
Like a serpent hidden in leaves and moss,
And life seemed hollow and gold was dross.
He scoffed at woman, and doubted God,
And died like a beast and went back to the sod.
The son of the labourer tilled the soil,
And thanked God daily for health and toil.
He wedded for love in his youthful prime,
And two lives chorded in tune and time.
His wants were simple, and simple his creed,
To trust God fully: it served his need,
And lightened his labour, and helped him to die
With a smile on his lips and a hope in his eye.
When all is over and all is done,
Now which of these men was the richer one?

Ella Wheeler Wilcox

Will We Heal with Living Water or Snake Oil?

Eric Potter (2016)

Samaritan Ministries, founded in 1994, is a voluntary association of over 200,000 Christians. Samaritan does not provide health insurance. Instead, members help each other pay their medical bills by sending a check each month to another member for a specific need assigned by the ministry. This article originally appeared in the Samaritan Ministries newsletter and on their blog (http://samaritanministries.org/will-we-heal-with-living-water-or-snake-oil-a-physician-reflects/). Eric Potter graduated from Vanderbilt Medical School in Nashville. He opened his current medical practice, Sanctuary Functional Medicine, in Middle Tennessee in 2014. Our purpose for including this article is not to endorse Samaritan Ministries, but rather to stimulate thinking about possible different approaches to the delivery of health care in our country.

Nearly every person touched by our health care system has a legitimate complaint concerning its dysfunction. The suffering complain that they feel like a number being shuttled through a hurried system. The doctors complain that they no longer have time to care for patients, but are instead filling out computer forms. The insurance companies complain that they must raise their rates. Conservatives complain that euthanasia and abortion are unhindered. Liberals complain that the poor go without care. There is truth to each of these and other complaints, yet I wonder how many of us really see the underlying source of the dysfunction.

We have all imbibed the snake oil of a humanistic approach to medicine. Clinically, financially, and ethically, we are drunk on this snake oil and wonder why we can't find our way out of the dark hole. Only a God-centered and God-directed approach can replace the snake oil with Living Water and bring Light to our path.

Before this Living Water can be appreciated, larger society, particularly those who follow Christ, must discern the reality of our broken system—a system broken to the core—rather than just complain about superficial symptoms. Compounded into the clinical care provided to each of us, we find at least two goal-oriented deceptions in the snake oil.

On the one hand, society desires to live autonomously, unheeding either Biblical truth or a natural understanding of health. We treat our being not as God's image, but solely as an instrument of self-pleasure. Stewardship rarely enters our thoughts or desires in regards to our personal health.

On the other hand, we look to medicine to be a savior of sorts, restoring the brokenness we suffer whether it comes from a fallen world or from our own actions. Even the seemingly noble patient-centered medicine where the doctor puts the patient into the driver seat, ultimately plays to the false notion that we can save ourselves. Humanistic medicine plays the part well, promising either a cure now or a glorious cure in the near future with a little more research.

Financial matters also play a leading role in producing the humanistic snake oil. Again we see the reflections of a false savior mentality. Insurance companies and government programs promise to care for us from cradle to grave, but ultimately they require more and more monetary sacrifices to keep them propped up.

Conventional medicine's economic model requires an assembly line system that often blames patients when the short visits and pharmaceutical miracles fail to fix the suffering. Drug companies market the latest and greatest costly medicine, guaranteed to fix your problems, at least until the next study shows how they are not quite as wonderful as the initial marketing campaign promised.

Pharmaceutical production line

The internet offers myriads of guaranteed cures, for the right price, to those left searching for hope after the conventional system scoots them out the door. These "natural" remedies, many of which restore true health more permanently, still may require submission to a higher authority overseeing their application and sale. At the lowest level of finances, the very startup of a Christian practice along Biblical principles faces looming financial obstacles if humanistic alliances are foregone.

Ethically, the snake oil is a bitter poison flavored with artificial sweeteners. Having lost sight of the core principles, a different type of medicine is promoted by society at large, either explicitly or implicitly through participation in the programs. Killing the weak is protected, whether at the end of life or its beginning. Sinful lifestyles are not only condoned but even applauded or legitimized. Condoned sin becomes "normal." Legitimized sin becomes a disease to be overlooked or medicated. Greed overrules the principles of loving God and loving neighbor, in board rooms, government gatherings, medical offices, and even our own homes. When the moorings of absolute truth are detached, we are left to drift about in any and all directions. The snake oil not only causes us to cut the anchor, but to lose sight of the very fact that we are adrift.

What are we to do? How can we restore such a broken system? Only a work of God according to His principles can reform, or even replace the humanistic snake oil with Living Water. Only a God-centered, Biblical, and whole-person approach can hope to be an antidote. Rather than focusing on either the physician or the patient, God must be acknowledged as the source of our health. Only in Him and according to His ways can shalom, the Hebrew word for wholeness or well-being, be approximated on earth.

If a whole-person Biblical model is practiced, the physician will be free to act and think differently. This actually allows him or her to serve God and to love the neighbor-patient across the table. The physician steps down from acting as a savior and the patient steps down from being an idol. After all, the patient finds greater security in a physician serving this higher goal than in a physician seeking to only serve the patient or physician's self-interests. Submission to God and His design for health blesses the suffering patient far more than a humanistic system focused primarily on maintaining itself.

How are we to know how to practice God-centered medicine? The truth and sufficiency of the Bible must be the highest authority, to have any hope of reforming medicine. The ethics of abortion and euthanasia may be the most obvious targets for Biblical application, but the Living Water must permeate much more deeply into the bowels of the system. The inherently dysfunctional economics of both corporate and socialistic policies must be ruthlessly measured by the Bible.

Furthermore, each individual must drink the Living Water, though it may initially taste bitter, because we must sacrifice something for the sake of supporting an alternative system. As long as Christians continue to gladly drink the snake oil, the snake oil industry will flourish. Not until we refuse the humanistic system's enticements and begin to sacrifice in support of a Godly alternative, will that alternative system have a hope of growing out of a thousand points of light.

What would this medicine look like in the exam room? Whole persons made in the image of God would be treated as such by the physician caring for them. The economic model would offer cost-efficient (avoiding bureaucratic waste and red tape), affordable care which simultaneously furnished a living for physicians and other caregivers who invested their lives into the healing arts. This model would supply adequate time, longer than a 12- to 15-minute visit, such that caregivers of all flavors could care for not only the physical, but the emotional and spiritual needs of their patients. The reality that we are embodied souls with feelings and relationships rather than just evolved animals or soulless robots would be evident to any observer of the process.

The Living Water of Kingdom Medicine practiced under a covenant before a sovereign Lord entails far more than can be described here. It must permeate every inch of our being, individually and corporately. When the caregiver covenants before God to tend to their patient according to God's ways for His glory and for the love of the neighbor-patient, Kingdom Medicine will be sought by the multitudes.

This vision is not impossible. One of the biggest hurdles is that oil and water cannot mix. We, as patients, doctors, pharmacists, third-party payers, nurses, family members, government leaders, and others must choose between Living Water or snake oil today rather than continuing to sip on some form of an eventually fatal mixture.

As I continue to strive toward a more Biblical approach to health care as a physician and for my family, the Lord has brought us to Sanctuary Functional Medicine and Samaritan Ministries.

I started the Sanctuary Functional Medicine practice along with fellow Christian doctors. It uses the Direct Primary Care model to prevent third parties from controlling health care, allowing the patient and doctor to remain free and follow their consciences. Health care sharing through Samaritan Ministries also leaves to the individual the responsibility of making health care decisions, and then brings the Body of Christ together to bear one another's large medical burdens.

I think this combination is a promising one more Christians should consider. However the Lord leads you, I hope you will join us in reforming the health care system for God's glory.

P.S. These ideas may stir some debate, but my greatest fear is not that some people will disagree but that no one will care enough to respond. Complacency, comfort, and diversion are the greater culprits convincing us to drink the snake oil. I look forward to questions, even challenges, but hope that each will first hear my undertones of repentance in having participated in the system. Let's all examine ourselves, repent of what God shows us, and begin to apply His principles to the entire system (Colossians 3:23).

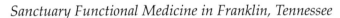

Sanctuary Functional Medicine in Franklin, Tennessee

Security in Your Old Age
Social Security Board (1936)

The U.S. government published this pamphlet to explain the new Social Security program to "employees of industrial and business establishments."

Beginning November 24, 1936, the United States Government will set up a Social Security account for you, if you are eligible. To understand your obligations, rights, and benefits you should read the following general explanation.

There is now a law in this country which will give about 26 million working people something to live on when they are old and have stopped working. This law, which gives other benefits, too, was passed last year by Congress and is called the Social Security Act.

Under this law the United States Government will send checks every month to retired workers, both men and women, after they have passed their 65th birthday and have met a few simple requirements of the law.

What This Means to You

This means that if you work in some factory, shop, mine, mill, store, office, or almost any other kind of business or industry, you will be earning benefits that will come to you later on. From the time you are 65 years old, or more, and stop working, you will get a Government check every month of your life, if you have worked some time (one day or more) in each of any 5 years after 1936, and have earned during that time a total of $2,000 or more.

The checks will come to you as a right. You will get them regardless of the amount of property or income you may have. They are what the law calls "Old-Age Benefits" under the Social Security Act. If you prefer to keep on working after

This poster was distributed during 1936 and 1937 to inform the public about the new Social Security program.

you are 65, the monthly checks from the Government will begin coming to you whenever you decide to retire.

The Amount of Your Checks

How much you will get when you are 65 years old will depend entirely on how much you earn in wages from your industrial or business employment between January 1, 1937, and your 65th birthday. A man or woman who gets good wages and has a steady job most of his or her life can get as much as $85 a month for life after age 65. The least you can get in monthly benefits, if you come under the law at all, is $10 a month.

If You Are Now Young

Suppose you are making $25 a week and are young enough now to go on working for 40 years. If you make an average of $25 a week for 52 weeks in each year, your check when you are 65 years old will be $53 a month for the rest of your life. If you make $50 a week, you will get $74.50 a month for the rest of you life after age 65.

If You Are Now Middle-Aged

But suppose you are about 55 years old now and have 10 years to work before you are 65. Suppose you make only $15 a week on the average. When you stop work at age 65 you will get a check for $19 each month for the rest of your life. If you make $25 a week for 10 years, you will get a little over $23 a month from the Government as long as you live after your 65th birthday.

If You Should Die Before Age 65

If you should die before you begin to get your monthly checks, your family will get a payment in cash, amounting to 3½ cents on every dollar of wages you have earned after 1936. If, for example, you should die at age 64, and if you had earned $25 a week for 10 years before that time, your family would receive $455. On the other hand, if you have not worked enough to get the regular monthly checks by the time you are 65, you will get a lump sum, or if you should die your family or estate would get a lump sum. The amount of this, too, will be 3½ cents on every dollar of wages you earn after 1936.

Taxes

The same law that provides these old-age benefits for you and other workers, sets up certain new taxes to be paid to the United States Government. These taxes are collected by the Bureau of Internal Revenue of the U. S. Treasury Department, and inquiries concerning them should be addressed to that bureau. The law also creates an "Old-Age

Reserve Account" in the United States Treasury, and Congress is authorized to put into this reserve account each year enough money to provide for the monthly payments you and other workers are to receive when you are 65.

Your Part of the Tax

The taxes called for in this law will be paid both by your employer and by you. For the next 3 years you will pay maybe 15 cents a week, maybe 25 cents a week, maybe 30 cents or more, according to what you earn. That is to say, during the next 3 years, beginning January 1, 1937, you will pay 1 cent for every dollar you earn, and at the same time your employer will pay 1 cent for every dollar you earn, up to $3,000 a year. Twenty-six million other workers and their employers will be paying at the same time.

After the first 3 years—that is to say, beginning in 1940—you will pay, and your employer will pay, 1½ cents for each dollar you earn, up to $3,000 a year. This will be the tax for 3 years, and then, beginning in 1943, you will pay 2 cents, and so will your employer, for every dollar you earn for the next 3 years. After that, you and your employer will each pay half a cent more for 3 years, and finally, beginning in 1949, twelve years from now, you and your employer will each pay 3 cents on each dollar you earn, up to $3,000 a year. That is the most you will ever pay.

Your Employer's Part of the Tax

The Government will collect both of these taxes from your employer. Your part of the tax will be taken out of your pay. The Government will collect from your employer an equal amount out of his own funds.

This will go on just the same if you go to work for another employer, so long as you work in a factory, shop, mine, mill, office, store, or other such place of business. (Wages earned in employment as farm workers, domestic workers in private homes, Government workers, and on a few other kinds of jobs are not subject to this tax.)

Old-Age Reserve Account

Meanwhile, the Old-Age Reserve fund in the United States Treasury is drawing interest, and the Government guarantees it will never earn less than 3 percent. This means that 3 cents will be added to every dollar in the fund each year.

Maybe your employer has an old-age pension plan for his employees. If so, the Government's old-age benefit plan will not have to interfere with that. The employer can fit his plan into the Government plan.

What you get from the Government plan will always be more than you have paid in taxes and usually more than you can get for yourself by putting away the same amount of money each week in some other way.

How Detroit's Automakers Went from Kings of the Road to Roadkill

Joseph B. White (2009)

Joseph B. White is a senior editor for the Wall Street Journal. *A graduate of Harvard University, he has worked for the* Journal *since 1987, and for most of that time he covered the auto industry, serving as Detroit bureau chief from 1998 to 2007. He won the Pulitzer Prize for reporting in 1993. The following is adapted from a speech Mr. White delivered at Hillsdale College during a seminar on "Cars and Trucks, Markets and Governments."*

I'd like to start by congratulating all of you. You are all now in the auto business, the Sport of Kings—or in our case, presidents and members of Congress. Without your support—and I assume that most of you are fortunate enough to pay taxes—General Motors and Chrysler would very likely be getting measured by the undertakers of the bankruptcy courts. But make no mistake. What has happened to GM is essentially bankruptcy by other means, and that is an extraordinary event in the political and economic history of our country.

GM is an institution that survived in its early years the kind of management turbulence we've come to associate with particularly chaotic Internet startups. But with Alfred P. Sloan in charge, GM settled down to become the very model of the modern corporation. It navigated through the Great Depression, and negotiated the transition from producing tanks and other military materiel during World War II to peacetime production of cars and trucks. It was global before global was cool, as its current chairman used to say. By the mid-1950s the company was the symbol

Above: M-10 tanks in production on a General Motors assembly line during World War II; Below: GM managers keep track of the flow of materials needed for wartime production.

of American industrial power—the largest industrial corporation in the world. It owned more than half the U.S. market. It set the trends in styling and technology, and even when it did not it was such a fast and effective follower that it could fairly easily hold its competitors in their places. And it held the distinction as the world's largest automaker until just a year or so ago.

How does a juggernaut like this become the basket case that we see before us today? I will oversimplify matters and touch on five factors that contributed to the current crisis—a crisis that has been more than 30 years in the making.

First, Detroit underestimated the competition—in more ways than one.

Second, GM mismanaged its relationship with the United Auto Workers, and the UAW in its turn did nothing to encourage GM (or Ford or Chrysler) to defuse the demographic time bomb that has now blown up their collective future.

Third, GM, Ford, and Chrysler handled failure better than success. When they made money, they tended to squander it on ill-conceived diversification schemes. It was when they were in trouble that they often did their most innovative work—the first minivans at Chrysler, the first Ford Taurus, and more recently the Chevy Volt were ideas born out of crisis.

Fourth, GM (and Ford and Chrysler) relied too heavily on a few, gas-hungry truck and SUV lines for all their profits—plus the money they needed to cover losses on many of their car lines. They did this for a good reason: When gas was cheap, big gas-guzzling trucks were exactly what their customers wanted—until they were not.

Fifth, GM refused to accept that to survive it could not remain what it was in the 1950s and 1960s—with multiple brands and a dominant market share. Instead, it used short-term strategies such as zero percent financing to avoid reckoning with the consequences of globalization and its own mistakes.

Competition from Overseas

In hindsight, it's apparent that the gas shocks of the 1970s hit Detroit at a time when they were particularly vulnerable. They were a decadent empire—Rome in the reign of Nero. The pinnacles of the Detroit art were crudely engineered muscle cars. The mainstream products

General Motors Headquarters in Detroit, Michigan

were large, V8-powered, rear-wheel-drive sedans and station wagons. The Detroit marketing and engineering machinery didn't comprehend the appeal of cars like the Volkswagen Beetle or the Datsun 240Z.

But it took the spike in gas prices—and the economic disruptions it caused—to really open the door for the Japanese automakers.

Remember, Toyota and Honda were relative pipsqueaks in those days. They did not have much more going for them in the American market prior to the first Arab oil embargo than Chinese automakers have today, or Korean automakers did 15 years ago. The oil shocks, however, convinced a huge and influential cohort of American consumers to give fuel-efficient Japanese cars a try. Equally important, the oil shocks persuaded some of the most aggressive of America's car dealers to try them. The Detroit automakers believed the Japanese could be stopped by import quotas. They initially dismissed reports about the high quality of Japanese cars. They later assumed the Japanese could never replicate their low-cost manufacturing systems in America. Plus they believed initially that the low production cost of Japanese cars was the result of automation and unfair trading practices. (Undoubtedly, the cheap yen was a big help.) In any case, they figured that the Japanese would be stuck in a niche of small, economy cars and that the damage could be contained as customers grew out of their small car phase of life.

They were wrong on all counts.

There were Cassandras—plenty of them. At GM, an executive named Alex Mair gave detailed presentations on why Japanese cars were superior to GM's—lighter, more fuel efficient, and less costly to build. He set up a war room at GM's technical center with displays showing how Honda devised low-cost, high-quality engine parts, and how Japanese automakers designed factories that were roughly half the size of a GM plant but produced the same number of vehicles.

Mair would hold up a connecting rod—the piece of metal in an engine that connects the piston to the crankshaft. The one made by GM was bulky and crudely shaped with big tabs on the ends. Workers assembling the engines would grind down those tabs so that the weight of the piston and rod assembly would be balanced. By contrast, the connecting rod made by Honda was smaller, thinner, and almost like a piece of sculpture. It didn't have ugly tabs on the end, because it was designed to be properly balanced right out of the forge. Mair's point was simple: If you pay careful attention to designing an elegant, lightweight connecting rod, then the engine will be lighter and quieter, the car around the engine can be more efficient, the brakes will have less mass to stop, and the engine will feel more responsive because it has less weight to move.

Another person who warned GM early on about the nature of the Japanese challenge was Jim Harbour. In the early 1980s, he took it into his head to try to tell GM's executives just how much more efficient Japanese factories really were, measured by hours of labor per car produced. The productivity gap was startling—the Japanese plants were about twice as efficient. GM's president at the time responded by barring Jim Harbour from company property.

By the late 1980s, GM's chairman, Roger Smith, had figured out that his company had something to learn from the Japanese. He just didn't know what it was. He poured billions into new, heavily automated U.S. factories—including an effort to build an experimental "lights out" factory that had almost no hourly workers. He entered a joint venture with Toyota to reopen an old GM factory in California, called New United Motor Manufacturing, Inc., or NUMMI. The idea was that GM managers could go to NUMMI to see up close what the "secret" of Toyota's assembly system was. Smith also launched what he promoted as an entirely new car company, Saturn, which was meant to pioneer both a more cooperative relationship with UAW workers and a new way of selling cars. None of these was a bad idea. But GM took too long to learn the lessons from these experiments—good or bad. The automation strategy fell on its face because the robots didn't work properly, and the cars they built struck many consumers as blandly styled and of poor quality. NUMMI did give GM managers valuable information about Toyota's manufacturing and management system, which a team of MIT researchers would later call "lean production." But too many of the GM managers who gained knowledge from NUMMI were unable to make an impact on GM's core North American business. Why? I believe it was because the UAW and GM middle managers quite understandably focused on the fact that Toyota's production system required only about half the workers GM had at a typical factory at the time. That was an equation the union wouldn't accept. The UAW demanded that GM keep paying workers displaced by new technology or other shifts in production strategy, which led to the creation of what became known as the Jobs Bank. That program discouraged GM from closing factories and encouraged efforts to sustain high levels of production even when demand fell.

GM and the UAW

This brings me to the relationship between Detroit management and the UAW.

It is likely that if no Japanese or European manufacturers had built plants in the U.S.—in other words if imports were still really imports—the Detroit carmakers would not be in their current straits, although we as consumers would probably be paying more for cars and have fewer choices than we do. The fact is that the Detroit Three's post-World War II business strategies were doomed from the day in 1982 when the first Honda Accord rolled off a non-union assembly line in Ohio. After that it soon became clear that the Japanese automakers—and others—could build cars in the U.S. with relatively young, non-union labor forces that quickly learned how to thrive in the efficient production systems those companies operated.

Being new has enormous advantages in a capital-intensive, technology-intensive business like automaking. Honda, Toyota, Nissan, and later BMW, Mercedes, and Hyundai, had new factories, often subsidized by the host state, that were designed to use the latest manufacturing processes and technology. And they had new work forces. This was an advantage not because they paid them less per hour—generally non-union autoworkers receive about what UAW men and women earn in GM assembly plants—but because the new, non-union companies didn't have to bear additional costs for health care and pensions for hundreds of thousands of retirees.

Moreover, the new American manufacturers didn't have to compensate workers for the change from the old mass production methods to the new lean production approach. GM did—which is why GM created the Jobs Bank. The idea was that if UAW workers believed they wouldn't be fired if GM got more efficient, then they might embrace the new methods. Of course, we know how that turned out. The Jobs Bank became little more than a welfare system for people who had nothing more to contribute because GM's dropping market share had made their jobs superfluous.

Health care is a similar story. GM's leaders—and the UAW's—knew by the early 1990s that the combination of rising health care costs and the longevity of GM's retired workers threatened the company. But GM management backed away from a confrontation with the UAW over health care in 1993, and in every national contract cycle afterwards until 2005—when the company's nearness to collapse finally became clear to everyone.

In testimony before Congress this December, GM's CEO Rick Wagoner said that GM has spent $103 billion during the past 15 years funding its pension and retiree health-care obligations. That is nearly $7 billion a year—more than GM's capital spending budget for new models this year. Why wasn't Rick Wagoner

Leaders of the United Auto Workers Union leave the White House in 1938 after urging President Franklin D. Roosevelt to appropriate $130 million for Michigan relief to avoid "mass starvation and mass misery."

making this point in 1998, or 1999, or even 2003? Even now, GM doesn't seem willing to treat the situation like the emergency it is. Under the current contract, the UAW will pay for retiree health-care costs using a fund negotiated in last year's contract—but that won't start until 2010. GM is on the hook to contribute $20 billion to that fund over the next several years—unless it can renegotiate that deal under federal supervision.

Toyota Assembly Plant in Bangkok, Thailand (2016)

Quality is Job One

Rick Wagoner told Congress: "Obviously, if we had the $103 billion and could use it for other things, it would enable us to be even farther ahead on technology or newer equipment in our plants, or whatever." Whatever, indeed.

This is a good place to talk about the Detroit mistake that matters most to most people: quality. By quality, I mean both the absence of defects and the appeal of the materials, design, and workmanship built into a car. I believe most people who buy a car also think of how durable and reliable a car is over time when they think of quality.

The failure of the Detroit automakers to keep pace with the new standards of reliability and defect-free assembly set by Toyota and Honda during the 1980s is well known, and still haunts them today. The really bad Detroit cars of the late 1970s and early to mid-1980s launched a cycle that has proven disastrous for all three companies. Poor design and bad reliability records led to customer dissatisfaction, which led to weaker demand for new Detroit cars as well as used ones. Customers were willing to buy Detroit cars—but only if they received a discount in advance for the mechanical problems they assumed they would have.

During the 1990s and the 2000s, a number of the surveys that industry executives accept as reliable guides to new vehicle quality began to show that the best of GM's and Ford's new models were almost as good—and in some cases better—in terms of being free of defects than comparable Toyotas, Hondas, or Nissans. But the Detroit brands still had a problem: They started $2,000 or more behind the best Japanese brands in terms of per-car costs, mainly because of labor and legacy costs, with a big helping of inefficient management thrown in. To overcome that deficit, GM and Ford (and Chrysler) resorted to aggressive cost-cutting and low-bid purchasing strategies with their materials suppliers. Unfortunately, customers could see the low-bid approach in the design and materials used for Detroit cars. So even though objective measures of defects and things gone wrong showed new Detroit cars getting better and better, customers still demanded deep discounts for both new and used Detroit models. This drove down the resale value of used Detroit cars, which in turn made it harder for the Detroit brands to charge enough for the new vehicles to overcome their cost gap.

GM, Ford, and Chrysler compounded this problem by trying to generate the cash to cover their health care and pension bills by building more cars than the market demanded, and then "selling" them to rental car fleets. When those fleet cars bounced back to used car lots, where they competed with new vehicles that were essentially indistinguishable except for the higher price tag, they helped drive down resale values even more.

So the billions spent on legacy costs are matched by billions more in revenue that the Detroit automakers never saw because of the way they mismanaged supply and demand. This is why the Detroit brands appear to be lagging behind not just in hybrids—and it remains to be seen how durable that market is—but also in terms of the refinement and technology offered in their conventional cars.

What to Build?

The recent spectacle of the Diminished Three CEOs and the UAW president groveling before Congress has us focused now on how Detroit has mishandled adversity. A more important question is why they did so badly when times were good.

Consider GM. In 2000 Rick Wagoner, his senior executive team, and a flock of auto journalists jetted off to a villa in Italy for a seminar on how the GM of the 21st century was going to look. Wagoner and his team talked a lot about how GM was going to gain sales and profit from a "network" of alliances with automakers such as Subaru, Suzuki, Isuzu, and Fiat—automakers into which GM had invested capital. They talked about how they were going to use the Internet to turbocharge the company's performance. And so on. But five years later, all of this was in tatters. Much of the capital GM invested in its alliance partners was lost when the company was forced to sell out at distressed prices. Fiat was the worst of all. GM had to pay Fiat $2 billion to get out of the deal—never mind getting back the $2 billion it had invested up front to buy 20 percent of Fiat Auto. GM said it saved $1 billion a year thanks to the Fiat partnership. Obviously, whatever those gains were, they didn't help GM become profitable.

At least GM didn't use the cash it rolled up during the 1990s boom to buy junkyards, as Ford did. But GM did see an opportunity in the money to be made from selling mortgages, and plunged its GMAC financing operation aggressively into that market. Of course, GM didn't see the crash in subprime mortgages coming, either, and now GMAC is effectively bankrupt.

GM's many critics argue that what they should have done with the money they spent on UAW legacy costs and bad diversification schemes was to develop electric cars and hybrids, instead of continuing to base their U.S. business on the same large, V8-powered, rear-wheel-drive formula they used in the 60s—except that now these vehicles were sold as SUVs instead of muscle cars. And indeed, Detroit did depend too heavily on pickup trucks and SUVs for profits. But they did so for understandable reasons. These were the vehicles that consumers wanted to buy from them. Also, these were the vehicles that government policy encouraged them to build.

When gas was cheap, big gas-guzzling trucks were exactly what GM customers wanted. Consumers didn't want Detroit's imitation Toyota Camrys. Toyota was building more than enough real Camrys down in Kentucky. GM made profits of as much as $8,000 per truck—and lost money on many of its cars. Federal fuel economy rules introduced in 1975 forced GM to shrink its cars so that they could average 27.5 miles per gallon. GM did this poorly. (Remember the Chevy Citation or the Cadillac Cimarron?) But federal laws allowed "light trucks" to meet a lower mileage standard. This kink in federal law allowed GM, Ford, and Chrysler to design innovative products that Americans clamored to buy when gas was cheap: SUVs. When Ford launched the Explorer, and GM later launched the Tahoe and the upgraded Suburban, it was the Japanese companies that were envious. In fact, one reason why Toyota is on its way to a loss for 2008—its first annual loss in 70 years—is that it built too many factories in the U.S. in order to build more SUVs and pickups.

GM vehicle on display in a hotel parking lot during a symposium on low pollution power systems development near Detroit, Michigan (1973)

One irony of the current situation is that the only vehicles likely to generate the cash GM and the others need right now to rebuild are the same gas-guzzlers that Washington no longer wants them to build. Even New York Times columnist Thomas Friedman has now come to realize that you can't ask Detroit to sell tiny, expensive hybrids when gasoline is under $2 a gallon. We have two contradictory energy policies: The first demands cheap gas at all costs. The second demands that Detroit should substantially increase the average mileage of its cars to 35 or even 40 miles per gallon across the board. How the Obama administration will square this circle, I don't know.

Thinking Anew

So now, where are we? GM has become Government Motors. With the U.S. Treasury standing in for the DuPonts of old, GM is going to try to reinvent itself. One challenge among many for GM in this process will be coming to terms with the reality that the U.S. market is too fractured, and has too many volume manufacturers, for any one of them to expect to control the kind of market share and pricing power GM had in its heyday. Today, according to Wardsauto.com, there are ten foreign-owned automakers with U.S. factories that assembled 3.9 million cars, pickups, and SUVs in 2007, before auto demand began to collapse. That's more than Ford's and Chrysler's U.S. production combined.

GM's efforts to cling to its 1950s self—with the old Sloanian ladder brands of Chevy, Pontiac, Buick, and Cadillac, plus Saturn, Saab, Hummer, and GMC—have led its management into one dark wood of error after another. Since 2001, GM's marketing strategy has come down to a single idea: zero percent financing. This was the automotive version of the addictive, easy credit that ultimately destroyed the housing market. Cut-rate loans, offered to decreasingly credit-worthy buyers, propped up sales and delayed the day of reckoning. But it didn't delay it long enough. The house of cards began tumbling in 2005, and I would say it has now collapsed fully.

Between 1995 and 2007, GM managed to earn a cumulative total of $13.5 billion. That's three-tenths of one percent of the total revenues during that period of more than $4 trillion-and those are nominal dollars, not adjusted for inflation. Between 1990 and 2007, GM lost a combined total of about $33 billion. The six unprofitable years wiped out the gains from 12 profitable years, and then some. But old habits die hard. Within hours of clinching a $6 billion government bailout last month, GMAC and GM were back to promoting zero-interest loans.

During the 1980s and 1990s, GM's leaders refused—and I believe some still refuse—to accept the reality of the presence of so many new automakers in the U.S. market, more than at any time since the 1920s. This hard truth means the company's U.S. market share going forward isn't going to return to the 40 percent levels of the mid-1980s, or the 30 percent levels of the 1990s, or even the mid-20 percent levels we have seen more recently. One thing to watch as GM tries to restructure now will be what assumptions the company makes about its share of the U.S. market going forward. If they call for anything higher than 15 percent, I would be suspicious.

Since all of you are now part owners of this enterprise, I would urge all of you to pay close attention, since what's about to unfold has no clear precedent in our nation's economic history. The closest parallels I can see are Renault in France, Volkswagen in Germany, and the various state-controlled Chinese automakers. But none of these companies is as large as GM, and none of these companies is exactly a model for what GM should want to become.

As I have tried to suggest, it's hard enough for professional managers and technicians—who have a clear profit motive—to run an enterprise as complex as a global car company. What will be the fate of a quasi-nationalized enterprise whose "board of directors" will now include 535 members of Congress, plus various agencies of the Executive Branch? As a property owner in suburban Detroit, I can only hope for the best.

After this speech was given, General Motors did declare bankruptcy. The U.S. Treasury invested about $50 billion to purchase a majority equity stake in GM. The reorganized company held an IPO in 2010. The U.S. Treasury sold its remaining shares in 2013 with a total loss of about $10 billion to taxpayers. GM has been running profitably since the bailout.

Reprinted by permission from Imprimis, *the national speech digest of Hillsdale College, www.hillsdale.edu.*

Ecology and the Economy: The Problems of Coexistence

James L. Buckley (1980)

James L. Buckley (born 1923) is a graduate of Yale and of Yale Law School. For many years he worked with a company that performed oil and gas exploration. In 1970 he was elected to the U.S. Senate from New York on the Conservative Party ticket in that state, and he served one term. He later was an Undersecretary for Security, Science, and Technology in the Department of State (1981-1982); president of Radio Free Europe (1982-1985); and then a judge on the U.S. Court of Appeals for the District of Columbia (1985-1996). Thus Mr. Buckley served in all three branches of the Federal government. He is the brother of the late conservative writer William F. Buckley Jr. This speech was given many years ago as environmental policy was in its early stages. Some of the specific questions he discusses have changed or been resolved, but the speech does a good job of presenting the issues involved in balancing economic growth with environmental responsibility.

I come before you as a conservationist who is also a political conservative. I try to make up for this apparent anomaly (and I haven't yet given up hope for my philosophical brethren) by being at the same time what might be styled a conservative conservationist; by which I mean to say that I see no particular virtue in turning the American environmental clock back to the year 1491. I am among those who view man as part of nature, with natural imperatives of his own which are not necessarily at odds with the rest of creation.

Over the centuries, in most parts of the world, man managed to live in a state of essential balance with nature, adjusting his agricultural practices by trial and error to meet the natural requirements of the land he tilled. Such pollution as his industries produced could usually be dissipated or reabsorbed into the environment without doing lasting harm. But over the past few decades, we have seen a dramatic change in the qualitative nature of man's impact on the world he lives in and on which he depends for his biological survival.

We are now producing vast varieties and volumes of exotic new chemicals which when released in the air and water as industrial wastes, or spread on the land as insecticides and pesticides, can inflict damage on a scale that no one could have anticipated a generation or so ago.

Unlike man's earlier wastes, which were derived from nature and in due course would be broken down by natural processes and recycled back into the soil, water or atmosphere, many of today's synthetics are proving virtually indigestible. We have learned that when such substances are used on any scale, there may be no such thing as "safe" concentrations. Radioactive materials and D.D.T., for example, are subject to biological concentration as they move up the food chain, and once injected into the environment they cannot be reclaimed.

DDT is sprayed in Thailand to kill mosquitoes.(2016)

In sum, our technology has propelled us into a new era where we have achieved an awesome power to disrupt the very rhythms of life and to inflict costs on society the full extent of which we have not yet learned to assess, costs that are no less real for having so long been either unsuspected or ignored.

It was a perception of the accelerating scale of the damage we were inflicting on the environment, and hence on ourselves, that sparked the environmental revolution of the past decade. One can question the appropriateness of the regulatory mechanisms we have set in place; one can question whether the costs exacted by them bear a rational relationship to the benefits gained; one can argue over the relative priority to be placed on certain environmental values whose importance few deny, but which no one has yet determined how to quantify; but no dispassionate person in possession of the facts, no one with an elementary grasp of biological cause and effect, can any longer deny that man has achieved the power to abuse his environment on a massive scale, or that there are formidable economic costs that flow from that abuse.

The challenge facing mankind, then, is not one of having to make a choice between economic welfare and ecological preservation, because our economic wellbeing ultimately depends on the health of our environment. The challenge, therefore, is to develop more effective techniques for bringing man's economic activities into equilibrium with the natural world of which he is an inescapable part.

As the saying goes, this is easier said than done. There is almost universal agreement on the need to do something about pollution. It is when one tries to suggest what should be done and at what cost that the discussion tends to degenerate into a brawl. Part of the problem is that the costs of implementing our existing anti-pollution laws are huge, and they fall on relatively few backs.

Until relatively recently public waters and the atmosphere were routinely considered to be available to all comers—industry, municipalities, individual households—as cost-free "dispos-alls." Thus the disposition of waste did not constitute a cost of production, and was not reflected in the price of goods. But the wastes discharged into our air and water nevertheless give rise to very real costs—costs measured in terms of corrosion, crop losses, doctor's bills, declines in fisheries, loss of recreational values, industrial absenteeism, and the like—that society as a whole has had to absorb.

Properly designed anti-pollution strategies will result not so much in added burdens on society as in what economists call the "internalizing" of external costs. This comes about as manufacturers incorporate the expense of cleaning up their wastes into the prices they charge for their products. Thus the ultimate consumer is required to pay the full cost of what he elects to use. Viewed from another perspective, if polluting is recognized as a form of public nuisance in which environmental freeloaders impose real costs on their downwind or downstream neighbors, then it is not entirely unreasonable for the neighbors to ask that the polluters be required to absorb those costs.

Therefore, what we ought to be asking ourselves is not whether we can afford a cleaner environment, but how we can best go about achieving one. Specifically, we need to determine whether the costs associated with our current pollution abatement strategies bear a reasonable relationship to the benefits to be derived from them. This, I admit, is a proposition far easier to state than to apply because of the exquisite difficulty of identifying all of the adverse effects of pollution in the first place, and of quantifying so many of them in the second.

Nevertheless, this is the rational context within which the current debate over our environmental laws ought to proceed. In comparing current costs with current benefits, however, one must keep in mind that our environmental effort today is rather like a football team that remains several touchdowns behind. It has to catch up before it can think of winning. As we have only recently awakened to the need for environmental protection, we are faced with a formidable backlog of pollution problems requiring immediate attention.

And make no mistake, the backlog is a massive one. Just the other day, the Environmental Protection Agency estimated that Federal programs to control environmental pollution will cost society some $360 billion in the decade between 1977 and 1986. That is an enormous figure—an average of some $36 billion for each of 10 years: and much of it will be required for the construction of such things as mutual sewerage treatment facilities that ought to have been in place years ago.

That figure reflects the fact that we have a lot of catching up to do, catching up that must be done sooner or later; but once we have caught up, once the capital investments required to achieve our stated goals have been completed, we can expect the annual cost of pollution abatement to decline. Furthermore, in assessing the E.P.A.'s estimates, we should keep in mind that they assume a continuation of the present system of control by regulation rather than through an alternative system of economic incentives that I shall discuss later; and they assume that no technological breakthroughs in pollution control will be achieved, which is certainly unrealistic—especially if such an alternative is adopted.

Perhaps our major problem in examining the environmental equation is in the assumption that both the benefits and the costs can be estimated with any degree of precision. I have seen enough cost-benefit analyses on dam and harbor projects to know that even when trying to compute so simple a benefit as flood protection for a particular town, the attempt to place a monetary value on that protection is anything but an exercise in precision; and it is apt to do little more than reflect the prejudice of the calculator. Time, however, seems to be on the side of those who argue the extent of the real economic costs that result from the indiscriminate discharge of manmade wastes. Too many examples are now surfacing where an ounce of pollution prevention could have saved a ton of environmental costs.

Our experience with the now notorious Love Canal in Niagara Falls, New York, is a case very much in point. This ironically-named ditch was originally intended to provide hydroelectric power for some nearby homes, but in the 1920s it was converted into a dumpsite. Over the years, dozens of chemicals—eleven suspected of producing cancer—

Love Canal area

were discovered to have oozed from their containers in the canal and percolated through the soil and into the basements of nearby homes, with a disastrous impact on the health of their inhabitants. The history of their illnesses included unusually high rates of miscarriages, abnormal births, and chronic illnesses.

At the time the Congress began work on the Clean Air Act of 1970, relatively little was known about the exact nature and extent of the harm done to human health by air pollution, although the fact of such harm was apparent to any one who had coughed and wheezed his way through a Los Angeles smog. Nor was much known about the probable cost of doing something about it or of the exact nature of the technology that would be required to bring air pollution under control. All that was known was that the situation was rapidly deteriorating, the costs to health undoubtedly soaring, and that something had to be done. But what?

Under Senator Edmund Muskie's leadership, the Congress came up with a strategy and a standard which at the time were entirely reasonable, especially as no one could have anticipated that they would take on something of the aura of the tablets handed down by a higher authority some millennia ago on Mount Sinai.

The strategy was to force the development of antipollution technology by legislative fiat; in the case of automobile emissions, by legislating stepped decreases in the principal pollutants—carbon monoxide, hydrocarbons, and nitrogen oxides over a specified period.

This was an admittedly crude approach; and it was acknowledged at the time to be nothing more than the initiation of a process that would have to be reassessed from time to time in the light of new knowledge and experience. The impact of this legislation has been formidable; and insofar as its initial goals are concerned, it has proven enormously effective.

Research conducted by the Council on Environmental Quality and others suggests that the achievement of current ambient air standards would result in savings of between $20 billion and $25 billion a year. This compares with a cost (as estimated by the E.P.A. in 1978) of $12 billion per year for the air pollution controls required to achieve those standards. And these studies have not taken into full account some of the unsuspected consequences of air pollution that are just now beginning to be perceived.

A few years ago, one of the popular proposals for handling emissions of sulfur dioxide was to build very tall stacks that would protect surrounding areas by dissipating the gas into the atmosphere. The strategy was first tested in England, where it achieved local

162

miracles. Shortly thereafter, however, German and Swedish scientists hundreds of miles to leeward began to notice a sharp increase in the sulphuric acid content of their rain water. Thus did the phrase "acid rains" enter our vocabulary.

Foresters working in our northeastern states subsequently noticed the same phenomenon and began to speculate as to the possible impact of changes in soil acidity on the rate of growth of timber. But hard evidence of the adverse environmental impact of acid rain is now coming to the fore. Just a few months ago, Canadian biologists found that over two hundred lakes in the province of Ontario have been rendered sterile; and the E.P.A. has now identified between ninety and one hundred lakes in the Adirondacks which no longer can support fish life. Apparently the acidity of their waters has reached levels where the fish fail to reproduce. In short, we have not yet reached the end of the catalog of damage attributable to air pollution. . . .

[We have learned some things about the marginal costs of pollution control] since our original landmark environmental laws were enacted. Whereas the great majority of our air and water pollutants can be brought under control at costs that most people will consider reasonable, it can become incredibly expensive to remove the last few percentages that existing legislation require to be removed within stated periods. Furthermore, the cost of such removal will vary by enormous margins depending on the particular industrial processes involved. Finally, there is increasing question as to whether the achievement of our necessary environmental goals really requires the uniform application of statutory standards irrespective of cost in specific localized instances; or for that matter whether it is possible to impose programs that will disrupt entire communities.

Let me illustrate by taking the celebrated case of Los Angeles and the ambient air goals legislated by Congress in 1970. Given the facts of the Los Angeles situation and the dependence of its people on the automobile, given the state of emission control technology, given the lack of adequate public transportation facilities and the impossibility of conjuring them up overnight, it became apparent by 1973 that there was no possible way of meeting statutory deadlines without closing down the city. When the E.P.A. decided to handle this dilemma by simply ignoring the explicit requirements of the law, environmentalists took the agency to court and a judge issued a decision which required the agency to promulgate a plan for the city that could in effect have declared a moratorium on the use of private automobiles during much of the year. This in turn left the Congress with little choice but to enact legislation extending the deadlines.

What becomes increasingly clear is the need for a greater flexibility in the application of our environmental laws so as to enable us to cope with the exceptional situation, but always under carefully defined safeguards. For example, if it should prove impossible, except at exorbitant cost, to achieve the incremental improvements in air pollution controls required to keep pollutants in the Los Angeles basin at national ambient standards during the periods of atmospheric inversions to which the city is prone, then perhaps we ought to allow Los Angeles the option to suffer under less than optimum conditions, perhaps requiring them to post signs along highways leading into the city warning travelers that "Breathing Los Angeles air may be dangerous to your health."

Beach closed due to pollution in Los Angeles, California (c. 1988)

None of this suggests that we should back away from our broadly-defined environmental objectives; rather, we should recognize that the time has come to take advantage of the substantial experience we have accumulated over the past decade and see how we can better achieve those objectives with a special eye to cost efficiency. Without pretending to cover the universe, let me suggest a few modifications in our present approach that I believe would go a long way toward dispelling the idea that there is a necessary conflict between environmental and economic goals.

The first and foremost problem posed by our environmental laws is the way they are structured—their almost total reliance on regulation for the achievement of stated goals. Because the regulatory approach to the implementation of public policy in any complex area requires the drafting of hundreds of detailed rules; because these in turn require the exercise of thousands of individual judgments by those charged with enforcing them; because our anti-pollution laws have tended to describe their policy objectives in the broadest terms; because of all these factors, the regulations drawn up and administered by the E.P.A. have proven in case after case to be inordinately complicated, their implementation needlessly costly, and the decisions made by individual E.P.A. administrators subject to infinite challenge.

And this in turn has converted our environmental laws into instruments for protracted litigation often entered into by environmentalist diehards whose primary goal is simply to obstruct. And so economically-important projects that have been cleared by all the relevant state and federal environmental agencies can nevertheless be delayed year after costly year until many of them are simply abandoned.

The answer to this regulatory morass is not to create an Energy Mobilization Board with the power to override the most important environmental safeguards by simple fiat, as the Congress is now in the process of doing. Such an approach is not only irresponsible, but it is apt to delay the kinds of revisions in our environmental laws and procedures which are so clearly needed.

We need, for example, to enact procedural reforms that will allow specific proposals to be submitted, considered, ruled upon, the rulings challenged, and the challenges adjudicated with an eye to achieving as expeditious a final determination of a particular matter as prudence will allow. We cannot permit the endless second guessing that is creating unconscionable delays and giving rise to confrontations and public frustration which in the end can only harm the environmental cause.

We should also move away from a reliance on regulations toward a strategy of economic incentives for the achievement of specific environmental goals. The fact is that no mechanism has yet been discovered that is as effective as the marketplace in harnessing human energy and ingenuity. Such a strategy offers the surest way to make pollution control less arbitrary, less costly, and less bureaucratic. Regulations are too often framed in terms of immutable standards to be universally applied, rather than in terms of innovative, cost effective, flexible controls.

We need to encourage the development of improved ways to control pollution; and the most promising way to do this is to move away from the present system of plant-by-plant regulation toward one that will rely on such incentives to innovation as taxes on specific pollutants or pollution permits that will encourage the marketplace to determine the most cost-effective ways to control pollution.

Before I left the United States Senate, I introduced an amendment to a revision of the Clean Air Act that would require the E.P.A. to study various ways of harnessing economic incentives for the abatement of nitrogen oxide emissions from stationary sources as a test of this approach to pollution control. Nitrogen oxides are produced in all combustion processes; but up to that time, efforts to control this particular pollutant had been limited to automobile emissions. My amendment survived my own tenure in the Senate, and became law in 1977.

The E.P.A. report mandated by the amendment is now close to completion, and its conclusions are more favorable than even I had anticipated. They show that such economic alternatives to regulation as a system of emission charges or pollution permits are likely to produce the same degree of nitrogen oxide control at anywhere from one-tenth to one-fourth the cost of the present system of regulation. In the words of the study: "Perhaps the greatest strength of economic approaches relative to the regulatory approaches is that they tend to locate decision-making responsibility with those who possess the information needed to make the best decision."

Another concept that I believe holds merit is what the E.P.A. terms its "offset" policy. Under this approach, a corporation wishing to locate or expand its operations in a polluted area may buy and retire the existing pollution from another company. An oil refinery, for example, might buy out a local dry cleaning plant and close it down rather than install a highly expensive, stringent pollution control system of its own. The refinery would thus obtain the degree of pollution reduction required to offset the pollution that its proposed facilities would generate.

Obviously, an offset purchase would only occur when it proved less costly than the alternative. Furthermore, this approach does not necessarily mean that the dry cleaning establishment would vanish from the area. If dry cleaners can handle their own pollution at a far lower cost per unit of pollutant than a refinery, then they can utilize the funds received from the refinery to install the necessary hardware and continue in operation at no net increase of pollution in the area. Thus flexibility replaces rigidity, and pollution abatement dollars are focused where they can achieve the greatest good.

Perhaps most important, these economic alternatives appear to be more likely than any other system to motivate the development of new pollution control technology. Under the present regulatory strategy, industry often balks at investing large sums in developing new technology because success is likely to mean that the industry will have to install that new technology even when to do so will significantly raise the overall costs of its operations. Under a system of economic incentives, however, the development of cost-efficient technology becomes a logical goal. In short, a move toward market incentives seems a far surer way of marrying economic and environmental objectives than the existing strategy of forcing technology to achieve fixed statutory goals.

Which brings me to another area for reform which would deal with what might be called the problem of environmental holy writ. The decision nine years ago to decrease each component of automotive pollution by 90% over a five- to six-year period was acknowledged at the time to be wholly arbitrary. Yet, it has fixed some totemic numbers in the statute books. Nitrogen oxide must be reduced to 0.4 parts per million because that was what was decreed in 1970 irrespective of what later studies may tell us as to the merits of such an objective.

If the necessary coexistence between economics and the environment is to be achieved, it is essential that specific goals be reviewed periodically in the light of developing knowledge, so that we may always be sure that the costs imposed by them are justified. Such reviews, of course, will apply the disciplines of cost-benefit analysis to the evaluation of pollution abatement strategies. But here I think we should keep in mind certain inherent limitations of this kind of exercise when applied to environmental problems. Reasonably reliable values can be assigned to the more obvious kinds of damage done by specific

Work of the Environmental Protection Agency (1974)

pollutants; and as I have suggested, I believe the case can be made that once in place, the costs of properly-structured pollution controls will more than pay for themselves in savings of a kind that the least imaginative cost accountant can recognize.

But inevitably there will be the cases at the margin, some of them involving substantial sums or important economic objectives, where the value to be placed on specific environmental benefits becomes more difficult or even impossible to quantify; and, of course, these are the cases that tend to become the focus of the most heated controversy. I do not suggest that the case for environmental protection is necessarily the weaker for having to deal at times with intangible values; only that at times this case may be more difficult to present and to understand. What value, for example, does one place on the Parthenon, whose facade is now being eaten away by the pollutants generated in modern Greece; what value on a pristine Grand Canyon, given its hydroelectrical potential; what value on the last great herd of migratory mammals left on earth, the protection of whose calving grounds would deny us access to potential oil reserves equivalent to perhaps five or ten days' consumption?

No legislation has focused more clearly on these less easily quantified aspects of environmental concern, and none in recent years has caused such apoplexy among so-called practical men of affairs, as the Endangered Species Act of 1973. This bill first burst upon the public consciousness two years ago when it was invoked to scuttle projected dams in Tennessee and Maine; the first to save a nondescript little fish called the snail darter and the other, an inconspicuous flower called the furbish lousewort.

It is idiotic, cry the practical men of affairs, to allow sentimentality over a few hundred weeds or minnows to stand in the way of progress. It is irresponsible, reply the conservationists, to destroy forever a unique pool of genetic material; and the conservationists can marshal a host of non-sentimental arguments in support of what many consider to be the most important environmental legislation of the decade.

Having said this, I can hear the P.M.O.A.'s swallow in disbelief as they ask, "Of what possible dollars-and-cents value is the snail darter?" To which conservationists will have to reply, "None that we know of." And that, paradoxically, is one of the major scientific justifications for the Endangered Species Act.

Our biological knowledge is still so pitifully small that it is less than likely that science can identify the immediate worth of any given species. It is therefore imprudent to allow such an estimate, as perceived by men trained to think in terms only of near-term goals, to be the basis for deciding whether a given species is to be preserved.

What good is a snail darter? As practical men measure "good," probably none; but we simply don't know. What value would have been placed on the cowpox virus before Jenner; or on penicillium molds before Fleming; or on wild rubber trees before Goodyear learned to vulcanize their sap? Yet the life of most Americans has been profoundly affected by these species.

Fully 40% of modern drugs have been derived from nature. Most of the food man eats comes from only about twenty out of the thousands of plants known to be edible. And even those currently being cultivated require the preservation of large pools of genetic material on which plant scientists can draw in order to produce more useful strains or to restore the vigor of the highly inbred varieties that have revolutionized agriculture in recent years.

Just a few months ago a front-page story in the *New York Times* announced: "In a remote mountain region in Mexico, a perennial plant that crossbreeds with corn has been discovered, awakening hopes for producing a perennial variety of that food crop with revolutionary implications for agriculture." This wild grass offers the prospect of a dramatic reduction in the cost of producing one of the world's most important foods. Had practical men of affairs been in charge of building dams in the Mexican Sierras, however, it might have been lost—forever.

This century has witnessed over half the extinctions of animal species known to have occurred during recorded history; and, largely because of the vast scale on which tropical rain forests are being cut around the world, it is estimated that by the year 2000 upwards of a million additional species—about 20% of those now in existence—may become extinct.

The Endangered Species Act was passed in order to slow down this accelerating rate of man-caused extinctions. Its purpose is not only to help save species that might prove of direct value to man, but to help preserve the biological diversity that, in America and on the rest of our planet, provides the fundamental support system for man and other living things.

As living creatures, the more we understand of biological processes, the more wisely we will be able to manage ourselves. Thus the deliberate extermination of a species can be an act of recklessness. By permitting high rates of extinction to continue, we are limiting the potential growth of biological knowledge. In essence, the process is tantamount to book-burning; but it is even worse, in that it involves books yet to be deciphered and read.

Grand Teton National Park, Wyoming

One might contend, of course, that our country's biological diversity is still so great and the land so developed—so criss-crossed with the works of man—that it will soon be hard to locate a dam anywhere without endangering some species. But as we develop a national inventory of endangered species, we certainly can plan our necessary developments so as to exterminate the smallest number possible, if not to preclude man-caused extinctions altogether. This, of course, is what the legislation is intended to accomplish.

This objective represents a quantum jump in man's acknowledgement of his moral responsibility for the integrity of the natural world he passes on to succeeding generations.

It is this which lends the Endangered Species Act its special significance. It recognizes values, be they ethical or aesthetic, that transcend the purely practical and admit to awe in the face of the diversity of creation. Not everyone will be moved by them, and they no more lend themselves to a cost-effective calculus than does a Bach chorale. But surely it is an act of unseemly arrogance to decree the extinction of a unique form of life without compelling justification.

Unfortunately, the Congress recently voted to override the procedures it itself had established for determining when such justification exists, and ordered the completion of the Tellico Dam despite detailed economic studies demonstrating it to be a costly boondoggle, a classic case of pork barrel legislation.

Nevertheless, I do believe that the history of the Endangered Species Act illustrates a growing awareness of the interrelationship between ecological preservation and economic well-being as well as the need for establishing mechanisms for mediating decisions in what I believe will in time be recognized as the relatively rare instances where the two are in genuine conflict.

I firmly believe that when all the facts are placed in their proper perspective, when we truly come to understand the full consequences of abusing the natural systems on which life depends, then it will be generally accepted that man cannot conduct his economic activities in an ecological void except at tremendous ultimate cost. If we care about the economic well-being of the next generation, then we must care more than we have in the past about the quality of the physical and biological world they will inherit.

As Edmund Burke reminded us years ago, the men and women of each generation are but "temporary possessors and life-renters" who "should not think it among their rights to cut off the entail or commit waste on the inheritance," lest they "leave to those who come after them a ruin instead of a habitation." I can think of no more appropriate perspective than Burke's as we work to establish a new harmony between man and the natural world he lives in.

Reprinted by permission from Imprimis, *the national speech digest of Hillsdale College, www.hillsdale.edu.*

The Rules of the Game and Economic Recovery

Amity Shlaes (2010)

Amity Shlaes is a syndicated columnist for Bloomberg, a director of the Four Percent Growth Project at the George W. Bush Presidential Center, and a member of the board of the Calvin Coolidge Memorial Foundation. She has served as a member of the editorial board of the Wall Street Journal *and as a columnist for the* Financial Times, *and is a recipient of the Hayek Prize and the Frederic Bastiat Prize for free-market journalism. She is the author of four books,* Germany: The Empire Within, The Forgotten Man: A New History of the Great Depression, The Greedy Hand: How Taxes Drive Americans Crazy and What to Do About It, *and* Coolidge. *This speech was presented at a Hillsdale College in 2010 during a conference on the New Deal.*

The Monopoly board game originated during the Great Depression. At first its inventor, Charles Darrow, could not interest manufacturers. Parker Brothers turned the game down, citing "52 design errors." But Darrow produced his own copies of the game, and Parker Brothers finally bought Monopoly. By 1935, the New York Times was reporting that "leading all other board games . . . is the season's craze, 'Monopoly,' the game of real estate."

Most of us are familiar with the object of Monopoly: the accumulation of property on which one places houses and hotels, and from which one receives revenue. Many of us have a favorite token. Perennially popular is the top hat, which symbolizes the sort of wealth to which Americans who work hard can aspire. The top hat is a token that has remained in the game, even while others have changed over the decades.

Monopoly board game with top hat token

One's willingness to play Monopoly depends on a few conditions—for instance, a predictable number of "Pay Income Tax" cards. These cards are manageable when you know in advance the amount of money printed on them and how many of them are in the deck. It helps, too, that there are a limited and predictable number of "Go to Jail" cards. This is what Frank Knight of the University of Chicago would call a knowable risk, as opposed to an uncertainty. Likewise, there must be a limited and predictable number of "Chance" cards. In other words, there has to be some certainty that property rights are secure and that the risks to property are few in number and can be managed.

The bank must be dependable, too. There is a fixed supply of Monopoly money and the bank is supposed to follow the rules of the game, exercising little or no independent discretion. If players sit down at the Monopoly board only to discover a bank that overreaches or is too unpredictable or discretionary, we all know what happens. They will walk away from the board. There is no game.

Relevance to the 1930s

How is this game relevant to the Great Depression? We all know the traditional narrative of that event: The stock market crash generated an economic Katrina. One in four was unemployed in the first few years. It resulted from a combination of monetary, banking, credit, international, and consumer confidence factors. The terrible thing about it was the duration of a high level of unemployment, which averaged in the mid teens for the entire decade.

The second thing we usually learn is that the Depression was mysterious—a problem that only experts with doctorates could solve. That is why FDR's floating advisory group—Felix Frankfurter, Frances Perkins, George Warren, Marriner Eccles and Adolf Berle, among others—was sometimes known as a Brain Trust. The mystery had something to do with a shortage of money, we are told, and in the end, only a Brain Trust's tinkering with the money supply saved us. The corollary to this view is that the government knows more than American business does about economics.

Another common presumption is that cleaning up Wall Street and getting rid of white-collar criminals helped the nation recover. A second is that property rights may still have mattered during the 1930s, but that they mattered less than government-created jobs, shoring up home-owners, and getting the money supply right. A third is that American democracy was threatened by the rise of a potential plutocracy, and that the Wagner Act of 1935—which lent federal support to labor unions—was thus necessary and proper. Fourth and finally, the traditional view of the 1930s is that action by the government was good, whereas inaction would have been fatal. The economic crisis mandated any kind of action, no matter how far removed it might be from sound monetary policy. Along these lines the humorist Will Rogers wrote in 1933 that if Franklin Roosevelt had "burned down the capital, we would cheer and say, 'Well at least we got a fire started, anyhow.'"

To put this official version of the 1930s in terms of the Monopoly board: The American economy was failing because there were too many top hats lording it about on the board, trying to establish a plutocracy, and because there was no bank to hand out money. Under FDR, the federal government became the bank and pulled America back to economic health.

When you go to research the 1930s, however, you find a different story. It is of course true that the early part of the Depression—the years upon which most economists have focused—was an economic Katrina. And a number of New Deal measures provided lasting benefits for the economy. These include the creation of the Securities and Exchange Commission, the push for free trade led by Secretary of State Cordell Hull, and the establishment of the modern mortgage format. But the remaining evidence contradicts the official narrative. Overall, it can be said, government prevented recovery. Herbert Hoover was too active, not too passive—as the old stereotypes suggest—while Roosevelt and his New Deal policies impeded recovery as well, especially during the latter half of the decade.

In short, the prolonged Depression can be put down to government arrogance—arrogance that came at the expense of economic common sense, the rule of law, and respect for property rights.

Arrogance and Discretion

Consider the centerpiece of the New Deal's first 100 days, the National Recovery Administration (NRA), which was in effect an enormous multisector mechanism calibrated to manage the business cycle through industrial codes that, among other things, regulated prices. The principles on which its codes were based appear risible from the perspective of microeconomics and common sense. They included the idea that prices needed to be pushed up to make recovery possible, whereas competition constrained recovery by driving prices down. They held that big firms in industry—those "too big to fail"—were to write codes for all members of their sector, large and small—which naturally worked to the advantage of those larger firms. As for consumer choice, it was deemed inefficient and an inhibitor of recovery. The absurdity of these principles was overlooked, however, because they were put forth by great minds. One member of the Brain Trust, Ray Moley, described the myopic credentialism of his fellow Brain Truster, Felix Frankfurter, in this way:

> The problems of economic life were to Frankfurter matters to be settled in a law office, a court room, or around a big labor-management bargaining table. . . . The government was the protagonist. Its agents were its lawyers and commissioners. The antagonists were big corporate lawyers. In the background were misty principals whom Frankfurter never really knew at first hand. . . . These background figures were owners of the corporations, managers, workers and consumers.

One family that was targeted by NRA bureaucrats was the Schechters, who were wholesale chicken butchers in Brooklyn. The NRA code that aimed to regulate what they did was called The Code of Fair Competition for the Live Poultry Industry of the Metropolitan Area in and about the City of New York. And according to this code, the Schechters did all the wrong things. They paid their butchers too little. They charged prices that were too low. They allowed their customers to pick their own chickens. Worst of all, they sold a sick chicken. As a result of these supposed crimes, they were prosecuted.

The prosecution would have been comic if it were not business tragedy. Imagine the court room scene: On one side stands Walter Lyman Rice, a graduate of Harvard Law School, representing the government. On the other stands a small man in the poultry trade, Louis Spatz, who is afraid of going to jail. Spatz tries

National Recovery Administration parade in New York City (1933)

to defend his actions. But he barely speaks English, and the prosecutor bullies him. Nevertheless, Spatz is now and then able to articulate, in his simple and common-sense way, how business really works.

Prosecution: But you do not claim to be an expert?
Spatz: No.
Prosecution: On the competitive practices in the live poultry industry?
Spatz: I would want to get paid, if I was an expert.
Prosecution: You are not an expert!
Spatz: I am experienced, but not an expert . . . .
Prosecution: You have not studied agricultural economics?
Spatz: No, sir.
Prosecution: Or any sort of economics?
Spatz: No, sir.
Prosecution: What is your education?
Spatz: None; very little.
Prosecution: None at all?
Spatz: Very little.

Then at one point this everyman sort of pulls himself together.

Prosecution: And you would not endeavor to explain economic consequences of competitive practices?

Spatz: In my business I am the best economist.

Prosecution: What is that?

Spatz: In my business I am the best economizer.

Prosecution: You are the best economizer?

Spatz: Yes, without figuring.

Prosecution: I wish to have that word spelled in the minutes, just as he stated it.

Spatz: I do not know how to spell.

President Franklin D. Roosevelt

This dialogue matters because little businesses like Schechter Poultry are the natural drivers of recovery, and during the Great Depression they weren't allowed to do that driving. They weren't allowed to compete and accumulate wealth—or, in terms of Monopoly, to place a house or hotel on their property. Instead they were sidelined. The Schechter brothers ultimately won their case in the Supreme Court in 1935. But the cost of the lawsuits combined with the Depression did not go away.

Regarding monetary policy, it is clear that there wasn't enough money in the early 1930s. So Roosevelt was not wrong in trying to reflate. But though his general idea was right, the discretionary aspect of his policy was terrifying. As Henry Morgenthau reports in his diaries, prices were set by the president personally. FDR took the U.S. off the gold standard in April 1933, and by summer he was setting the gold price every morning from his bed. Morgenthau reports that at one point the president ordered the gold price up 21 cents. Why 21, Morgenthau asked. Roosevelt replied, because it's 3 x 7, and three is a lucky number. "If anyone knew how we set the gold price," wrote Morgenthau in his diary, "they would be frightened."

Discretionary policies aimed at cleaning up Wall Street were destructive as well. The New Dealers attacked the wealthy as "money changers" and "Princes of Property." In 1937, after his re-election, Roosevelt delivered an inaugural address in which he described government as an instrument of "unimagined power" which should be used to "fashion a higher order of things." This caused business to freeze in its tracks. Companies went on what Roosevelt himself resentfully termed a "capital strike."

These capital strikers mattered because they were even more important to recovery than the Schechters. Consider the case of Alfred Lee Loomis, who had the kind of mind that could contribute significantly to Gross Domestic Product and job creation. During the First World War, he had improved the design of firearms for the U.S. Army. In the 1920s, he became wealthy through his work in investment banking. He moved in a crowd that was developing a new form of utility company that might finally be able to marshal the capital to bring electricity to the American South. But when Loomis saw that the Roosevelt administration was hauling utilities executives down to Washington for hearings, he shut down his business, retreated to his Tudor house, and ran a kind of private think tank for his own benefit. We have heard a lot about a labor surfeit in the 1930s. Here is a heresy: What if there was a shortage of talent brought on by declarations of class warfare?

Another challenge to the Depression economy was tax increases. While these increases didn't achieve the social equality at which they aimed, they did significant damage by confiscating too much individual and corporate property. As a result, many individuals and businesses simply reduced or halted production—especially as the New Deal wore on. In the late 1930s, banker Leonard Ayres of the Cleveland Trust Company said in the New York Times: "For nearly a decade now the great majority of corporations have been losing money instead of making it."

As for big labor, the Wagner Act of 1935 proved to be quite destructive. It brought on drastic changes at factories, including the closed shop—the exclusion of non-union members. Another innovation it helped bring about was the sit-down strike, which threatened the basic property right of factory owners to close their doors. Most importantly, it gave unions the power to demand higher wages—and they did. A wage chart for the 20th century shows that real wages in the 1930s were higher than the trend for the rest of the century. This seems perverse, considering the economic conditions at the time. The result was high paying jobs for a few and high unemployment for everyone else. The reality of overpriced labor can be seen in several stock phrases coming out of the Great Depression—"Nice work if you can get it," for example, was the refrain of a Gershwin song performed by Fred Astaire in *The Damsel in Distress*, a film released in 1937 at the zenith of union power.

To return to the Monopoly board metaphor, the problem in the 1930s was not that there was no bank. It was that there was too much bank—in the form of the federal government. The government took an arbitrary approach to the money supply and made itself the most powerful player. It shoved everyone else aside so that it could monopolize the board. Benjamin Anderson, a Chase economist at the time, summed it up in a book about the period: "Preceding chapters have explained the Great Depression of 1930 to 1939 as due to the efforts of the governments and very especially the government of the United States to play god."

Relevance for Today

It is not hard to see some of today's troubles as a repeat of the errors of the 1930s. There is arrogance up top. The federal government is dilettantish with money and exhibits disregard and even hostility to all other players. It is only as a result of this that economic recovery seems out of reach.

The key to recovery, now as in the 1930s, is to be found in property rights. These rights suffer under our current politics in several ways. The mortgage crisis, for example, arose out of a long-standing erosion of the property rights concept—first on the part of Fannie Mae and Freddie Mac, but also on that of the Federal Reserve. Broadening FDR's entitlement theories, Congress taught the country that home ownership was a "right." This fostered a misunderstanding of what property is. The owners didn't realize what ownership entailed—that is, they didn't grasp that they were obligated to deliver on the terms of the contract of their mortgage. In the bipartisan enthusiasm for making everyone an owner, our government debased the concept of home ownership.

Property rights are endangered as well by the ongoing assault on contracts generally. A perfect example of this was the treatment of Chrysler bonds during the company's bankruptcy, where senior secured creditors were ignored, notwithstanding the status of their bonds under bankruptcy law. The current administration made a political decision to subordinate those contracts to union demands. That sent a dangerous signal for the future that U.S. bonds are not trustworthy.

Three other threats to property loom. One is tax increases, such as the coming expiration of the Bush tax cuts. More taxes mean less private property. A second threat is in the area of infrastructure. Stimulus plans tend to emphasize infrastructure—especially roads and railroads. And after the Supreme Court's *Kelo* decision of 2005, the federal government will have enormous license to use eminent domain to claim private property for these purposes. Third and finally, there is the worst kind of confiscation of private property: inflation, which excessive government spending necessarily encourages. Many of us sense that inflation is closer than the country thinks.

If the experience of the Great Depression teaches anything, it is that property rights must be firmly established or else we will not have the kind of economic activity that leads to strong recovery. The Monopoly board game reminds us that economic growth isn't mysterious and inscrutable. Economic growth depends on the impulse of the small businessman and entrepreneur to get back in the game. In order for this to happen, we don't need a perfect government. All we need is one that is "not too bad," whose rules are not constantly changing and snuffing out the willingness of these players to take risks. We need a government under which the money supply doesn't change unpredictably, there are not too many "Go to Jail" cards, and the top hats are confident in the possibility of seeing significant returns on investment.

Recovery won't happen from the top. But when those at the top step back and create the proper conditions, it will happen down there on the board—one house at a time.

Reprinted by permission from Imprimis, *the national speech digest of Hillsdale College, www.hillsdale.edu.*

Speech on the Economic Bailout Proposal

George W. Bush (2008)

President George W. Bush delivered this televised address on September 24, 2008, outlining the economic crisis that the country faced and the bailout legislation that he was proposing to Congress.

Good evening. This is an extraordinary period for America's economy. Over the past few weeks, many Americans have felt anxiety about their finances and their future. I understand their worry and their frustration. We've seen triple-digit swings in the stock market. Major financial institutions have teetered on the edge of collapse, and some have failed. As uncertainty has grown, many banks have restricted lending. Credit markets have frozen. And families and businesses have found it harder to borrow money.

We're in the midst of a serious financial crisis, and the federal government is responding with decisive action. We've boosted confidence in money market mutual funds, and acted to prevent major investors from intentionally driving down stocks for their own personal gain.

President George W. Bush

Most importantly, my administration is working with Congress to address the root cause behind much of the instability in our markets. Financial assets related to home mortgages have lost value during the housing decline. And the banks holding these assets have restricted credit. As a result, our entire economy is in danger. So I've proposed that the federal government reduce the risk posed by these troubled assets, and supply urgently-needed money so banks and other financial institutions can avoid collapse and resume lending.

This rescue effort is not aimed at preserving any individual company or industry—it is aimed at preserving America's overall economy. It will help American consumers and businesses get credit to meet their daily needs and create jobs. And it will help send a signal to markets around the world that America's financial system is back on track.

I know many Americans have questions tonight: How did we reach this point in our economy? How will the solution I've proposed work? And what does this mean for your financial future? These are good questions, and they deserve clear answers.

First, how did our economy reach this point?

Well, most economists agree that the problems we are witnessing today developed over a long period of time. For more than a decade, a massive amount of money flowed into the United States from investors abroad, because our country is an attractive and secure place to do business. This large influx of money to U.S. banks and financial institutions—along with low interest rates—made it easier for Americans to get credit. These developments allowed more families to borrow money for cars and homes and college tuition—some for the first time. They allowed more entrepreneurs to get loans to start new businesses and create jobs.

Unfortunately, there were also some serious negative consequences, particularly in the housing market. Easy credit—combined with the faulty assumption that home values would continue to rise—led to excesses and bad decisions. Many mortgage lenders approved loans for borrowers without carefully examining their ability to pay. Many borrowers took out loans larger than they could afford, assuming that they could sell or refinance their homes at a higher price later on.

Optimism about housing values also led to a boom in home construction. Eventually the number of new houses exceeded the number of people willing to buy them. And with supply exceeding demand, housing prices fell. And this created a problem: Borrowers with adjustable rate mortgages who had been planning to sell or refinance their homes at a higher price were stuck with homes worth less than expected—along with mortgage payments they could not afford. As a result, many mortgage holders began to default.

"Fannie Mae stole my job because I told the truth. Fannie Mae owes me money. I told the truth. Fannie Mae lied. Fannie Mae got billions. I lost everything."
Washington, D.C. (2008)

These widespread defaults had effects far beyond the housing market. See, in today's mortgage industry, home loans are often packaged together, and converted into financial products called "mortgage-backed securities." These securities were sold to investors around the world. Many investors assumed these securities were trustworthy and asked few questions about their actual value. Two of the leading purchasers of mortgage-backed securities were Fannie Mae and Freddie Mac. Because these companies were chartered by Congress, many believed they were guaranteed by the federal government. This allowed them to borrow enormous sums of money, fuel the market for questionable investments, and put our financial system at risk.

The decline in the housing market set off a domino effect across our economy. When home values declined, borrowers defaulted on their mortgages, and investors holding mortgage-backed securities began to incur serious losses. Before long, these securities became so unreliable that they were not being bought or sold. Investment banks such as Bear Stearns and Lehman Brothers found themselves saddled with large amounts of assets they could not sell. They ran out of the money needed to meet their immediate obligations. And they faced imminent collapse. Other banks found themselves in severe financial trouble. These banks began holding on to their money, and lending dried up, and the gears of the American financial system began grinding to a halt.

With the situation becoming more precarious by the day, I faced a choice: To step in with dramatic government action, or to stand back and allow the irresponsible actions of some to undermine the financial security of all.

I'm a strong believer in free enterprise. So my natural instinct is to oppose government intervention. I believe companies that make bad decisions should be allowed to go out of business. Under normal circumstances, I would have followed this course. But these are not normal circumstances. The market is not functioning properly. There's been a widespread loss of confidence. And major sectors of America's financial system are at risk of shutting down.

The government's top economic experts warn that without immediate action by Congress, America could slip into a financial panic, and a distressing scenario would unfold:

More banks could fail, including some in your community. The stock market would drop even more, which would reduce the value of your retirement account. The value of your home could plummet. Foreclosures would rise dramatically. And if you own a business or a farm, you would find it harder and more expensive to get credit. More businesses would close their doors, and millions of Americans could lose their jobs. Even if you have good credit history, it would be more difficult for you to get the loans you need to buy a car or send your children to college. And ultimately, our country could experience a long and painful recession.

Fellow citizens: We must not let this happen. I appreciate the work of leaders from both parties in both houses of Congress to address this problem—and to make improvements to the proposal my administration sent to them. There is a spirit of cooperation between Democrats and Republicans, and between Congress and this administration. In that spirit, I've invited Senators McCain and Obama to join congressional leaders of both parties at the White House tomorrow to help speed our discussions toward a bipartisan bill.

I know that an economic rescue package will present a tough vote for many members of Congress. It is difficult to pass a bill that commits so much of the taxpayers' hard-

New York Stock Exchange on Wall Street (2009)

earned money. I also understand the frustration of responsible Americans who pay their mortgages on time, file their tax returns every April 15th, and are reluctant to pay the cost of excesses on Wall Street. But given the situation we are facing, not passing a bill now would cost these Americans much more later.

Many Americans are asking: How would a rescue plan work?

After much discussion, there is now widespread agreement on the principles such a plan would include. It would remove the risk posed by the troubled assets—including mortgage-backed securities—now clogging the financial system. This would free banks to resume the flow of credit to American families and businesses. Any rescue plan should also be designed to ensure that taxpayers are protected. It should welcome the participation of financial institutions large and small. It should make certain that failed executives do not receive a windfall from your tax dollars. It should establish a bipartisan board to oversee the plan's implementation. And it should be enacted as soon as possible.

In close consultation with Treasury Secretary Hank Paulson, Federal Reserve Chairman Ben Bernanke, and SEC Chairman Chris Cox, I announced a plan on Friday. First, the plan is big enough to solve a serious problem. Under our proposal, the federal government would put up to $700 billion taxpayer dollars on the line to purchase troubled assets that are clogging the financial system. In the short term, this will free up banks to resume the flow of credit to American families and businesses. And this will help our economy grow.

Second, as markets have lost confidence in mortgage-backed securities, their prices have dropped sharply. Yet the value of many of these assets will likely be higher than their current price, because the vast majority of Americans will ultimately pay off their mortgages. The government is the one institution with the patience and resources to buy these assets at their current low prices and hold them until markets return to normal. And when that happens, money will flow back to the Treasury as these assets are sold. And we expect that much, if not all, of the tax dollars we invest will be paid back.

A final question is: What does this mean for your economic future?

The primary . . . purpose of the steps I have outlined tonight is to safeguard the financial security of American workers and families and small businesses. The federal government also continues to enforce laws and regulations protecting your money. The Treasury Department recently offered government insurance for money market mutual funds. And through the FDIC, every savings account, checking account, and certificate of deposit is insured by the federal government for up to $100,000. The FDIC has been in existence for 75 years, and no one has ever lost a penny on an insured deposit—and this will not change.

Once this crisis is resolved, there will be time to update our financial regulatory structures. Our 21st century global economy remains regulated largely by outdated 20th century laws. Recently, we've seen how one company can grow so large that its failure jeopardizes the entire financial system.

Earlier this year, Secretary Paulson proposed a blueprint that would modernize our financial regulations. For example, the Federal Reserve would be authorized to take a closer look at the operations of companies across the financial spectrum and ensure that their practices do not threaten overall financial stability. There are other good ideas, and members of Congress should consider them. As they do, they must ensure that efforts to regulate Wall Street do not end up hampering our economy's ability to grow.

In the long run, Americans have good reason to be confident in our economic strength. Despite corrections in the marketplace and instances of abuse, democratic capitalism is the best system ever devised. It has unleashed the talents, and the productivity, and entrepreneurial spirit of our citizens. It has made this country the best place in the world to invest and do business. And it gives our economy the flexibility and resilience to absorb shocks, adjust, and bounce back.

Our economy is facing a moment of great challenge. But we've overcome tough challenges before—and we will overcome this one. I know that Americans sometimes get discouraged by the tone in Washington, and the seemingly endless partisan struggles. Yet history has shown that in times of real trial, elected officials rise to the occasion. And together, we will show the world once again what kind of country America is—a nation that tackles problems head on, where leaders come together to meet great tests, and where people of every background can work hard, develop their talents, and realize their dreams.

Thank you for listening. May God bless you.

President George W. Bush stands with Federal Reserve Chairman Ben Bernanke, left, SEC Chairman Chris Cox, right, and Treasury Secretary Hank Paulson as he delivers a statement on the economy in the Rose Garden of the White House five days before delivering this speech (2008)

What Makes for Success?

Dave Thomas (1996)

Dave Thomas (1932-2002) started working in a restaurant when he was twelve and became a millionaire when he was 35. He founded the Wendy's restaurant chain in 1969. In this speech Thomas shares the principles that guided his life and business.

There are all kinds of success and all kinds of ways to achieve it. I know bus drivers who are as successful as bankers. I know anonymous computer programmers who are now more successful than some of the biggest sports celebrities. I also know glamorous Hollywood stars and leading political figures who are failures. Sometimes you can spot true success. Sometimes you can't. Success can take many forms, but one thing's for sure: There are certain ingredients that are necessary in any recipe for success, and they may be applied by anyone.

Wendy's restaurant in Plainville, Connecticut (2014)

In other words, success comes through doing the right things—developing proper skills, attitudes, and values. As I've thought this through from an ordinary guy's perspective (which, above all else, I am; Lord knows, I'm no scholar), I have come to identify twelve ingredients. We know them as "character traits" or "values" or "virtues." People have been making lists of these ingredients ever since the Bible was written—and even before then. I've seen lists that are longer and some that are shorter, but twelve feels just about right to me. They are the ones that have made the most sense and have proved most valuable in my walk through life. But I should warn you, making lists is not enough to achieve success. You have to show people what success is. For example, I don't think that we really need to define generosity; we need to show what it means to be more generous—with our time, our talents, and our treasures.

My list of ingredients for success is divided into four basic groups:

- Inward—these have to do with getting your own act together successfully.

- Outward—these are all about treating people right.

- Upward—these are skills you need to know if you want to go beyond just doing an okay job and truly excel.

- Onward—these are attitudes you need to have in order to put yourself second and other people first. I think that onward values may be the toughest and the most rewarding values of all.

Added on to these ingredients are some others. Since I'm a hamburger cook, I call them "toppings." They are the pickles and onions of how I look at success:

- Anything is possible within the laws of God and man.

- You can't cut corners on quality.

- Give back—early and often.

- When you help someone, you really help yourself.

- Pay attention to the basics.

- You can't make much progress walking forward if you don't keep your balance, and that means balance in every part of your life.

- Have a sense of urgency about most things you do, and you won't end up as the caboose.

- Focus on only one thing at a time, and on just a few things in a lifetime.

- Don't waste time trying to do things you know nothing about: Either learn the basics or steer clear.

- Remember that life is short and fragile. Live it as if you don't know if you are going to be around for the next breath.

- Don't take the people of our nation—or their freedom—for granted.

- Be yourself—don't take yourself too seriously.

- Do the right thing—even when it may seem like the hardest thing in the world.

- Put more into life than you get out of it.

Inward: Getting Your Own Act Together

Success starts inside. Unless your own attitude and beliefs are right, you can never be a success. That goes for being successful in raising your family or helping to lead your church or synagogue or just making a buck. People never really have their act together unless they are honest, they believe in something, and they develop basic discipline.

Honesty

Many good people may look at honesty backwards. They think that it's okay if they don't come forward with the whole truth until someone challenges them with the right questions. But honesty doesn't mean hiding in the weeds; it means stepping out and telling the whole truth. Honesty means being sincere. It also means being fair in all your dealings with others.

Honesty is the number-one ingredient for success. I learned this the way most people do: through trial and error. I was born out of wedlock in New Jersey in 1932. A Michigan couple adopted me just after I was born. My adopted mother died when I was only five, but I had the good fortune to have a wonderful adoptive grandmother, Minnie Sinclair, who looked out for my welfare and helped shape my beliefs. I did not discover that I was adopted for many years, and, I have to admit, this made me angry and resentful for some time. I wish I had known from the beginning.

Yet after I learned the truth, I didn't always share it with others. One day, an African-American Wendy's manager buttonholed me and said, "Dave, when you gave your speech today, you left out the part about being adopted. Why did you do that? I always related to that because I was adopted myself." The comment hit home. From that point on, I made it a practice to be fully honest—and proud—about my past.

Faith

Honesty doesn't come from out of nowhere. It is a product of your moral convictions. But what do you do when your convictions are challenged? It is faith that gives you the strength to go on believing. . . . I don't support convictions or cults that are negative and lead only to hatred and fanaticism. Faith must be positive.

Live your faith. Don't wear it on your sleeve; roll up both sleeves and do something about it. When I was eleven years old, my adoptive grandmother took me to Michigan's Gull Lake to be baptized by immersion. I really felt that I was accepted by God when I was baptized. But what I remember most about my baptism was that my Grandma Minnie made it happen. For her, Christianity meant more than doctrine you talked about on Sundays. It meant working hard in a restaurant, seeing to the lodgers she rented rooms to, tending a big garden, doing the canning, and taking care of the farm animals every morning. And it meant teaching her grandson about faith.

At night we would listen to a gospel radio station that broadcast out of Chicago, and on Sundays before church we would listen to shows like the Cato Tabernacle out of Indianapolis. The public praying and singing part of her faith might not have stuck with me all that much, but I got baptized into the roll-up-your-sleeves kind of faith of Grandma Minnie. And I believe in it to this day.

Discipline

Routine lies at the heart of discipline. Routine is what keeps us focused on the main things in life. But routine doesn't have to mean boring. Unless you have a strong, healthy routine, I doubt that you can live a successful life. Discipline means keeping things and people in their proper places. For example, I think that taxpayers should discipline their politicians so that they don't get too uppity! Children need discipline, too—plenty more than most of them get—and that's the fault of their parents. Discipline means direction— clear and firm direction—not physical or mental abuse. Discipline helps you keep track of your own thinking and also keeps such thinking simple and to the point so that you don't mess up by dreaming up fancy, big-shot thoughts when you shouldn't.

Roy Tuggle, one of the pioneers of the modern restaurant business, is a classic in discipline as far as I'm concerned. When he was fourteen years old, Roy—the sixth of twelve children—left Ravenna, Kentucky, during the Great Depression. With only two years of school under his belt, nine pennies in his pocket, and cardboard soles in his shoes, he hopped a freight train to Columbus, Ohio. After unloading stoves and refrigerators and working as a dishwasher, he became a fry cook. By sheer will and discipline he built his career and a great restaurant business while he and his wife Mary raised their family.

When Roy started out, hamburgers were only a nickel and a small restaurant operator had to scrimp for every penny. Years later, when Roy sold his business, he became a millionaire. But the dollar signs never changed Roy. He's never been driven by money. As you'll hear Roy often put it today, "I never wanted to be the richest man in the graveyard," to which I'll generally chime in, "You got it, Roy. You've never seen a hearse with luggage racks." Roy's is the kind of discipline that keeps success from going to your head once you have had the good fortune to achieve your goals.

Outward: Treating People Right

Success may start inside, but it doesn't mean anything until you draw other people into the picture. The key is whether you are going to be fair to other folks—will you treat people right? If you are to treat people right, you have to master three fundamentals: caring, teamwork, and support. Most of us are lucky enough to learn these basic ideas

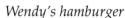
Wendy's hamburger

from our parents and should be pros at them by the time we are in nursery school. (But I have met some Ph.D.s and millionaires who have never learned the words or have forgotten what they mean, and I bet that you know people like that, too.) Not taking people for granted is a great way to steer a straight outward course and to do right by your fellow human beings.

Wendy's in Tokyo, Japan (2008)

Caring

Caring is the rock that love is built upon. Caring is feeling what another person feels. Some people call it "empathy." Genuinely caring about people usually leads to success. And really successful people widen the circle of people they care about more and more as they grow older. Mary Kay Ash, founder of Mary Kay Cosmetics, once told me something I'll never forget. She said the one suggestion she got in life that helped her most was to "pretend that every single person you meet has a sign around his or her neck that says, 'Make me feel important.'"

Why aren't we just nice to people? One year, shortly before Christmas, I went to a Wendy's restaurant in Albuquerque to film a television program about adoption with two youngsters. The little girl, who was about seven, had a fresh scar where her father had walloped her with a beer bottle. That scar wasn't going to go away. As we ate lunch along with a friend of mine, the girl and her older brother, who was about nine, finally started to look us in the eyes, and that was none too easy for them. We talked about how important it is to stick together when you don't have other family. And then the boy said: "I don't want to be adopted with her. Just look at her ugly scar!"

It may seem cruel, but he was right. The boy knew his sister's appearance would turn off many possible adoptive parents. And before you condemn him, think back for a minute: Were you any less selfish when you were nine? I doubt that I was. My friend— who is smart in a low-key way and who made it big-time by building a big business over the years—reached into his wallet and pulled out two crisp one hundred dollar bills. "You kids," he said in a real quiet voice, "don't have any money to buy Christmas presents. It's plain to see that. So I want you to buy some Christmas presents, but there's a catch. You can't buy anything for yourself. Think hard about what your brother or sister might like or need and buy that instead. Finally, you have to write me a letter about what you got each other."

That five-minute course in caring outdid the best universities anywhere. The brother and sister made up. In January, my friend received a letter reporting what they bought each other, and he sent a copy to me. Then we learned that they had been adopted by a family. As I hear it, they're quite a team, and their new parents are proud to have them—because of the way that they care for each other and for lots of other reasons, too.

Teamwork

Teamwork is the starting point for treating people right. Most people think that teamwork is only important when competing against other teams. But competition is only part of the picture. In most things we do in life, people have to work with rather than against each other to get something done. Win-win situations and partnerships are the most important results of teamwork. The best teams in the world are the ones that help people become better and achieve more than they ever thought they could on their own.

One place people learn teamwork from is their families. Children get their first lesson watching how their parents behave toward each other. So, if you're a parent, you are also a teacher of teamwork—for good or ill—every day. Your sons and daughters learn from what you do. For me, the people I've worked with have become my family, too. Throughout my career, my "second family" has taught me a whole lot about teamwork.

There are little teams and there are big teams. Your community is a team, for example. My daughter Pam organizes volunteer work for the city of Columbus, so she knows a lot about how to get different kinds of teams to work together, on projects ranging from recreation centers to hospital boards. Teams can work together, and teams can compete, too, even when they are not rivals. Why aren't Pam's kids jealous when she spends so much of her time on community work? There is a simple answer: The kids are all involved in community work themselves, and they have been from an early age. Pam and her husband, Steve, endorse it and encourage it. The community team isn't a rival or an opponent of the family team—it's an extension of it. Neat idea, don't you think?

Support

Many people believe that support is something you give to someone you feel sorry for or that it means propping someone up who would fail unless you were there to give him a boost. But that's not the way I see it. Support is the boost you give someone who can help himself but who needs a partner to open a window or to push aside a roadblock. Support isn't a bunch of reckless advice, either. It's real help—commitment and effort. Support is "teamwork plus." Support is also sharing feelings and insights with other people. It's helping others with their level of awareness and making your own awareness stronger at the same time.

The best way to get support is to give it. Wendy's President Gordon Teter likes to remind people of a saying that Jack Mollenkopf, his college coach at Purdue, often used: "Meet me halfway, and it's amazing what can happen." It is amazing what can be done when you treat people with respect. Respect goes both ways, too. Just as the players need it from the coach, the coach needs it from the players.

Support is also easier if things aren't too complicated. Gordon believes in what he calls "The Law of the Lowest Common Denominator," and it has nothing to do with arithmetic. It goes like this: "The simpler you can keep it, the better you can execute it." It's that way for a department and its boss, for a congregation and its minister, and for a volunteer group and its chairperson. If you want to give and get support, it's a lot more likely to come and keep coming if the rules are simple and clear.

Upward: Going for Excellence and Beyond

When you have your own act together and get along well with others, you're ready to reach for another goal, that of excellence. Nothing is as tricky in the world of success as excellence. From our earliest days, we are taught that it is snazzy, glossy, bigger than life. It's that three seconds of glory when a major leaguer puts one out of the park or a figure skater completes a triple jump, not the constant training or workouts. But that's just false. Most people think excellence in business is sitting at a big desk and making power decisions, but true excellence is really the years beforehand making little and big decisions and learning from mistakes when things go wrong.

No one can excel in everything. In fact, excellence in any one little thing is hard enough. And don't forget: It's easy to become selfish when you "go for the gold." The graveyards of the world are loaded with people who lost it all at the same time they thought they were winning it all.

Motivation

Without a doubt, motivation is a key ingredient of success. Know what motivates you, and prove to yourself that this motivation is honest and worthwhile. But don't let too many different things motivate you, or you'll be tangled up in a maze of all kinds of conflicts. Stay focused. Figure out what your motivations are going to be in the next step of your life before you arrive at it. Keep dreaming, but don't daydream. And don't do anything just to earn praise, or you are likely to short-change yourself in the end. Look at success firsthand so that you really know how it works and what it costs to achieve.

It may be corny, but I'm big on lapel pins. Some people hand out business cards; I give away lapel pins. Wendy's gives out pins to employees, and to customers, too—they're just as much a part of the family as anyone else. As I said, I don't believe in wearing your beliefs on your sleeve; but I do believe in wearing them on your lapel. Yep, I'm one of those guys who'll wear an American flag pin on my lapel from time to time; it shows I'm proud to be an American. In the same way, by wearing Wendy's lapel pins, our employees show they're proud to be a part of the Wendy's team. Does having a little symbol that means they're part of the Wendy's family motivate employees to work a little harder, or customers to come in more often? A little bit, I'll bet. And success in life is made up of a lot of little things that keep you motivated and that motivate others too.

Examples of Wendy's pins

Creativity

Creativity means change, but if you don't use common sense when you change things around, you are likely to end up farther behind than when you started. Not everybody can be creative. Accept it as a fact of life that if you aren't creative yourself your challenge is to learn how to work with people who are. And being creative doesn't always mean doing new things. Sometimes, it's using a creative idea that worked in one instance and applying it to another. I'm a disciple of reality. Successful creative dreams have to be realistic—within man's laws as well as God's—and within the realm of common sense.

What makes people creative? Sometimes, it's having your life shaken up. George Valassis is a pal of mine. For nineteen years he worked as an advertising salesman for his father's brother. One day his uncle decided to retire and his cousin took over the business. The cousin fired him. Without warning, George lost a modest though comfortable job, and he realized then and there that job security could vanish like a puff of smoke. So, he put his nineteen years of experience to use in order to come up with an innovative idea. He knew that advertisers like Procter and Gamble and General Foods were having a really tough time delivering coupons to customers quickly, so he came up with the idea of inserting books filled with coupons in newspapers. To this day, when you open the Sunday edition of your newspaper and see a book of coupons inside, you're looking at what the ad industry calls a "Valassis Insert." George sold the company he built for big bucks. If he hadn't gotten fired, would he have come up with this great idea? George doesn't think so. To this day, he says he just played the hand he was dealt. Pretty creative though, wasn't it?

Leadership

Everybody is saying that we need to stop putting leaders on pedestals. I'm not so sure. The real problem is finding leaders who truly deserve to keep their pedestals. What knocks off more leaders than anything else is failing to practice what they preach. Of all the things leaders are supposed to do, nothing is more important than setting a good example. Ben Franklin had it right when he wrote in Poor Richard's Almanac, "Well done is better than well said." I don't think we should do away with pedestals; we ought to be putting a lot more "little people"—people who have really achieved something—on them so that ordinary folks have a better, clearer idea of who's doing the job and who's setting the pace.

J. B. Fuqua died in 2006. The Fuqua School of Business at Duke University is named in his honor.

J. B. Fuqua is a titan of industry who built a huge conglomerate and broadcast empire. J. B. is also a guy who still knows the meaning of being humble. Born to a poor family, his mother died when he was two months old, and his grandparents adopted him. When J. B. was out on his own and wanted to learn about radio electronics, the only library he knew about was Duke University's. The library staff decided to loan him the books he needed even though he was not a student. It wasn't a bad deal for Duke: After J. B. hit the bull's-eye in his own companies, he invested $15 million in the Duke University business school, helping put it in the front ranks of all business schools in the U.S.

First and foremost, J. B. is a leader. In addition to the donations he's made to Duke, he's donated $4 million to train managers in Russia and Ukraine as these nations attempt to put at least a few true free enterprise principles into practice. And then there's the $10 million that he's giving to Prince Edward County, Virginia, to help turn around the educational system for youngsters in kindergarten through twelfth grade. It will be a model of doing the right thing for rural school systems throughout the United States.

It's not the money that makes J. B. successful as a leader. It's the fact that he won't let go. J. B. will tell you that leadership doesn't stop with giving but begins there. He's well past retirement age, yet you'll find him all over—from Farmville to Kiev—giving to others, passing on his own experience and wisdom. J. B.'s style is real leadership—letting go in the doing, but not letting go in the guiding.

Onward: Putting Yourself Second and Others First

If going upward and reaching for excellence is where success gets tricky, going onward by putting yourself second and others first is where success really gets tough. Most books on success tell you that you have really "arrived" when you win the race. That's wrong. Truly successful people are the ones who help others cross the finish line. People who make this last big step toward success really have three things: responsibility, courage, and generosity. Onward is the direction Success Soldiers follow—Christian or any other kind.

Responsibility

We try to teach children responsibility, and that's good, but, as I have already said, most of us don't learn the full meaning of responsibility until we are older and have gained solid experience, made some decisions, and learned from our mistakes—not the simple mistakes we make when "following orders" but mistakes we make when trying to do something really hard or trying to excel. Making these sorts of mistakes teaches us judgment, and it helps toughen our backbone.

Mature responsibility means realizing that no single person can be responsible for everything. You can't be successful if you are stumbling around trying to juggle the whole world on your shoulders. Responsible people refuse to take shortcuts, even though they are almost always available. They make sure that others with duties act responsibly, too. And they use whatever recognition or honor they may have earned not to further their own ends but on behalf of good causes. Instead of stealing the limelight, they allow it to shine upon a good cause.

My son Kenny says that the most important piece of advice I ever gave him came in 1979 as the two of us were driving over the Oakland Park Bridge in Ft. Lauderdale. He was thinking about becoming a Wendy's franchisee. I gave him my opinion; I was against it. I didn't come out and say why, but my feeling was that he wasn't ready for that kind of responsibility, and I didn't want to see him fail. When he told me his mind was made up, I said, "Don't ever forget how you got here, and don't ever let yourself become complacent." Kenny went on to become pretty successful in the restaurant business. He says my advice really helped him. But I could have summed up everything I said that day in just two words: Be responsible.

Courage

We tend to make courage too dramatic. Courage is often doing something simple, unpleasant, or boring again and again until we get it down pat. People who are physically challenged and who have the determination to get around their handicaps are great examples because their courage makes them test their limits every day in a way that the rest of us write off as small-time or insignificant. Lois Gruenbaum grew up in Cleveland and went to work in a hospital kitchen when she was fifteen. During World War II, she became a nurse's aide and worked in an army hospital. After a shift, she would say to herself, "Hey, things are bad, but there's always someone who is worse off. All you need to do is find out what you can and can't do and then go ahead and do what you can do."

Great lesson—Lois learned it not long before she needed to put it to use. In 1955, she was diagnosed with cancer. Operation after operation followed, but the cancer always came back. Finally, she lost one leg and half of the pelvic bone and was forced to drag herself around on crutches. She came home from the hospital faced with the challenge of taking care of her husband, a seven-year-old, a four-year-old, and two-year-old twins. She says she cut a deal with the Lord: "I promised that if He let me live to raise my children, I would not vegetate. I would be a contributing person." It was a good deal. Forty years later, the family is flourishing, and Lois is one of the most active and happy people you could ever hope to meet. And there are thousands of such quiet, unsung heroes in every town. I'll bet you know lots of people with the courage of Lois Gruenbaum.

Generosity

A person who has modest means and won't share may be considered stingy. But rich people can give 'til they're purple and still not be truly generous. You have to give of yourself, not just of your wallet. One of the things I'm proudest about in the Wendy's family is that so many franchisees make significant donations to the community—and they contribute leadership as well as dollars. Another old friend, the late Kenny King, was a generous guy who had a real knack for how he gave. He really took pleasure in it, was modest about it, and often gave anonymously. But even more important was the fact that he really tried to learn what giving was all about. Whether he was giving people moral or financial support, he would always say, "I'm really getting a lot more out of this than you are." I can't tell you how many times he said that same thing to me. Later, when I tried to do for others what Kenny had done for me, I learned what he meant. When you give people help and understanding, you truly learn what they are like. And those who understand others better are certainly the most likely to succeed. The giving and the getting become all mixed up—which is great.

The Proud Beggar

In February of 1991, I had to travel to Memphis. It wasn't a trip I wanted to make. There's a church there I'll never forget; you don't forget places where you say good-bye to your best friends. It's plenty bigger than Calvary Church in Kalamazoo where I had my first memories of going to church. In fact, it's a cathedral—the Cathedral of the Immaculate Conception. It looks Spanish and it's mighty big and fancy. On the day I was there, every seat was filled, and a huge crowd stood outside. A lot of other people—not just me—had lost a friend.

Oh, Danny boy, the pipes, the pipes are calling,
From glen to glen and down the mountainside,
The summer's gone—all the roses falling,
'Tis you, 'tis you must go, and I must bide.

A song you'd expect to hear in an Irish pub, not in a cathedral. You wouldn't expect it to be sung by a Metropolitan Opera soprano like Marguerite Piazza either. Maybe you'd think that it was honoring an Irish cardinal, but who would expect that it was in memory of a Lebanese entertainer of humble origins? Many eyes were tearing before the music started, but when they heard the first notes of that song—Danny Thomas's theme song for decades—everybody choked up. A little girl and an older couple near me were crying, and I don't know what sound seemed bigger to my ears—the crying or the music.

Danny was a great friend. He was [a great] showman. But, most of all, he was a success—not just as an entertainer but as a human being. An obsession drove him—the St. Jude's Children's Hospital in Memphis. He'd do anything for that hospital. No man or woman I know ever got over every inch of the false pride that we are all born with more than Danny Thomas did. He called himself the "Proud Beggar."

If Danny Thomas hadn't forgotten a promise, St. Jude would never have been built. Back in 1943, Danny was still playing five-dollar-a-week gigs. His wife was pregnant with their first child, Marlo, and they needed money to raise a family. Danny's uncle by marriage was a butcher who offered him a job cutting meat, but he wanted to stay in show business. Danny stopped at a church and, according to the Catholic tradition, prayed to St. Jude for direction. He promised he would show his gratitude if guided to the right path: Should he be a comedian or a butcher? Not much later, Danny's act was booked at Chez Paris in Chicago. He had made it to the big time. The booking lasted for five years, and it helped launch his television career.

Until well into his stint at Chez Paris, Danny had forgotten all about his promise. Forgetting to make good on a promise was about the worst thing a person could do, in Danny's book. When he finally remembered, he went to see an old friend, Cardinal Stritch, and he asked what he should do. The cardinal told him that there were already enough churches and enough statues in the world. Recalling his first parish in Memphis, he proposed the idea of starting a children's hospital there.

That's what Danny did. He built the best children's hospital in the world. Why is the place named after St. Jude? St. Jude is the saint in charge of impossible acts. Danny felt that "no child should die in the dawn of life," so he declared a personal war against the killer diseases that strike the young. He started funding the hospital in Memphis in 1957. Great names in medicine led the research. Plenty of impossible things were made possible because Danny stuck to his mission like a bulldog. In 1962, only 4 percent of the victims of acute lymphocytic leukemia survived the disease; in 1991, 73 percent survived. Only 7 percent of patients with non-Hodgkin lymphoma recovered; now, about 80 percent do. The list goes on and on. When people tell you about the "impossible," just think of St. Jude's Hospital.

In 1991, Danny Thomas was promoting his new book, the proceeds of which were earmarked for St. Jude. He always did fund-raising for the hospital before taking on jobs that would put money in his own pocket. One night, worn out, he got home late. At 2:30 a.m., a massive heart attack killed him. He was not buried in some grassy cemetery. He was laid to rest in a mausoleum inside St. Jude's Hospital. All around the mausoleum, Danny's favorite sayings are inscribed—sayings like: "Blessed is the man who knows why he was born," and "He who denies his heritage has no heritage." Danny gave of himself. He taught others to give of themselves, too, and to forget their selfish side. I remember his response to a donor who had put down a large hunk of change: "The deepest thank-you I can offer is to pray that you and yours will never need the help of St. Jude's."

St. Jude Children's Research Hospital in Memphis, Tennessee, serves about 8,000 patients per year. Its research programs also improve treatments for other patients around the world.

Well done, Danny boy!

Danny Thomas's example is worth remembering anytime the temptation arises for "me" to take over "we." Everything that made him a success was based on simple principles:

- Keep your word. Danny kept his word to God.

- Let a good cause that's bigger than you take over your life. What is your St. Jude? There ought to be one. Think about it, and support it.

- Don't get scared by the word impossible. In fact, get together the best talents you can find to tackle the impossible.

- Do it through people. Danny got people to work together. That's the way it should be, isn't it?

- Whether you are passing the hat for a good cause, defending your beliefs, teaching your children, helping your community, or starting a business, be a proud beggar. Real proud.

Reprinted by permission from Imprimis, *the national speech digest of Hillsdale College, www.hillsdale.edu.*

The Art of Money Getting

P. T. Barnum (1880)

Phineas Taylor "P. T." Barnum (1810-1891) was a sensational showman who created a traveling circus during the mid-1800s. In his later life, he served in the Connecticut state legislature and as mayor of Bridgeport, Connecticut. His 1880 book The Art of Money Getting, or Golden Rules for Making Money *contains good advice. Here are some excerpts.*

In the United States, where we have more land than people, it is not at all difficult for persons in good health to make money. In this comparatively new field there are so many avenues of success open, so many vocations which are not crowded, that any person of either sex who is willing, at least for the time being, to engage in any respectable occupation that offers, may find lucrative employment.

Those who really desire to attain an independence, have only to set their minds upon it, and adopt the proper means, as they do in regard to any other object which they wish to accomplish, and the thing is easily done. But however easy it may be found to make money, I have no doubt many of my hearers will agree it is the most difficult thing in the world to keep it. The road to wealth is, as Dr. Franklin truly says, "as plain as the road to the mill." It consists simply in expending less than we earn; that seems to be a very simple problem. Mr. Micawber, one of those happy creations of the genial Dickens, puts the case in a strong light when he says that to have annual income of twenty pounds per annum, and spend twenty pounds and sixpence, is to be the most miserable of men; whereas, to have an income of only twenty pounds, and spend but nineteen pounds and sixpence is to be the happiest of mortals. Many of my readers may say, "we understand this: this is economy, and we know economy is wealth; we know we can't eat our cake and keep it also." Yet I beg to say that perhaps more cases of failure arise from mistakes on this point than almost any other. The fact is, many people think they understand economy when they really do not. . . .

True economy consists in always making the income exceed the out-go. Wear the old clothes a little longer if necessary; dispense with the new pair of gloves; mend the old dress: live on plainer food if need be; so that, under all circumstances, unless some unforeseen accident occurs, there will be a margin in favor of the income. A penny here, and a dollar there, placed at interest, goes on accumulating, and in this way the desired result is attained. It requires some training, perhaps, to accomplish this economy, but when once used to it, you will find there is more satisfaction in rational saving than in irrational spending. Here is a recipe which I recommend: I have found it to work an excellent cure for extravagance, and especially for mistaken economy: When you find that you have no surplus at the end of the year, and yet have a good income, I advise you to take a few sheets of paper and form them into a book and mark down every item of expenditure. Post it every day or week in two columns, one headed "necessaries" or even "comforts", and the other headed "luxuries," and you will find that the latter column will be double, treble, and frequently ten times greater than the former. The real comforts of life cost but a small portion of what most of us can earn. Dr. Franklin says "it is the eyes of others and not our own eyes which ruin us. If all the world were blind except myself I should not care for fine clothes or furniture." . . .

Don't Mistake Your Vocation

The safest plan, and the one most sure of success for the young man starting in life, is to select the vocation which is most congenial to his tastes. Parents and guardians are often quite too negligent in regard to this. It is very common for a father to say, for example: "I have five boys. I will make Billy a clergyman; John a lawyer; Tom a doctor, and Dick a farmer."

P. T. Barnum (c. 1862)

He then goes into town and looks about to see what he will do with Sammy. He returns home and says "Sammy, I see watch-making is a nice genteel business; I think I will make you a goldsmith." He does this, regardless of Sam's natural inclinations, or genius.

We are all, no doubt, born for a wise purpose. There is as much diversity in our brains as in our countenances. Some are born natural mechanics, while some have great aversion to machinery. Let a dozen boys of ten years get together, and you will soon observe two or three are "whittling" out some ingenious device; working with locks or complicated machinery. When they were but five years old, their father could find no toy to please them like a puzzle. They are natural mechanics; but the other eight or nine boys have different aptitudes. I belong to the latter class; I never had the slightest love for mechanism; on the contrary, I have a sort of abhorrence for complicated machinery. I never had ingenuity enough to whittle a cider tap so it would not leak. I never could make a pen that I could write with, or understand the principle of a steam engine. If a man was to take such a boy as I was, and attempt to make a watchmaker of him, the boy might, after an apprenticeship of five or seven years, be able to take apart and put together a watch; but all through life he would be working up hill and seizing every excuse for leaving his work and idling away his time. Watchmaking is repulsive to him.

Unless a man enters upon the vocation intended for him by nature, and best suited to his peculiar genius, he cannot succeed. I am glad to believe that the majority of persons do find their right vocation. Yet we see many who have mistaken their calling, from the blacksmith up (or down) to the clergyman. You will see, for instance, that extraordinary linguist the "learned blacksmith," who ought to have been a teacher of languages; and you may have seen lawyers, doctors and clergymen who were better fitted by nature for the anvil or the lapstone. . . .

Whatever You Do, Do It With All Your Might

Work at it, if necessary, early and late, in season and out of season, not leaving a stone unturned, and never deferring for a single hour that which can be done just as well now. The old proverb is full of truth and meaning, "Whatever is worth doing at all, is worth doing well." Many a man acquires a fortune by doing his business thoroughly, while his neighbor remains poor for life, because he only half does it. Ambition, energy, industry, perseverance, are indispensable requisites for success in business.

Fortune always favors the brave, and never helps a man who does not help himself. It won't do to spend your time like Mr. Micawber, in waiting for something to "turn up." To such men one of two things usually "turns up:" the poorhouse or the jail; for idleness breeds bad habits, and clothes a man in rags. The poor spendthrift vagabond says to a rich man:

"I have discovered there is enough money in the world for all of us, if it was equally divided; this must be done, and we shall all be happy together."

"But," was the response, "if everybody was like you, it would be spent in two months, and what would you do then?"

"Oh! divide again; keep dividing, of course!" . . .

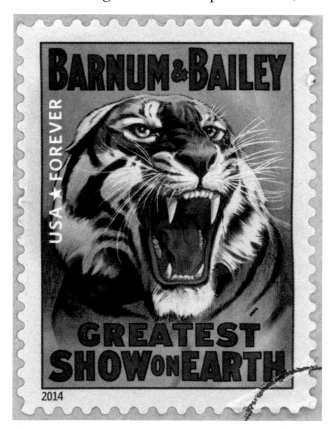

Vintage circus poster on a United States Postal Service Stamp (2014)

Don't Get Above Your Business

... "In England, the business makes the man." If a man in that country is a mechanic or working-man, he is not recognized as a gentleman. On the occasion of my first appearance before Queen Victoria, the Duke of Wellington asked me what sphere in life General Tom Thumb's parents were in.

"His father is a carpenter," I replied.

"Oh! I had heard he was a gentleman," was the response of His Grace.

In this Republican country, the man makes the business. No matter whether he is a blacksmith, a shoemaker, a farmer, banker or lawyer, so long as his business is legitimate, he may be a gentleman. So any "legitimate" business is a double blessing—it helps the man engaged in it, and also helps others. The Farmer supports his own family, but he also benefits the merchant or mechanic who needs the products of his farm. The tailor not only makes a living by his trade, but he also benefits the farmer, the clergyman and others who cannot make their own clothing. But all these classes often may be gentlemen.

The great ambition should be to excel all others engaged in the same occupation.

The college-student who was about graduating, said to an old lawyer:

"I have not yet decided which profession I will follow. Is your profession full?"

"The basement is much crowded, but there is plenty of room up-stairs," was the witty and truthful reply.

No profession, trade, or calling, is overcrowded in the upper story. Wherever you find the most honest and intelligent merchant or banker, or the best lawyer, the best doctor, the best clergyman, the best shoemaker, carpenter, or anything else, that man is most sought for, and has always enough to do. As a nation, Americans are too superficial—they are striving to get rich quickly, and do not generally do their business as substantially and thoroughly as they should, but whoever excels all others in his own line, if his habits are good and his integrity undoubted, cannot fail to secure abundant patronage, and the wealth that naturally follows. Let your motto then always be "Excelsior," for by living up to it there is no such word as fail.

Learn Something Useful

Every man should make his son or daughter learn some useful trade or profession, so that in these days of changing fortunes of being rich to-day and poor tomorrow they may have something tangible to fall back upon. This provision might save many persons from misery, who by some unexpected turn of fortune have lost all their means.

Let Hope Predominate, But Be Not Too Visionary

Many persons are always kept poor, because they are too visionary. Every project looks to them like certain success, and therefore they keep changing from one business to another, always in hot water, always "under the harrow." The plan of "counting the chickens before they are hatched" is an error of ancient date, but it does not seem to improve by age.

Do Not Scatter Your Powers

Engage in one kind of business only, and stick to it faithfully until you succeed, or until your experience shows that you should abandon it. A constant hammering on one nail will generally drive it home at last, so that it can be clinched. When a man's undivided attention is centered on one object, his mind will constantly be suggesting improvements of value, which would escape him if his brain was occupied by a dozen different subjects at once. Many a fortune has slipped through a man's fingers because he was engaged in too many occupations at a time. There is good sense in the old caution against having too many irons in the fire at once. . . .

Read the Newspapers

Always take a trustworthy newspaper, and thus keep thoroughly posted in regard to the transactions of the world. He who is without a newspaper is cut off from his species. In these days of telegraphs and steam, many important inventions and improvements in every branch of trade are being made, and he who don't consult the newspapers will soon find himself and his business left out in the cold. . . .

Be Polite and Kind to Your Customers

Politeness and civility are the best capital ever invested in business. Large stores, gilt signs, flaming advertisements, will all prove unavailing if you or your employees treat your patrons abruptly. The truth is, the more kind and liberal a man is, the more generous will be the patronage bestowed upon him. "Like begets like." The man who gives the greatest amount of goods of a corresponding quality for the least sum (still reserving for himself a profit) will generally succeed best in the long run. This brings us to the golden rule, "As ye would that men should do to you, do ye also to them" and they will do better by you than if you always treated them as if you wanted to get the most you could out of them for the least return. Men who drive sharp bargains with their customers, acting as if they never expected to see them again, will not be mistaken. They will never see them again as customers. People don't like to pay and get kicked also. . . .

Barnum and Bailey Circus Poster (1897)

Be Charitable

Of course men should be charitable, because it is a duty and a pleasure. But even as a matter of policy, if you possess no higher incentive, you will find that the liberal man will command patronage, while the sordid, uncharitable miser will be avoided.

Solomon says: "There is that scattereth and yet increaseth; and there is that withholdeth more than meet, but it tendeth to poverty." Of course the only true charity is that which is from the heart.

The best kind of charity is to help those who are willing to help themselves. Promiscuous almsgiving, without inquiring into the worthiness of the applicant, is bad in every sense. But to search out and quietly assist those who are struggling for themselves, is the kind that "scattereth and yet increaseth." But don't fall into the idea that some persons practice, of giving a prayer instead of a potato, and a benediction instead of bread, to the hungry. It is easier to make Christians with full stomachs than empty. . . .

Preserve Your Integrity

It is more precious than diamonds or rubies. The old miser said to his sons: "Get money; get it honestly if you can, but get money:" This advice was not only atrociously wicked, but it was the very essence of stupidity: It was as much as to say, "if you find it difficult to obtain money honestly, you can easily get it dishonestly. Get it in that way." Poor fool! Not to know that the most difficult thing in life is to make money dishonestly! Not to know that our prisons are full of men who attempted to follow this advice; not to understand that no man can be dishonest, without soon being found out, and that when his lack of principle is discovered, nearly every avenue to success is closed against him forever. The public very properly shun all whose integrity is doubted. No matter how polite and pleasant and accommodating a man may be, none of us dare to deal with him if we suspect "false weights and measures." Strict honesty, not only lies at the foundation of all success in life (financially), but in every other respect. Uncompromising integrity of character is invaluable. It secures to its possessor a peace and joy which cannot be attained without it—which no amount of money, or houses and lands can purchase. A man who is known to be strictly honest, may be ever so poor, but he has the purses of all the community at his disposal—for all know that if he promises to return what he borrows, he will never disappoint them. As a mere matter of selfishness, therefore, if a man had no higher motive for being honest, all will find that the maxim of Dr. Franklin can never fail to be true, that "honesty is the best policy."

To get rich, is not always equivalent to being successful. "There are many rich poor men," while there are many others, honest and devout men and women, who have never possessed so much money as some rich persons squander in a week, but who are

Vintage circus posters on United States Postal Service Stamps (2014)

nevertheless really richer and happier than any man can ever be while he is a transgressor of the higher laws of his being.

The inordinate love of money, no doubt, may be and is "the root of all evil," but money itself, when properly used, is not only a "handy thing to have in the house," but affords the gratification of blessing our race by enabling its possessor to enlarge the scope of human happiness and human influence. The desire for wealth is nearly universal, and none can say it is not laudable, provided the possessor of it accepts its responsibilities, and uses it as a friend to humanity.

The history of money-getting, which is commerce, is a history of civilization, and wherever trade has flourished most, there, too, have art and science produced the noblest fruits. In fact, as a general thing, money-getters are the benefactors of our race. To them, in a great measure, are we indebted for our institutions of learning and of art, our academies, colleges and churches. It is no argument against the desire for, or the possession of wealth, to say that there are sometimes misers who hoard money only for the sake of hoarding and who have no higher aspiration than to grasp everything which comes within their reach. As we have sometimes hypocrites in religion, and demagogues in politics, so there are occasionally misers among money-getters. These, however, are only exceptions to the general rule. But when, in this country, we find such a nuisance and stumbling block as a miser, we remember with gratitude that in America we have no laws of primogeniture, and that in the due course of nature the time will come when the hoarded dust will be scattered for the benefit of mankind. To all men and women, therefore, do I conscientiously say, make money honestly, and not otherwise, for Shakespeare has truly said, "He that wants money, means, and content, is without three good friends."

The Wanamaker Name

Philip Ryken (1995)

John Wanamaker (1838-1922) was a pioneering businessman in Philadelphia, creating a successful chain of department stores. The Wanamaker Family Trust sold the company in 1978, and the remaining Wanamaker stores were rebranded by new owners in 1995. Philip Ryken delivered this sermon while serving as a pastor at Tenth Presbyterian Church in Philadelphia. He gave credit to William Allen Zulker's book John Wanamaker: King of Merchants *for many details. Ryken became president of Wheaton College in 2010.*

Christmas is not quite the same this year. You cannot go to Wanamaker's to see the Wanamaker's Light Show. You can go to Hecht's to see the Hecht's Light Show, but the Wanamaker name has vanished.

If you had lived in Philadelphia around the turn of the century, it would have been different, for you could hardly have avoided the Wanamaker name.

Shortly before Christmas in 1850, a twelve-year-old boy named John Wanamaker entered a jewelry store to buy a gift for his mother. Just as the storekeeper was wrapping

Wanamaker building in New York City (2011)

the gift, he saw something else he liked better. "It's too late," the storekeeper said, "you've already bought this." It was then that the young John Wanamaker made his vow: "Some day I'll own a store and I'll treat my customers kindly and fairly."

And so he did. John Wanamaker was a gifted merchant. He established four cardinal principles of business that became the "platform of modern business":

- First, Return of money if buyer returns goods in ten days uninjured,

- Second, The guarantee to each buyer stating terms of sale,

- Third, No second price,

- Fourth, Any article may be exchanged if desired, within two weeks of purchase.

Although it was opened during the difficult years of the Civil War, his store's annual sales surpassed $2 million by the end of its first decade. (That was back when $2 million was a lot of money). Seventy thousand customers came to Wanamaker's when the new store was first opened at 13th and Market, a sign that in time, the store that offered

"Everything from Everywhere to Everybody" would become the largest retail store in America. It was the first to send buyers to foreign markets, the first to have electric lights, the first to have air conditioning, the first to use newspaper advertisements, the first to have a profit-sharing plan to employees, the first to offer two-weeks free summer vacation, and, believe it or not, the first to offer daily weather forecasts to the general public.

Much of Wanamaker's commercial success came from the integrity of his business practices. This advertisement was typical of Wanamaker's honesty: "Men's ties. They're not as good as they look. But they're good enough. 25 cents." The store couldn't buy enough 'good enough' ties to keep up with the demand!

John Wanamaker was a churchman. When he was appointed Postmaster General of the United States by President Harrison, he traveled more than 100,000 miles in order to be present at worship every Sunday. In all, he founded and built four different Presbyterian churches. For sixty years he was the Superintendent of the Sunday School he established. By 1900 the Bethany Mission School, as it was called, had an average attendance of more than 5,000 young people every Sunday, 4,000 of whom Wanamaker knew by name.

John Wanamaker was an evangelist. This is what he had to say about helping someone to "receive the Savior," as he usually called conversion:

> If you once have the joy and sweet pleasure of bringing one soul to Christ, you will be hungry to get to another. Do not argue, do not be rebuffed, be patient and gentle and keep on with a prayer in your heart and drop a good word here and there as you go along. Oh, what a pleasure it will be to you to have a newborn soul beside you at the next Supper of the Lord.

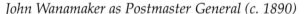

John Wanamaker as Postmaster General (c. 1890)

Wanamaker organized, hosted, and paid for the Dwight L. Moody evangelistic meetings in Philadelphia in 1875. In order to do so, he delayed the opening of his new store, saying "The new store can wait for a few months for its opening, the Lord's business comes first." More than a million people attended the Moody meetings in all.

Wanamaker also established the Bethany Brotherhood, a group of nearly a thousand men who promised to "pray daily for the spread of Christ's kingdom among men" and to "make an earnest effort to bring at least one man or one boy within the hearing of the Gospel of Jesus Christ." The epitaph given to Wanamaker at Bethany Collegiate Presbyterian Church is a suitable one: "By reason of him many went away and believed on Jesus."

John Wanamaker was a missionary statesman. At the age of 20, he began to provide leadership to the fledgling Philadelphia Y.M.C.A., back in the days when it really was the Young Men's Christian Association. He was first introduced to the Philadelphia Y.M.C.A. as "the young man with the funny name that no one has ever heard of." They became familiar with the name soon enough. Wanamaker organized hundreds of open-air summer evangelistic meetings held all over Philadelphia. Over the years, he also provided by himself the money to build Y.M.C.A. facilities in Madras, Calcutta, Seoul, Kyoto, Peking, and Russia.

John Wanamaker was a peacemaker. His contacts with African-American clergy in Philadelphia led to the foundation of the "Colored Branch" of the Y.M.C.A. Wanamaker himself served on the First Interracial Committee of the organization and provided the funds for them to purchase their own building.

John Wanamaker was a patriot. During his brief tenure as Postmaster General, he initiated the parcel post, rural free delivery, and commemorative postage stamps. He also trained some 1,400 of his employees for military service in World War 1.

John Wanamaker was a patron of the arts. He brought the famed Wanamaker Organ to Philadelphia in 1911. He also displayed massive paintings of Christ Before Pilate and Christ on Calvary in his store during Easter. The paintings have since been sold, of course.

John Wanamaker was a man of personal godliness. His testimony was that he "gave his heart and life to God at fifteen." As far as one is able to tell, he walked with God ever after. When the financial markets faltered in 1907, and it was rumored that his business was about to fail, he wrote in his diary: "I am just going on day after day with a heart strong in the belief that the Heavenly Father has me in his keeping and will guide me to do for me what is best." This is how he prayed for his Sunday School students:

> We will make heart-room for Jesus, Thy Son, the name to sinners most dear. We live in the grace of His redeeming love and our only hope is the finished salvation of Calvary. Empty-handed, full of sin; sad of heart and conscious of aggravated wickedness, we cast ourselves at thy feet, O Christ. God be merciful to me a sinner.

John Wanamaker even had something helpful to say about Christmas: "Christmas is a Man born, not a sentiment."

From these details of the life of John Wanamaker I want to make three practical observations. . . .

The Wanamaker Organ in Philadelphia, Pennsylvania, is the largest fully functional pipe organ in the world.

First, we could sure use a few men and women of the caliber of John Wanamaker. In a time of declining godliness, we could use a few men and women who are vigorous in their work, generous with their money, loyal to the church, affectionate towards children, and zealous for the gospel.

Second, names do not last very long on this earth. None of us is very likely to attain anything like the cultural influence or civic renown of John Wanamaker. Among his pallbearers were the Senators and Governor of Pennsylvania, the Mayors of New York and Philadelphia, Chief Justice William Taft, William Jennings Bryan, and Thomas Alva Edison. The Philadelphia public schools were closed on the day of his funeral. Nevertheless, just 75 years later, the Wanamaker name has all but disappeared. Soon, the only place you will be able to read it is on his statue on the east side of City Hall, unless Hecht's has taken care of that as well. Be assured that your name, too, will one day vanish from this earth.

Third, the Lord remembers the names of the righteous. Even when the names of godly men and women have disappeared from all earthly remembrance, they are carefully and perfectly marked and remembered by the living God in the Book of Life. Surely this promise from Psalm 112 was true for John Wanamaker, and can be true for you as well: Good will come to him who is generous and lends freely . . . a righteous man will be remembered forever.

Image Credits

Images marked with one of these codes are used with the permission of a Creative Commons Attribution or Attribution-Share Alike License. See the websites listed for details.

CC-BY-2.0   creativecommons.org/licenses/by/2.0/
CC-BY-3.0   creativecommons.org/licenses/by/3.0/
CC-BY-SA-1.0   creativecommons.org/licenses/by-sa/1.0/
CC-BY-SA-2.5   creativecommons.org/licenses/by-sa/2.5/
CC-BY-SA-3.0   creativecommons.org/licenses/by-sa/3.0/
CC-BY-SA-4.0   creativecommons.org/licenses/by-sa/4.0/

1	windu / Shutterstock.com	74	Allen.G / Shutterstock.com
2	TFoxFoto / Shutterstock.com	77	JSvideos / Shutterstock.com
3	SylvainB / Shutterstock.com	79	HUANG Zheng / Shutterstock.com
4	Northfoto / Shutterstock.com	80	clearviewstock / Shutterstock.com
5	Lee Prince / Shutterstock.com	82	Department of Homeland Security
6	Mega Pixel / Shutterstock.com	83	Department of Homeland Security
8	JASPERIMAGE / Shutterstock.com	85	Library of Congress
10	Milton E Porter / Library of Congress	86	Sheila Fitzgerald / Shutterstock.com
11	Andrew Roland / Shutterstock.com	87	New York Public Library
12	Zvonimir Atletic / Shutterstock.com	88	defotoberg / Shutterstock.com
15	Heartland Arts / Shutterstock.com	89	Library of Congress
16	Susan Montgomery / Shutterstock.com	90	New York Public Library
19	Dimitrina Lavchieva / Shutterstock.com	91	Library of Congress
20	John McGraw / Shutterstock.com	92	Paul Sequeira / NARA
23	FlavoredPixels / Shutterstock.com	93	A.M. Cassandre / Library of Congress
25	Everett Historical / Shutterstock.com	95	dcwcreations / Shutterstock.com
26	Georgios Kollidas / Shutterstock.com	97	ChaiyonS021 / Shutterstock.com
29	Andrey N Bannov / Shutterstock.com	98	Joseph Sohm / Shutterstock.com
31	Ruslan Iefremov / Shutterstock.com	100	Dream79 / Shutterstock.com
32	Syukri Shah / Shutterstock.com	102	edella / Shutterstock.com
36	Library of Congress	103	Library of Congress
37	Public Domain	105	Everett Historical / Shutterstock.com
39	Arturo Espinosa / Flickr / CC-BY-2.0	107	a katz / Shutterstock.com
40	pcruciatti / Shutterstock.com	108	Karin Hildebrand Lau / Shutterstock.com
42	Mark Van Scyoc / Shutterstock.com	110	EQRoy / Shutterstock.com
43	Mieszko9 / Shutterstock.com	112	Library of Congress
45	Library of Congress	115	Karin Hildebrand Lau / Shutterstock.com
46	Library of Congress	116	Olga Popova / Shutterstock.com
49	Everett Historical / Shutterstock.com	117	Library of Congress
50	Everett Historical / Shutterstock.com	119	James R. Martin / Shutterstock.com
52	Everett Historical / Shutterstock.com	121	Everett Historical / Shutterstock.com
53	National Park Service	122	Library of Congress
56	Sarine Arslanian / Shutterstock.com	123	Joseph Sohm / Shutterstock.com
59	Sorbis / Shutterstock.com	124	Dennis A. Crumrin / Shutterstock.com
60	Jubal Harshaw / Shutterstock.com	127	Matt Ragen / Shutterstock.com
63	Mikhail Pogosov / Shutterstock.com	128	Edwin Verin / Shutterstock.com
64	FSAOWI Collection / Library of Congress	131	Andrew Babble / Shutterstock.com
67	cybercrisi / Shutterstock.com	133	Leena Robinson / Shutterstock.com
69	Theodore Trimmer / Shutterstock.com	134	Goncharenya Tanya / Shutterstock.com
70	balounm / Shutterstock.com	135	DW labs Incorporated / Shutterstock.com
73	Leonard Zhukovsky / Shutterstock.com	137	Library of Congress

Also Available from Notgrass History

Exploring America by Ray Notgrass

Your child can earn one year of credit in American history, English (literature and composition), and Bible. Engaging history lessons, combined with primary sources, provide a rich understanding of our nation's past. High school.

Exploring World History by Ray Notgrass

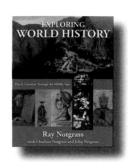

Engaging lessons, combined with primary sources, survey history from Creation to the present. Your child can earn one year of credit in world history, English (literature and composition), and Bible. High school.

Exploring Government by Ray Notgrass

This one-semester course provides a half-year credit in government and English (literature and composition). Learn about the operations of government and about issues facing our nation today. High school.

America the Beautiful by Charlene Notgrass

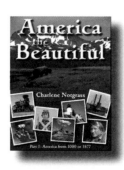

This one-year American history, geography, and literature course combines the flexibility and richness of a unit study with the simplicity of a textbook-based approach to history. Engaging, fascinating, and fun. Ages 10-14.

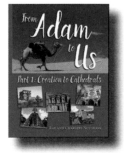

From Adam to Us by Ray and Charlene Notgrass

This one-year world history and literature course combines narrative lessons, full-color photographs, primary sources, literature, and hands-on activities to help the student connect with world history in a personal way. Ages 10-14.

Uncle Sam and You by Ray and Charlene Notgrass

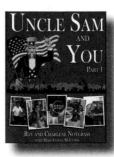

This one-year civics and government course has daily lessons that teach your child about the foundations of American government, the elections process, and how Federal, state, and local governments work. Ages 10-14.

For more information about our resources, call 1-800-211-8793 or visit notgrass.com.